BLESSED

The Life and
Edward C. !

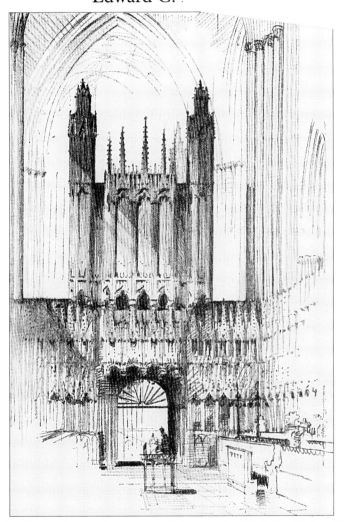

York Minster Organ, from a pencil drawing by W. D. Suddaby, 1929

*Cover photograph from York Minster Library by kind permission
of the Dean and Chapter of York*

Sir Edward Bairstow

Blessed City
The Life and Works of Edward C. Bairstow
1874-1946

Francis Jackson

William Sessions Limited
York, England

ISBN 1 85072 192 0

First (hardback) edition
issued October 1996

This revised second edition
issued February 1997

Printed in 11 on 12½ point Plantin Typeface
from Author's disk
by Sessions of York
The Ebor Press
York, England

Contents

* Chapters I-V are Sir Edward's own autobiographical writings

List of Illustrations

Captions in quotation marks are as written by E.C.B. in his photograph album

Preface

A S HE APPROACHED HIS 70th year, Sir Edward Bairstow, in a
letter, told me that he had begun to write his reminiscences
and was enjoying doing so. At the time of his death some two and
a half years later he had reached page 106 and had got as far as
describing York Minster as he found it on moving there from Leeds
in 1913. What would have followed is, of course, mere conjecture.
No doubt there would have been many pages crowded with incident, instruction and philosophy, and we can only regret that he
did not live to complete what would have become a document of
considerable interest.

The fact that it was incomplete, and that it was said by some
at the time to be of purely local interest, seemed to preclude any
chance of its being of use for publication, and all thought of that
was dropped. Others, however, thought more highly of ECB's writing and were of the opinion that an attempt could be made to make
it available to the public in some form. The obvious person to complete Bairstow's draft lived in York: H.Percy Dixon, a sub-editor
on the Yorkshire Evening Post, a poet as well as a journalist, and a
musician and pupil of Sir Edward. He tackled the task with relish
but had not gone far with it before he was taken ill and, unfortunately, died. (The first two paragraphs on page 159 are his work,
as are the start of chapter VI, the insertion of the account of the
memorial service for Edward VII on page 79 and the line on page
135 which begins with Sir Edward's initials). It was still felt, however, that, with the help of Sir Edward's pupils and the use of his
scrap-book, (the remaining one of two to which he refers – the
other, prior to 1907, having disappeared) some form of completion might be achieved. The problems did not seem insuperable.
What was envisaged was a collection of tributes and assessments,

brought together with information from the scrap-book and other sources.

There was much willing co-operation from his family, pupils and friends who held his memory in affection and gratitude, especially from the two persons nearest to him, his daughter Nancy Brown and Sir Ernest Bullock. Their writings seemed to embrace the whole basis of his personality, and to provide an introduction and an epilogue to the book. The final result appears in the pages that follow. Whatever its merits or failings, it is hoped that more than an inkling is portrayed of the great deal that he meant to those whose lives he enriched.

Of his 106 pages, 103 are in typescript, and the final three are in his own handwriting. These are his first thoughts and have been subjected to no revision whatever, by himself or anyone else. It seemed best, then, to leave it like that and to make no attempt to alter or correct anything – not that there is any great need to do so, even in places such as page 84 where events at Sandsend in 1918 are followed by Leeds matters of some years before. It seemed important to retain the freshness of his first utterance, capturing his characteristic way of expressing himself – without any punch-pulling and often in vivid terms. All the letters quoted are ones he wrote to me, abroad on active service, with the exception of that to David Hird on page 226 and, of course, those from him to William Wolstenholme. And I have tried to keep my own contribution as unobtrusive as possible (seeing my rôle as that of editor and co-ordinator) and, I hope, clearly delineated, sometimes in italics or within brackets.

I have received, also, a great deal of help and co-operation from many willing friends, and can now express my gratitude to them all for many and varied services. First, to those who contributed their recollections of Sir Edward, chief among them the late Sir Ernest Bullock; others of his pupils, Alice Knight, Harold Aubie Bennett and Doctor George Gray, who are unfortunately no longer with us, David Hird, Doctor Lionel Dakers, Doctor David Swale of Adelaide, and many former York choristers, notably George Budden, one of Bairstow's finest solo boys of the immediate post-war years.

Many aspects of research were undertaken: by Maurice Johnstone of the BBC, Gerald Temple of the Hallé Orchestra, David Cutter of Wigan Parish Church (one of ECB's successors there) and his Rector, Canon K. M. Forrest, Doctor Michael Smith of Llandaff Cathedral, Paul Hale of Southwell Cathedral, the Reverend Jonathan Boston, Doctor Harry Bramma, David Lang, Richard Popple and Mrs. Willis Grant who, between them, discovered the date of the Sonata's début, Martin Monkman for the recording dates of 1927 by courtesy of the Gramophone Company; Doctor Bernard Rose who furnished the Latin oration in the Sheldonian and persuaded Bishop Peter Walker to translate it; Andrew Carter, James Lancelot of Durham Cathedral, Robin Langley, Philip Lowe, Edward Singleton, Malcolm Smart, Robert Holtby (Dean Emeritus of Chichester) and his wife Mary who made valuable suggestions before the proof-reading stage; Ramsay Silver whose interest in the book dates from its beginnings; Roger Norris of Durham University library, and Derek W. Downes, whose efforts to trace in the university archives any documentary evidence of Bairstow's appointment to the Durham professorship, though exhaustive, proved fruitless: to Malcolm Riley, Tim Storey, Anthony Boden (author of the history of the Three Choirs Festival), and to Douglas Carrington for a great deal of help and information from the Wolstenholme archive under his care in Blackburn Central Library, and to his wife Linda. Dean Milner-White's Christmas letter (p. 197) was found still within the pages of the book when it was bought in a second-hand bookshop by Mr. Nelson Walmsley, whose permission to include it is greatly appreciated. Special appreciation is accorded for the articles by Gordon Pullin and by Doctor Donald Webster for the benefit of their specialist knowledge, of songs and hymns respectively: to Michael Gillingham and Donald Findlay who tracked down photographs of All Saints Norfolk Square in the National Monuments Archive. Of particular value has been the thesis written by Robert Stevens for his librarian's diploma, a work of the minutest detail exploring many unsuspected byways involving untold hours of patient probings, which greatly eased this editor's task and for which he is more than grateful.

Likewise to Lord Coggan, whose particular aptitude for spotting printing errors was deployed to great effect, in fulfilment of his offer made more than twenty years earlier, to read the proofs. My warmest thanks go to him for this invaluable service, all unsolicited and rapidly carried out.

Due acknowledgment is made – and gratefully expressed – for the newspapers and periodicals which have provided so much of value; to the university library at Cambridge, the archive of Leeds university and to the Royal College of Organists in which Sir Edward delivered four addresses during his presidency – talks which contain a great deal of his thought and wisdom and have been freely drawn upon. To the rest of the home team: Philip Moore, the present holder of Bairstow's York office; to Richard Shephard, Head of the Minster School, whose generous practical help in the way of office equipment and computer expertise is quite inestimable, great thanks are due: as also to his ever willing and utterly patient secretary, Jane Wegelius whose tolerance, time after time, reached epic proportions as an incompetent, untutored tyro wrestled in electronic waters too deep for him, and retained her sunny calm and composure through it all. Not only that, for many of the pages were typed by her own hand during intervals of her school secretarial work when periods of easeful quiescence might have been more to her liking. To my wife Priscilla for her perpetual help, forbearance and encouragement, and, to our daughter Alice whose typing skills, as those of her mother, were always available, it is impossible to give adequate thanks.

Finally, an explanation for the book's delayed appearance. A busy and varied schedule caused the work to be continually pushed into the background, even after one had relinquished Minster duties. But the fiftieth anniversary of Sir Edward's death gave the opportunity which I felt should not be missed to present an account of his life and works to the public. I owe Mrs. Brown, her son Stephen George Bairstow Brown, and others of Sir Edward's family, some very warm thanks indeed for their patience, and for the privilege of being allowed to undertake such an important commission.

FRANCIS JACKSON, East Acklam   July 1996

Preface to the Revised Second Edition

M Y VERY WARM GRATITUDE goes to the Friends of York Minster
and the Dean and Chapter for their willingness to undertake the sponsorship of this book, without which it might never
have achieved publication. The fact that the first print run of 600
sold out almost immediately has been of great encouragement. The
reprinting has also provided me with the opportunity to make some
minor revisions and to include additional commentary in Chapter
XIX. I am grateful, once more, to Mr. Nelson Walmsley for bringing to my notice the two hymn tunes *St. Oran* and *Memento Mori*
of whose existence I was unaware: also to Derek Sutton (Minster
chorister 1935-42 and former Headmaster of St. Paul's Cathedral
Choir School) whose meticulous observance revealed several errors
in the first edition which had escaped detection at the proof stage.

The book's title was an eleventh-hour decision and has received
a good deal of commendation. It is the idea of Philip Lowe, organist of Rochdale Parish Church, who, in July of 1996, mounted a
concert commemorating Sir Edward under the title 'Blessed City',
and he graciously allowed its use for the present work. The programme on that occasion, incidentally, as well as featuring the
anthem of the same name, contained Philip Lowe's own arrangement for S.A.T.B. of the unison service in E flat, with accompaniment for strings and organ.

FRANCIS JACKSON, East Acklam   January 1997

Introduction

by Sir Ernest Bullock

A T THE BEGINNING OF THIS century Sir Edward Bairstow (then Dr. Bairstow) was the organist and choirmaster at Wigan Parish Church, and I was a small boy in his choir. He must have discovered that I had some music in me, because he very soon began to teach me at that early age, and also gave me some little jobs cataloguing the music in the library at the church. So began for me a life-long love, respect and admiration of E.C.B., by which initials I always spoke of him and to him.

In 1906 he was appointed to Leeds Parish Church, which had an acknowledged high standard of music, dating from the tenure of Dr. S.S. Wesley as organist. So it was arranged with my mother that I should go to Leeds as his articled pupil, and Mrs. Bairstow agreed to allow me to live with them in their house. Consequently, their kindness and understanding from that time inevitably caused me to regard them both as a second father and mother.

Anyone who knew E.C.B.'s artistic temperament and integrity could not fail to realise that he was a perfectionist. He would not tolerate bad, clumsy, slovenly craftsmanship either in life or music; by his example he inspired discipline and especially self-discipline. He always expressed his ideas and opinions in a straightforward way, and had courage to do so, in spite of consequences. Perhaps above all, he could not take 'humbug', as he called it, and he was short and almost ruthless with those suspected of insincerity, and of similar devious devices. In these days, these qualities are, by some, largely despised and disregarded, as I write in this year of grace 1971. But do not imagine these unrelenting attitudes go to give a picture of E.C.B., for he also had an innate kindness and

1

generosity, and an unfailing genuine sympathy for those really deserving. He had a keen sense of humour, of the ridiculous, and he delighted to shock and indeed mock pompous and pretentious folk by attacking their weaknesses with blunt words, causing them to deflate. Like a number of artists, he was moody and sometimes difficult, but many a crisis was averted by the wonderful way in which Lady Bairstow managed him. She tackled every emergency with love and understanding in a practical, commonsense way together with great gentleness and calm which never failed ultimately in its objective.

Another side of his character I well remember. When Stephen, the eldest of the family, was a young boy, E.C.B. bought for him a model railway. In a short space of time, the railway had been built up, having a length of lines, crossings, points, signals, stations and several mechanical engines together with carriages and trucks. Whenever there was a short free time, E.C.B. and I set out the lines etc., and played with the railways, ostensibly for Stephen, who certainly enjoyed seeing the trains in action, and especially delighted when engines collided and there was an accident. Both E.C.B. and I got a great deal of fun out of the working of the model railway. It was interesting to plan and design a variety of shapes for the lines, placing the points and crossings and necessary signals at the correct places, then starting off trains at various speeds and on different routes, moving points and signals in order to avoid a breakdown. Childish, you might think, but, at the same time, giving thought and quick action for each person playing the game.

When first we got to Leeds, E.C.B. worked very hard for, after Sunday services, he left early on Monday morning to travel to Blackburn, there to teach and train the local Choral Society. On Tuesday he did similar work at Preston with teaching and their Choral Society. Wednesday morning was spent in Wigan teaching, and then returning to play choral evensong at Leeds Parish Church. During the remainder of the week, he was teaching and taking rehearsals and playing the church services. Anyone would consider this a full week, but not E.C.B., for even in the train he would spend time composing music or reading proofs. For example, he wrote in the train a work for two pianos entitled Variations on an Original Theme, afterwards published by the Oxford University Press. This he dedicated to two* Leeds musicians who practised together regularly and gave concerts in various towns and cities in Yorkshire. I well remember reading proofs with him as we travelled in a train; one piece, in particular, I recollect, *Scherzo in A flat* for the organ.

He was truly a great teacher of music, and not only as a specialist in one branch but many, as can be seen by the names of some of his pupils who later became well-known. There were singers like Elsie Suddaby, George Parker, Etty Ferguson and Stephen Manton; organists and choirmasters Gordon Slater, George Gray, Lionel Dakers, and Francis Jackson; Willis Grant, Professor of Music at Bristol, the late Gerald Finzi, and the late Lt.Colonel Jaeger, Director of Military Bands and finally of Kneller Hall. Not many teachers can be cited who have assisted the developmental advancement of music by having so many pupils of distinction in so many varying branches of the art.

As a teacher, he had no particular set method, but he passed on to his pupils his ideals and principles, and a knowledge of the value of disciplined hard work. He had that uncanny gift of being able to present the subject in the right way to suit the particular pupil he was teaching. He was quick to understand the character of his pupil, and had an intuition of how best to guide each one. He had a knowledge of the necessary techniques, backed up by a wide repertory of music, in order to help the pupil to tackle styles and problems connected with different periods in the history of music.

But what impressed me most of all was his profound and unfailing love of music which one instinctively recognised as sincere. He had much sympathy with an enthusiastic pupil who worked well and achieved a result according to his ability, but woe betide a pupil who was apathetic and did not attempt to take his full share of work needed to maintain progress. For example, he would set a goal and would expect a pupil to reach it. If a personal instance can be mentioned, I remember an occasion when an organist, who had been asked to play Brahms' "German Requiem" for a performance by the augmented choir, was unable to do it, either on account of

---

* The dedication on the published copy of 1932 - over 20 years after its composition - is 'to H. Percy Richardson' who was organist of St. Chad's, Far Headingley. FJ (see page 300).

illness or some other cause. E.C.B. told me that I must do it, and I had only three days to prepare for the performance. Of course it was done, but with what result, I have no idea. A challenge, and one had to meet it.

He was a successful choir trainer both of small groups, such as church choirs, or large bodies like choral societies. Some singers in the latter type found that they could not take what they considered to be his rough treatment of them. But, in my experience, the rough treatment only lasted until he had got rid of the passengers, leaving a keen and enthusiastic membership from which he could have a body of singers sufficiently malleable and responsive to his interpretative wishes required by the music in hand. There must still be many people who can remember the excellent standard of singing of the church choirs at Wigan and Leeds, finally reaching the highest level at York Minster. One cannot forget his choral society work during the early days in Lancashire, and later with Yorkshire choirs, especially with the Leeds Philharmonic, York Musical Society, and particularly the memorable performances of J.S. Bach's *St. Matthew Passion* during Lent at York Minster. Incidentally, he was no mean conductor of orchestras as well as choruses. During the early days in Lancashire, members of the Hallé orchestra were engaged to play for the choral societies, and these experienced professional players tried to take advantage of the young conductor. However, E.C.B. soon made these men realise that he would not be trifled with or accept such treatment, with the result that they began to pay him respect.

Another important work that he did, was after he was appointed to the Chair of Music at Durham University. The duties were to give a few lectures, and to be in charge of the musical degree examinations. It was a part-time appointment and could be carried on with his work at York. The musical examinations were open and the candidates non-residential for the most part.He had obtained a music degree at Durham himself and, prior to his appointment to the chair he had been an examiner, so now he felt a change of style was needed in the examinations in order to increase the efficiency of the candidates and thus improve their professional work for music in general. Over a period of time, the requirements of the examinations and the questions asked had become stereotyped, consequently those teachers who prepared the candidates were able to anticipate the questions asked, and devise methods to gain the desired result. In other words, it was a happy hunting ground for "crammers", as the vulgar phrase goes. Whilst keeping to the syllabus, E.C.B., with the help of his examiners, formulated questions from which to assess the candidate's musical talent and craftsmanship and technique together with his knowledge of history and musical scores. The questions were no longer stereotyped, but allowed candidates scope to show their musical talents and their technical ability, all within the strict bounds of the syllabus. In this way, the standard of the examinations rose and was generally acknowledged to be as high as possible with non-residential candidates.

But to turn back to the Leeds days, E.C.B. was selected to be the organist for the Leeds Festivals and, at that time, Sir Charles Stanford was its chief conductor, and eventually they became friends. Stanford was the adviser on musical matters to Macmillan and Co.Ltd., and he asked E.C.B. to write a text book, and the work was completed and published in 1937 under the title *Counterpoint and Harmony*. Also during the Leeds days, the City Fathers set up a Municipal School of Music, with Percy Scholes as its Registrar. The best teachers of music in the area joined the staff, including E.C.B., and whilst the School lasted a great deal of first rate work was done, and much enthusiasm created for the advancement of serious music-making. Like many another similar institution, it had to rely on financial backing, which in this case was from the Corporation and, after a few years, the financial support was withdrawn and the School was forced to close.

In 1913, E.C.B. was appointed to York Minster, and he devoted the rest of his life to the work there, and could not be tempted to leave, although I know that he was invited to become Organist and Master of the Choristers at Westminster Abbey in 1927.

Of E.C.B.'s character there are many examples which could be given, but I will mention only a few. Let us take first his courage, concerning which two examples can suffice. Soon after E.C.B. began work at Leeds Parish Church, it was discovered that a wealthy churchwarden had greatly contributed to the cost of the choir, and had been allowed to say how and what music should be done. Soon it was clear that there was a difference of view and, after much discussion, the final outcome was that the Vicar at that time, the Reverend Canon Samuel Bickersteth, supported E.C.B., and the churchwarden withdrew his financial support for the choir. It needed great courage on E.C.B.'s part, especially at the beginning of his work at Leeds Parish Church, but it was not only at the church, for this particular man also had great influence on the musical life of the City.

Another example of E.C.B.'s courage is still vivid in my mind, although it is many, many years ago. He was judging at a Music Competition Festival, and he allowed me to sit with him in order to be introduced to and instructed in that type of work. The class was for Male Voice Choirs, and after several had sung, on came a choir that was obviously accustomed to these competitions, and its members were quite pleased with their efforts. The choir sang well, but the sole effect and object was to "play to the gallery", as the phrase goes. At the end of this effort, the audience responded with thunderous applause. Several other choirs sang, including one which sang most beautifully, most movingly, technically well done, and showing great artistic merit, and yet the audience only gave it a polite response. When E.C.B. gave his remarks and decision, he paid due respect to the precision, ability and experience of the choir which had captured the applause, yet reminded the choir that the interpretation of the music should come first, their efforts directed with taste and sincerity, with no thought of capturing the applause of the audience, "stunting" in order to do so rather than putting the music first. His decision was clear and reasoned, but, of course, did not please that particular choir or many of the audience. To me, it was an important lesson, for it will be generally agreed that it took courage in a crowded hall and against the expressed preference of the majority of the audience, to give his unpopular verdict.

Between the two World Wars, E.C.B. was much in demand to judge at Musical Competition Festivals, for the movement was helping enormously to encourage, instruct, and raise the standard of amateur music-making, not only in this country but in certain other countries overseas. When at these Festivals, E.C.B. was not content merely to admire and praise the efforts of the competitors – although he was appreciative if he felt it was deserved – but he felt it a duty to give constructive criticism and give the advantage of his experience as a teacher to improve their performances. His remarks were welcomed by those who wished to improve, and enjoy the music for its own sake, but those who merely wanted congratulations and first place in the class were disgruntled. E.C.B. would always go straight to the point, and give his opinions clearly, perhaps too bluntly for some folk. He was out to help them, and to him it was the music and the advancement of the art that was of first importance. I well remember him saying, a little sadly, to me after having judged for many years: "I have judged at almost all important Music Competition Festivals in the United Kingdom and in Canada" (then he waited to emphasize the last word) "once!!"

As I have indicated, E.C.B. was a compulsive teacher, it was in his nature, and he could not help giving the benefit of his gift to others. My mind goes back to a visit to Leeds of a friend who had been an articled pupil of Sir Frederick Bridge at Westminster Abbey at the same time as E.C.B. This friend had become well-known as the composer of ballads, popular at that time, and vulgarly known by the music profession as 'pot-boilers'. This friend wished to have E.C.B's opinion of a song-cycle he had written, but E.C.B. tried to dissuade him. However, he was persistent, and finally the songs were played through. Then E.C.B. turned to me and said: "Remember, you cannot touch pitch without being defiled." That was a lesson I can never forget.

This brings forward the question of E.C.B's attitude to money, for when I was with him in Leeds I looked after his accounts. To E.C.B. his first consideration was music, and he used to quote: "Seek ye first the kingdom of God and all these things shall be added unto you." I do not remember that he ever expressed a wish to make a great deal of money, and he clearly had faith that as money was not the primary purpose of his life, what was needed would be available when required.

After visiting Canada, where he had judged at Musical Competition Festivals, he was invited to New York by his predecessor Mr Thomas Noble, who had become organist at St. Thomas Church, and whose wealthy congregation had provided a choir school and every musical facility needed to start a tradition similar to an English Cathedral Musical Foundation. When E.C.B.

came home I asked him whether he would like to go to America to work and found a similar musical tradition. His reply left me in no doubt; he said: "I would rather go to the Devil."

He enjoyed a joke, even if the laugh was against himself. He told me about a visit to York of members of an Organists' Association. They came from one of the Yorkshire towns, and this was to be their summer outing. E.C.B. suggested that they should attend evensong at the Minster, and afterwards he would give an organ recital. All went according to plan, and then the time came for the chairman to propose a vote of thanks. He concluded by saying something like this: "I was sitting for the service in a bad draught, I went out to get some warmth of the sun, so I missed the recital, but them as 'eard it, said it was very good." Faint praise, if you like, but E.C.B. enjoyed to hear it.

On another occasion, when he was on holiday in Sandsend, he was asked to give an organ recital for charity at Lythe Church. As you probably know, Lythe is a village at the top of a steep hill outside Sandsend. He toiled up the hill on the afternoon of the recital to practise, and discovered that the organ was hand-blown, with an old man there to do the job. When the playing began, the blower pumped vigorously and overfilled the wind reservoir, consequently the escaping air made an unpleasant hissing noise. Very patiently, E.C.B. went and instructed the old man how to maintain a steady pressure of wind, after which all went well. At the evening recital, during the first piece, there was a repetition of the afternoon experience of bad blowing, vigorous pumping, and hissing escaping wind. E.C.B. was angry and went round to the blower, not realising that he was a different old boy, pitched into him and gave him the edge of his tongue. An official of the church came to see what was the trouble, and said to E.C.B.: "It's no good talking to him, he's stone deaf!" E.C.B's anger left him, and he enjoyed the laugh.

Soon after the First World War, and I had been at Exeter a little time, I stayed at 1 Minster Court. Going through some church music with E.C.B., we read an advertisement on the back of a piece, naming a cantata entitled "Balaam and Balak". E.C.B. said: "I wonder if there is a part for the ass?" "No," said I. He asked how did I know, and I told him that recently I had played for a performance of that work in Exeter. E.C.B. was both surprised and greatly amused.　　　　　　　　　　　　　　　　　　　　　　　　E.B.

Childhood (1874-1891)

"And when you look back, it's all a puff,
Happy and over, and short enough."

THE EVENTS WHICH EMERGE from the misty memories of the past are mostly musical. I can still recall the quiet, unemotional, yet sweet tones of my mother's voice when she sang to me Doddridge's hymn, *See Israel's gentle Shepherd stand* to the carol tune of the *Seven joys of Mary*. She told me in later days that I was emphatic in my dislike of certain tunes; that I used to protest, "please not cupper cow" when she sang "Gentle cow that brings me milk" to the tune usually associated with "Conquering kings their titles take."

Another early remembrance still clear in my mind is of sitting at my father's side on a long duet stool while he improvised or sang songs to his own accompaniment. He was self taught and had a pleasant tenor voice. However imperfect his efforts he enthralled me, and it was not long before I began to try myself to draw sweet sounds from the piano. When I was about six I found one day that I had succeeded in more or less mastering my first little piano piece. My father and mother were out, and so the two maids were summoned as audience. No doubt they thought I was showing off, but no idea of that kind entered my head. The thrill of the music was such a joy to me that I felt I must share it with somebody, and the two maids were the only people available. This is the one incident of all the memories of my childhood which is most pleasing to me, for it shows that I had been born with that most precious gift, the 'sense of message': the feeling that what you do is done for others. The other extreme is well illustrated by a man past middle age who came to me for piano lessons years ago. When he used an impossible fingering and I corrected it he would say, "Well you see I only play for my own amusement, so that it doesn't really matter." Then he would tell me he didn't like the music I had given him to learn. My answer to this was that he couldn't play it. Then his parrot cry would be renewed: "As I only play to amuse myself, what's the use of bothering to learn something I don't like?" Finally I said, "Why pay my fee and your railway fare to York if you only wish to potter about for your own amusement and won't accept my ruling either in regard to what you play or how you play it?" That finished him.

One more very early recollection is of a large wardrobe. To my childish mind the doors seemed very like those which enclosed the manuals of the organ in the chapel at which I gazed on a Sunday. When they were opened the shelves resembled the keyboards, and the drawers, with white knobbed handles, looked very like drawstops. I was allowed to sit on a high stool and play this 'organ' to my heart's content, for it was a silent game.

My parents were ardent Wesleyan Methodists. They read every word of the Bible *au pied de la lettre*. It was a sin not to believe every syllable; it was a sin even to question a single word. But that narrow form of religion had two salient points; the first was its intense sincerity, and the second, which hinged on the first, was that as theirs was the only safe road to heaven, it behoved them to go out into the highways and hedges, and compel any wanderers, or, as they would have put it, 'sinners', to join the flock. This they did for many years without a thought for their own personal comfort. I never remember seeing my mother the slightest bit out of temper. My father was very different. He was intolerant. If he discovered any wickedness he informed the police at once. He was somewhat of a handful for my mother. It has always been a source of wonder to me how she could live amongst poverty and wickedness for so many years, coax my father, and yet preserve her sunny calm coupled with a real sense of humour.

You can imagine that the life of a musician for their only son was anathema to my parents. Most musicians were in their opinion drunken scamps on the sure way to hell. Still they paid for my musical instruction. This was of a mixed quality, and I never seemed to be very long with the same teacher. I used to stay for long and very happy periods with my maternal grandmother at Nottingham. Here I got quite good teaching, and my practising was overlooked by a musical aunt who also played Haydn's symphonies with me as duets. When I went back to my native town of Huddersfield I was given lessons by an elderly female, a distant relation in poor circumstances. She was both dull and inefficient. After a few lessons, when the time for the next one came round, I retired to the bottom of the garden and bolted myself in a certain place, refusing to come out until the lady had gone. That was my only personal experience of the type of woman whose one object in life seems to be to give children a lasting hatred of learning to play the piano. The race is not quite extinct; specimens of it are still to be found, chiefly in girls' schools. But they are nothing like so numerous as they were when I was a boy.

It was in these days that I loved to hear the bands in Greenhead Park, Huddersfield; to get as near as possible to them, and 'drink in the utmost sound I could'*; to walk round the bandstand so that I might distinguish the individual timbre of the various instruments. Even now I love to soak in sound if it is beautiful; to sit in the cross of the Minster facing the screen, and wallow in the rich tones of the full organ when an accomplished pupil is playing; to revel in a glorious climax of orchestra and chorus when I conduct them, and when one's own enthusiasm has warmed them to give a hundred per cent spontaneously.

The Nottingham visits were a great joy. They began when I was a baby, but I can remember my grandfather who died in 1879. He was a grand old man with the manners of a duke. He had a draper's shop on the Long Row and supplied all the little village shops for miles around. I was allowed to drive round with my uncle in a spanking dog-cart to take their orders. The old shop on the Long Row had rock cellars beneath the ordinary cellars. They were never used and were full of rats. It was said that Nottingham was honeycombed with ancient cellars and passages cut in the sandstone on which the city stands. In the great kitchen behind the shop

---

* From Walter de la Mare, *The Bells*

was a huge fireplace with an open hearth. A clock-work spit twirled in front of this, cooking an enormous joint for the mid-day dinner of the employees. The house where my grandparents lived was in New Basford. It was a double fronted house with a garden in front, in the corner of which was an arbour where we played games in the summer. Behind this was an orchard and a hen run. Along the back of the house were outhouses with stables at the opposite end to the orchard. Across the road running in front of the house was a large field and kitchen garden. In this was a great tree that I could climb with a book and read unmolested in a comfortable fork, high and screened from the prying eyes of aunts. Every day grandmother had to be read to sleep after the mid-day meal. I and my sister shared this duty. I often tried a very gradual diminuendo, creeping towards the door at the same time, and attempting a silent exit. But she invariably woke up at the critical moment and the process had to be started all over again.

The last visit to Nottingham was in the severe winter of 1889-90. I and two friends – brothers – made up our minds one Saturday afternoon to skate on the Nottingham and Grantham canal to a farm house where these boys had spent their summer holidays. Unfortunately the canal did not follow the crow, and instead of the farm being 'about four or five miles' it turned out to be more than twice that distance. There was only a narrow path of smooth swept ice, the rest was rough frozen snow. Every now and then we came to a lock where the ice had been broken. At one place a factory had been running warm water into the canal. Here the ice was as thin as cardboard. We reached the farm about five p.m. and were given a glorious high tea with an enormous pork pie which we finished entirely. Then we made for the railway station, only to discover, with a boy's usual improvidence, that we had not enough cash to pay the fare home. There was nothing for it but returning to the canal, screwing on our skates, and making our way back to Nottingham in the dark. The younger brother was only twelve and was soon fagged out. Luckily one of us had a walking stick. The youngster grasped the middle and we two elders took the ends and pulled him back to Nottingham. He was on the smooth path (when we did not lose it in the dark) but we were floundering on the ice hummocks. We nearly had a catastrophe at the factory, the ice

Sir Edward's parents

cracking all round us. How we avoided the locks in the pitch dark I don't know. It was nearly midnight when we approached the town to be met by a very anxious father with helpers and lanterns. We slept till the middle of Sunday, but were none the worse.

In 1939, when I was President of the Incorporated Association of Organists, their annual conference took place at Nottingham. I made a special journey to see the old house again. But it was a sad spectacle, built up on all sides and looking shabby and melancholy.

My father became more and more restless to give up business life in Huddersfield and try to find some religious work. His desire was fulfilled in 1889 when he joined for a while the Salvation Army. They employed him chiefly on the business side to advise them where to place contracts for uniforms. As he had been a wholesale clothier for years he was able to help them. After that he joined the South London Wesleyan Mission.

My schooling was as disjointed as my musical instruction. I was at Nottingham High School for a short time and then went to the Grocers' Company's School on Hackney Downs. After that I was with a private coach, working for London matriculation. I found it

very difficult to do regular, concentrated work at home, nor was I
interested in the subjects which the coach selected for me. I wasn't
very much surprised when I failed for the examination.

*In 1887 for about two years, out of school hours, he had organ and
pianoforte lessons from Mr Arthur Page, one of the best-known members
of the profession in the city.*

Farmer (see page 15) *had a studio at Steinway Hall, and thither the
youth repaired for three years, working chiefly at the pianoforte, and in
a less ordered way at composition, for Farmer, whatever his musical gifts,
was not to the manner born as an expert in the art of teaching composition. He set Bairstow to work at harmonizing chorales, and thus at
least laid a solid foundation of harmonic progression, around which other
developments could be built, and fortunately for the young student,
Farmer's taste in pianoforte music was strongly in the direction of Bach.
Bairstow took a prominent part in the musical activities of the Grocers'
School by deputising at the organ at the services and playing pianoforte
solos at the school concerts, and he was also concerned in the performance
of Sullivan's operas, which were produced at the school with extraordinary completeness and ability under the direction of Mr Broughton Black,
who was then one of the masters of the School. (Musical Times, May
1914).*

The question of my future now loomed up large with my
parents, but not with me. I knew I was better fitted to be a musician than for any other pursuit both by inclination and natural gifts.
They took me to play to various people whom they considered to
be authorities. Some were favourable, others were not, but it made
no difference to me. I have often described my own situation at this
time to the many aspirants who have come to me asking my advice
as to whether they should enter the profession of music, telling
them how my parents disliked the idea of my becoming a musician,
and how some of the people to whom I was taken for an audition
did not recommend it. My contention is that if you have a strong
inner consciousness that music is your job, and an equally strong
feeling that you have a musical message for the community, either
as composer or performer or both, then nothing will deter you from
becoming a musician.

My parents gradually came to see that I could not be dissuaded. In the late eighties and early nineties I had lessons from John Farmer who visited Steinway Hall to teach the piano at the time when he was organist of Balliol College, Oxford. He taught me to love the best in music and was a rare enthusiast, but I cannot remember very much instruction in the foundations of piano technique and none in harmony and counterpoint. However, he encouraged me and prophesied for me a successful future.

Youth (1891-1899)

"Youth is full of pleasure"

IT NOW BECAME ESSENTIAL that I should earn money. A chance came for me to join the staff of a private school at Windsor as assistant music master. I was to get my board and coaching for another shot at London Matriculation in return for my services in teaching little boys to play the piano and teaching ordinary subjects in the junior school during the morning. I believe there was a small salary as well. The headmaster, known to us as 'Pecksniff', used to marshal the boys and line them up on either side of the road leading up to the Castle to welcome Queen Victoria when she returned after a sojourn at Balmoral or elsewhere. Pecksniff stood at the head of the line in an immaculate frock coat and shiny top hat which he doffed with a flourish as the Queen drove past. She never took the slightest notice. It was here I met Ackworth Stuart, another member of the staff. He was an athlete; a fine soccer player and a good cricketer. He was fond of music and appreciated the beautiful in all things. He also had a fine sense of humour. Many a time on a Sunday afternoon did he and I go to St. George's Chapel to listen to Sir Walter Parratt and his choir. I shall never forget one Sunday when we could not get into the choir, but listened in the north aisle to Mendelssohn's *Hear my prayer*. I was absolutely ravished by it. I often wonder whether such youthful experiences at a very impressionable age are in danger of warping one's judgement as to the absolute value of the music. *Hear my prayer* appeals to the man in the street, but there must be other things endeared to the cathedral organist by youthful associations which leave him cold.

The masters' room at the Windsor school was up a ricketty old staircase. It contained some ricketty old chairs and a ricketty old piano. At one end was a boot box with compartments. In this room many international cricket matches were played – England *v* Scotland. The boot box was the wicket, the bat was the leg of a chair, the ball was made of paper and string. Runs were scored entirely by boundaries. Marvellous snap catches were made. The bowling was difficult, for a lively finger-spin made the ball break in the most disconcerting way.

A few Frenchmen aged between eighteen and twenty came to the school to learn English. They were too old to mix with the boys and therefore were anxious to make free with our common room. This we all resented. One of them was specially offensive to us. Last of all he challenged us to fight. We drew lots to settle who should meet him. Luckily the odd man out was the athletic Stuart. I should have been knocked out in the first round for I was by no means muscularly strong and knew nothing of boxing. After mid-night we cleared one of the class rooms. The headmaster's son acted as second for the Frenchman and I acted for Stuart, knowing nothing of the rules. However, it mattered very little for the Frenchman was soon *hors de combat* with a black eye, to which beef steak was immediately applied.

It soon became evident to me that I could not stay at Windsor very long. The coaching for the London matriculation consisted of getting up at 6.30 and having lessons with the elder Miss Pecksniff. But as I had to work in school all the morning and teach piano for the rest of the day, these lessons were of no use. Moreover my piano and organ practice were neglected. The year or so that I spent there was a very happy time. This was chiefly due to Stuart who gave me a taste for athletics and a healthier outlook on life in general. We had many long walks together, mostly on Sunday evenings. I remember well the impression made on my north-country, town-bred mind by the song of the nightingales in the springtime and the sound of the stags bellowing in the Great Park in the autumn.

My mother had a lifelong friend, a Mrs Robertson, always known as 'Bidie'. She had two fine sons, the elder of whom, by the way, was knighted about the same time as I was. When she and my mother got together, as they often did, for intimate conversation, the subject was nearly always sons. Bidie had known the first wife of Dr J. F. Bridge, organist of Westminster Abbey, and it was she who suggested that I should go to Dr Bridge as a pupil. How the money was forthcoming I do not know, for my parents had an income of between two and three hundred a year, but in July, 1892, I went to the Abbey. Dr Bridge suggested that I should go up to Durham for the entrance examination for music students and the first examination for bachelor of music which could then be taken on consecutive days. The entrance examination was fairly easy in those days, for the Durham music degrees had only just been started, and were designed to attract musicians already earning their living by music, many of whom had never had the time or opportunity for an elaborate education. The Cambridge musical degrees were only open to resident students; Oxford followed suit a year or so after I went to Durham, after considerable opposition from certain musicians including Dr Bridge. At London University the stiff matriculation was the bugbear. Therefore, especially in those first years, many men went to Durham for their degrees. Looking through the great book wherein are entered the names of all successful candidates, such well-known names occur from time to time as Walter Alcock, Ernest Bullock, John Ireland, Malcolm Sargent and W.G. Whittaker. Though the preliminary examination was easy the music examinations have always kept up a standard quite as high as other English Universities. And so it was settled that I should go to Durham in September, although I knew practically nothing of the harmony and counterpoint in four parts required in the syllabus. Bridge gave me some specimen papers to work out for his inspection, but, truth to tell, I did these by the light of nature. He was just off for his annual stay in Scotland, and left me to work with Russell, one of his numerous assistants. It was not long before that Bridge had married his second wife who had been his pupil. She was a Miss Amphlett and her people had for a time been strongly opposed to the marriage. She had been brought up in an atmosphere of 'huntin', shootin' and fishin', and to please

her Bridge did his best to become a sport. He often took one of the
pupils with him to a shooting school. I never went, but the story
circulated that every man on the place lay down flat when Bridge
fired at the clay pigeons. This may have been an exaggeration – it
probably was – but I can vouch for the truth of the following story.
One day, to his great delight, he received an invitation to stay with
some of Miss Amphlett's relations in Ireland to go deer stalking.
He was determined not to disgrace himself, and was doing his best
to crawl along silently on his tummy as they approached a stag,
when a violent desire to sneeze overtook him. In desperation he
buried his head in the heather. The extraordinary noise he made
was so like that of another stag that the victim, instead of running
away, came nearer to investigate and was shot. One year when
Bridge had returned from Scotland to his work in September, leaving his wife to enjoy a little more sport, some venison arrived. It
had not been bled and looked such a sanguinary mess that Bridge
told the cook to cut it up and give it to the pupils. When the blood
began to ooze through the newspaper wrappings most of them
threw their parcels over Westminster Bridge. With an extra newspaper or two I managed to get mine home respectably. It was so
delicious when cooked that when I went to the Abbey next morning my heart was full of gratitude and I carried with me the thanks
of the whole family. "Yes", said Bridge when he heard this, "I only
kept a small piece for myself and it was so good that I was sorry I
had given any away."

To return to the examinations: I worked hard with Russell who
knew the ropes well. In those days it was a matter of conforming
strictly to the textbooks; any musicianship found its way into the
exercises despite, not because of, the cramping strait-jacket of for-
mality imposed. My work for the London matriculation helped me
to pass the easy Durham examination, and, rather to my surprise,
I was lucky enough to get through the first Mus.B. also. But the
hurried work of that summer and the lack of background made it
difficult for me later on. At that time the next procedure was the
writing of a composition as an 'exercise'. Only one type was allowed,
a cantata for chorus and string orchestra consisting of four movements – a chorus, a solo quartet, a vocal solo and a choral fugue.
Mine was returned to me with instructions to rewrite certain parts;

it was then duly passed. In these days it would certainly have been ploughed. Although the whole of the curriculum for degrees was in written music, and although the exercise was the one and only example of extended composition required, the other examinations being entirely short melodies to harmonize or figured basses given for the addition of the upper parts, or dull counterpoints with semibreve *canti fermi* the second examination followed the composition of the exercise. It was not until comparatively recently that this was altered. Now the exercise is the final test and the two other examinations are devised to lead up to it as far as possible, by setting fewer questions, but making them longer and more musical and stimulating to the candidates, and by asking them for a certain amount of original work.

In September, 1893 I was sent up for the final examination, but the hurry of the first examination and the scramble to rewrite the exercise prevented me from gaining enough knowledge of music in general and practising counterpoint and fugue sufficiently. I could not do the work in the allotted time. Stainer gave me my *viva voce* and asked me whether classical recitative usually remained in one key or modulated freely. Not knowing, I, silly-like, said classical recitatives were diatonic. "What about 'Thy rebuke hath broken my heart' from *Messiah*?" said Stainer. I had only worked at piano and organ music and had never heard a complete performance of *Messiah*. This cooked my goose; I failed. I had to wait a year until September, 1894. This time I made sure. J.R. Dear, a fellow pupil, and I worked together under ideal circumstances, for his parents lived at Ventnor. In the August of that year we did our work in the mornings and enjoyed ourselves for the rest of the day all over that lovely Isle of Wight, cycling, walking, bathing and playing tennis. I walked through the examination, finishing all the papers before time.

Bridge was an adept at making other people do his work for him. Personally I welcomed any opportunity of helping him. I believe my parents only paid him one year's fee. After that, owing to his kindness and partly also because I did my best to be useful to him, he kept me on at the Abbey until May, 1899. During this time I 'devilled' for him; took rehearsals of the choristers, corrected examination papers, went to the British Museum to hunt up material for his Gresham lectures, and occasionally played the organ in the Abbey. All this was worth far more to me than lessons in any subject. The old adage, 'Experientia docet', is absolutely true. The knowledge a teacher imparts to his pupils is less important than the right experience he provides for them.

Bridge, as I have said, deputed the paper-work instruction to Russell. The organ and piano lessons were given by Walter Alcock, now (1945) Sir Walter Alcock, M.V.O., organist of Salisbury cathedral. Bridge turned up unexpectedly every few weeks and heard a few of us play. We were turned on suddenly at his request, to the discomfiture of some of the weaker players.* One evening in 1893 Bridge suddenly made his appearance at organ lessons and told me to play first a piece, then a psalm and finally to improvise. I was rather over-whelmed with all this attention and quite at a loss to account for it until a parson appeared in the organ loft. He was the Rev. William Boyd, vicar of All Saints, Norfolk Square, Paddington. In a few minutes he had appointed me his organist. After leaving Windsor I played for a few months at a Congregational Church at Upper Norwood. The minister requested me to "play gently after Sunday morning service, for the congregation like to indulge in a little gossip, that being in some cases their only opportunity of meeting." I was very glad, therefore, to go to All Saints. Moreover the vicar was musical and wanted a beautiful service. The increase in salary was also a great consideration in those days. Boyd was a very good friend to me. At that time we lived a stone's throw from the Old Kent Road to be near my father's work. It was an hour's journey on a horse-bus to Paddington. I was offered luncheon on a Sunday at the Vicarage and was thankful to accept. The vicar certainly loved music and was much moved by it, but his favourite composers were Gounod and Mendelssohn. He had mixed a lot with the music world and had been a professional accompanist for a time between leaving Oxford, where he was organ scholar of Exeter, and taking orders. He was the composer of the tune to 'Fight the good fight' called 'Pentecost' in Hymns Ancient and Modern, and produced several other tunes of a similar type

---

* He well remembers Sir Frederick saying, "No doubt you think you are a little Beethoven, but there are plenty of fellows as clever as you are." (M.T. 1914)

whilst I was his organist. After service he would keep the choir on their knees quite a long time if he thought I had struck a good vein of improvisation. After luncheon, if the choir had sung really well, he would say, "Have a cigar, my boy." If the music had been just normal, it would be, "Have a cigarette." But if things had gone badly he would say in a lugubrious voice, "Have you brought your pipe with you?" I was much happier at All Saints than a fellow-pupil who was sent to his first post at a small church in South London. He was brimful of zeal; he held extra practices for the choristers, and the choirmen caught some of his enthusiasm and began to sing with confidence and intelligence. When this had gone on for about a year he received a letter from the Vicar just after Easter. It ran something like this:-

"Dear Mr.–,

The churchwardens and myself are so pleased with your hard and successful work with the choir, with the extra rehearsals you have taken and with the improvement in the music generally, that we have determined to raise your salary from twenty pounds a year" (here he turned over a page) "to twenty-one pounds a year."

The Church of All Saints, Norfolk Square
(Photo courtesy of the Royal Commission on the Historical Monuments of England)

One morning I arrived at the Abbey for nine o'clock rehearsal and was hailed by a fellow-pupil with, "I say, Bairstow, do you know your church has been burnt down?" I jumped into a bus and made my way post-haste to Norfolk Square to find only the walls standing. The previous evening I had kept two choir boys back after evensong to blow the organ whilst I practised. They blew in a cubby hole that I very rarely visited. It turned out that their custom was to light a candle, turn it upside down, and then stick it in the accumulated candle grease. This particular evening they had forgotten to blow it out.

It was not more than a year before a new church was built, a far more attractive one than the dark and gloomy edifice of Victorian gothic which was burnt. A new organ was built by Hill with three manuals instead of two, pneumatic action and a hydraulic blowing apparatus. The latter was not altogether successful, for it was found that on Sundays, especially in the evening, the water pressure was not heavy enough to keep the wind in the organ. The organ and the blower were raised about twenty feet on the north side of the choir. To remedy the low pressure, instead of removing both wind reservoirs and motor into the basement, only the motor was moved, and two, long, wooden arms installed to actuate the bellows above. They worked through wooden bearings and squeaked if not constantly treated with mutton fat. Even when well greased they uttered loud groans for a moment or two when first started. I used to stop the motor during the sermon. If it was a very long one I am afraid I started them too soon, for it was so easy to say to the protesting vicar, "Sorry, but I thought you were just finishing."

Hill Shop Book 4, p.56   All Saints Norfolk Square   job no.2160   1894
Gt CC-A   DD. Op i. Op ii. HohlFl. Prin. HarFl. 12. 15. Tr.
Sw CC-A   Bdn. Op. Sal. VCel [ten]C. RohrFl. Prin. Mix3.
                                    ConFag(large). Horn. Ob. Tremt.
Ch CC-A   Dul. Vl di G. Ged. SuabeFl. Clarnt.
Ped F   Open. Bdn. BassFl. Trombone slide.
Cplrs   Sw-Gt. Sw 8ve. Sw-Ch. 3 Ped [cplrs]
6 comps – Gt to act on Ped (direct mechanical action)
pneu to Gt   tubular drawstops & pedal touch
hydraulic blowing 20 to 55 lbs   no case

Detail from the Hill Shop Book 4, p. 56

About this time an incident occurred which I have never forgotten, for at that time I thought the bottom had dropped out of my world. In those days the music needed for the boys' rehearsals was carried to and from the Abbey by the boys themselves. It naturally suffered considerably in the process. After numerous tragedies, such as dropping the old first editions of Croft, Greene and Boyce in the mud and tearing the music, Bridge ordained that I should be responsible. This meant being present at the Abbey every day and having a large slice of my working hours eaten up. But I could not refuse. I was dependent on him to a large extent for any future advancement, and already owed him much for his kindness. Then came a day when I had a wedding to play with a good fee at All Saints. I got one of the other pupils to promise to "do librarian" for me at the Abbey, but he forgot, and there was no music put out for evensong. Next morning when I arrived Bridge said he never wished to see my face again, and would listen to no explanation. The situation was difficult because I could not explain without giving the other fellow away. I was dismissed, and can still recall my feelings of utter misery. But I went straight away to All Saints and did three hours solid practice on the organ, feeling much better at the end of it. I spent a few very miserable days, however, until Bridge, feeling that he had been hasty and unjust, took me back again.

I think it must have been 1895 when the cycling boom reached its zenith. Everyone rode a bicycle. My friend Dear and I looked down with contempt on all these mere fashion-followers and 'park wobblers'. We were old hands who thought nothing of sixty miles after lunch on a Saturday, and often rode the seventy-two miles to Portsmouth, caught the boat to Ryde and did the last and hardest twelve miles to Ventnor in the cool of the evening. Bridge caught the fever and bought a fine new bicycle. "But," said he, "I'm not going to learn on it. You must teach me on yours, Bairstow." Accordingly we started up and down the central drive in the Westminster College garden. There were two old stone statues at one end, and when he had reached the stage of being able to balance himself precariously, these statues acted on him like magnets. A triumphant career along the drive would end in a crash into one or the other. When I got home I found both the front forks cracked nearly through. Two pounds of my precious money went in replacing them. As a reward Bridge gave me a complimentary copy of the music to be sung at the Purcell bicentenary. I still have this, with the inscription, "To my master in cycling, from J. Frederick Bridge." I was also rewarded by being allowed to use his new and shining bicycle for some of our Saturday excursions.

The first mention of my doings in the public press had nothing to do with music, but with cycling. One day I was battling with a head wind down Parliament Street on my first clumsy bicycle that weighed forty pounds and had no brake, when just ahead of me a policeman held up his hand signalling me to stop. This I did easily. "Are you in a hurry?" he said, "Yes, I'm in a beastly hurry," said I, innocently, for, having been at the three o'clock evensong at Westminster, I had to go round to Novello's shop, then in Berners Street, and make All Saints before five. He took my name and address, and before long I was summoned to Bow Street. Before the magistrate he swore I was doing eighteen miles an hour! The magistrate asked me if I had any questions to ask the officer. Yes," I said. "How far from you was I when you first saw me?" "Twenty yards," said Robert. "Then how could I pull up in that distance on a heavy old bicycle without a brake?" But the magistrate said, "Fourteen shillings or a fortnight." When I paid the money to the clerk he said I should have got off cheaper if I had not delayed the court by asking questions. It turned out that an old woman had been knocked down in Parliament Street the day before my rencontre, and the police had been warned to stop anything like furious riding. The headline of the Star that evening was: "Paddington Organist in a beastly hurry."

Some of Lady Bridge's relations (Bridge was knighted in 1897) lived near Petworth in Sussex. A number of county folk in the district conceived the idea of forming a choral society. Bridge was asked to recommend a conductor and sent me. The prime movers were Lady Leconfield and Lady Bartelot (sic), and the rehearsals were held at their houses alternately, Petworth House and Stopham Hall. This was my first experience of conducting, of teaching people to sing, and my introduction to Society. All three – the technique of the baton, the knowledge of the voice, and manners – had to be picked up by the light of experience. The only attribute I could lay

Sir Edward, aged about 21, at Petworth

claim to was enthusiasm. Of this I had an unlimited supply. Having lived in London since 1889 I fondly imagined that I had lost all trace of North-Country speech. But at the close of the first rehearsal a curate who had been singing tenor came up to me and said, "You come from Yorkshire." "How do you know that?" I asked. "You said 'uz' instead of 'us'!" Nor could I deny it. When I travelled down from London to the rehearsals there was a change at Pulborough into a train with a funny little engine that puffed its leisurely way to Petworth station. The journey was not quite over even then, for the peer reigning at the time the railway was constructed would not allow it to come within sight of his mansion, and so the last mile or so was made in a queer little horse-drawn bus. It was a great thrill to see the wonderful Inigo Jones house, and to conduct rehearsals in the picture gallery with Turner's pictures of Petworth Park looking down from the walls. Some of the men in the choir came from an army coach's establishment at Storrington. They were supplemented by a few parsons. There were always plenty of women. They all got so keen that they would give up hunting to attend the rehearsals. Bridge told two of his wife's relations in the chorus that they would be asked to sing solos at the concerts. I backed up his subterfuge, and the two girls were kept in a state of trepidation for some weeks. It was strange that I at the age of twenty-one could make these people, so far above me in social station, stand up for hours and work very hard at learning the notes. It never occurred to me that they could do the preliminary practice sitting down. But stand up they did from 2.30 to 4.30 and seemed to enjoy it. The concerts took place at three places – Petworth, Pulborough and Storrington. Lord and Lady Leconfield gave hospitality to many people at these small festivals. I never stayed at the House, for the local doctor, who was also my first violin, used to put me up. Those who did described to me the old-world scene when the host and hostess, standing at the foot of the magnificent staircase, said good-night to the guests, each one of whom took a silver candlestick from a large table, and, lighting it, formed a picturesque procession upstairs.

I spent many an hour boiling down the full scores for the tiny orchestra, and writing out the missing parts for piano and harmonium, the latter being played by my friend Dick Dear. I remember on one occasion after a rehearsal at Pulborough we were proceeding in carriages and wagonettes to Storrington for the concert, when a motor-car made its appearance. One old dowager with a carriage-and-pair made the coachman get down from his seat, cover the horses' heads with a rug and lead them, whilst she clambered up on to the box and drove. All these good folks were kindness itself to me, often asking me for a meal, or putting me up for the night.

The Secretary was a keen musician and played the viola in the band. But he was somewhat vague and absent-minded. After the final concert, when I was leaving London and could no longer conduct, the choir gave me a silver sovereign purse and a present of money. The leading soprano made a pretty little speech and handed me a small parcel. This I naturally began to open. But frantic signs were made to me, so I put it in my pocket and returned thanks. Afterwards I was told it contained nothing but brown paper, the Secretary having given the order for it too late. When it did arrive my initials were engraved on it, but in the wrong order.

The two outstanding occasions at the Abbey during my time there were the Purcell Bi-centenary in 1895 and Gladstone's funeral in 1898. Partly because Purcell was one of our greatest musicians and partly because he was organist of Westminster Abbey, Bridge quite rightly determined that his bi-centenary should be suitably celebrated. A Purcell anthem was sung every week during the year (not many of them appeared after that) and a great service was held in the Abbey in the Spring. Some time before this a man had appeared out of the blue with what turned out to be the original manuscript of the great Te Deum and Jubilate that Purcell wrote for St. Cecilia's day. This had been sung previously to a mutilated version edited by William Boyce. He, like many another editor even until recent years, eliminated many of Purcell's prophetic discords, just as he did with some of the anthems which appear in his collection of Cathedral music. He also inserted some passages of his own. Bridge was a man who, after he had embarked on an undertaking, never left a stone unturned to bring it to a successful fruition. The Te Deum and all the great anthems were sung as Purcell wrote them with full orchestra, first-rate soloists and an excellent choir.

Gladstone's funeral gave me a grand opportunity of seeing a host of celebrated personages, for I was one of the choir stewards. The choir was a union of all the most celebrated London choirs, together with St. George's Chapel, Windsor. It was drawn up in two long lines in the nave. Between these lines passed a long procession of royalties, peers and commons. Finally the choir preceded the coffin, carried by renowned bearers, into the sanctuary. The wonderfully solemn yet simple burial sentences of William Croft (1678-1727) sung unaccompanied by that great choir impressed me very deeply. Although I have heard them scores of times since it was this performance before this vast and representative congregation that made the greatest impression.

The music at the Abbey during the time I worked there was a curious mixture. The majority of the great treasures of the Tudor composers were unknown, for there had been no modern reprints of them. Those that had been included in Boyce's collection were sung, but in the keys in which they were written, for no-one seemed to have discovered that Elizabethan pitch was higher than contemporary pitch. These anthems and services (Gibbons in F, for instance) were sung at the same strength and pace throughout, with all Boyce's bowdlerisms. Naturally they were regarded by all of us as very dull and inexpressive. We admired the counterpoint but felt them to be partly a penance and partly a duty. Post-restoration and Georgian music was well represented and well sung, but there was no discrimination. For instance, large numbers of anthems by Greene and others were included, with florid solos, duets and trios, most of which were poor copies of Handel. I remember one afternoon at evensong, when a somewhat aged male alto was warbling through one of these solos with a little-falsetto-pipe of a voice. A pigeon got in through one of the clear-story (sic) windows and fluttered down, fascinated I suppose by the cooing of the soloist. It perched on the glass candle shade just in front of him, and cocking its head on one side, looked up at him as if to say, "How does he do it?" This was too much for the soloist, who collapsed.

To return to the repertory, there were large excerpts from English nineteenth-century oratorios which were not really anthems at all, and most of them, like Sullivan's "Light of the world", never ought to have seen the light of the world. Then there was a great quantity of contemporary music without distinction, punctiliously conventional, and often sentimental to a degree. No-one seemed to feel the incongruity when, for instance, the service was a pretentious and noisy effusion, perhaps composed by a vulgar and showy London organist, and the anthem was one of Purcell's greatest inspirations.

Some years before I left London I determined to live with my friend Dick Dear in some very comfortable rooms we found in West Hampstead just opposite the church of St. James where Dick had recently been appointed organist. I did this partly because my father's house was so far from my work, and partly because my mother spoiled me. For instance, if I left a room grossly untidy in the morning, when I came home in the evening it had been straightened and not a word was said. At Hampstead, I was obliged to be tidy for the sake of the other man. The Saturday evening before Dick's first Sunday at St. James's he went in to practise the organ, when to his dismay two pedals stuck down. He had the address of the organ-tuner in Camden Town, and dashed off on his bicycle to find him. But Saturday night is not a likely time to find an organ

tuner beside his own hearth, and it was some time before Dick
discovered the particular hostelry he affected. A good deal of persuasion was needed before he would turn out. Late at night he
arrived at St. James's and pulled a piece of chalk from between the
two offending pedals which at once sprung up and worked
normally. Language then flew thick and fast. The moral is, of
course, that an elementary knowledge of organ mechanism is a
useful thing for an organist.

Life in London in those days was very pleasant. There was
plenty of work for Bridge and at All Saints, together with daily piano
and organ practice, youthful efforts at composition and a little
teaching. The bicycle provided most of the recreation. We were
experts, and could ride along the tram-lines on a wet night rather
than jolt over the rough stone setts forming the paving of the road.
Distances of over a hundred miles did not tire us unduly: we saw
a great deal of beautiful country. But this pleasant life was leading
nowhere. There was a church at the corner of every street; organists were as common as leaves in autumn. Bridge was anxious that
I should go to High Wycombe, where his brother-in-law had a
school. I went to spy out the land (on a wet day) and thought the
place would turn out to be a backwater. In fact another pupil who
took the post instead of me stayed for many years and died there.

One morning in the spring of 1899, when I reached the Abbey,
Bridge took me on one side and said, "Bairstow, there is a post
going in the provinces which would just suit you." "Where is it, Sir
Frederick?" said I. "Wigan," said he. Before I could express an
opinion, he said, "Let's see; the living of Wigan is in the gift of the
Bridgeman family. Now I know a Bridgeman in the Colonial Office.
He'll know all about it. I'll give you a note to him." Before 9.30
a.m. I was on my way to the Colonial Office and it was only a short
time after that I journeyed to Wigan to interview the Rector at his
request, and was very soon appointed organist of the old parish
church. All this was typical of Bridge. He may not have been a wonderful composer, conductor or organist, but he had his oar in and
had begun to pull before the other fellow had made up his mind.
(*The musical adviser in choosing the man for the post was Sir Walter
Parratt of St. George's Chapel, Windsor.*)

Bridge gave a dinner to the various assistants and pupils in my honour by way of farewell. As usual, he did the occasion proud; it was a first-rate dinner and a very happy evening. I little thought that day that in years to come I should visit the old house in the Little Cloisters as a guest of my own pupil who was to be organist of Westminster Abbey. Bridge taught me a great deal outside music, but not much of music itself. Dear Walter Alcock taught me the organ splendidly, I have always been unfeignedly thankful to him for his precept and example. Russell taught me harmony and counterpoint in a rigid, unmusical way. The rest I picked up for myself.

(James Richard Dear – 1872–1953 – became organist of St. Saviour's church, Eastbourne, and later of St. Peter's. As well as the chants mentioned on page 101, music for the Pevensey Pageant and Songs of the Open air, *he composed a* Communion Service in F, *a work of character which was for many years in the York repertoire during Bairstow's time.)*

Manhood

"I am the master of my fate,
I am the captain of my soul."

WHAT A CONTRAST TO London! I had taken on the rooms of
my predecessor, C.H. Moody, now (1945) and for the last
forty years organist of Ripon Cathedral. In Hampstead we had as
landlady a woman who had been a servant in a good family. She
was not voluble, knew how to set a table and how to wait, and
studied our needs. At Wigan in the evening of the day of my arrival
I was trying to get my sitting room straight when in comes my landlady inquiring as to the identity of a girl whose photograph I was
just placing on the mantelpiece. She was a school friend of my
sister's and was herself a schoolmistress. "You young men should
be very careful of school teachers and girls in the post office," says
the landlady, "they'll entangle you if they can." She had five sons
and three daughters and no doubt spoke from bitter experience.
They all lived at home with the exception of one married son. How
they all crammed into that little house I don't know, for I had the
two best rooms. The husband was a clever harness-maker.
Unfortunately he changed every few months from a somewhat
pedantic critic of other men's vices to a dipsomaniac for a week or
two. His employer always took him back when he was sober again
because he was such a good craftsman. The landlady kept everything as clean as a new pin, and the whole family was kindness itself
to me. But the food left a good deal to be desired and badly upset
my digestion. When the family had a joint I had a cut from it, but

in the ordinary way someone was sent out in a hurry to the little shop round the corner to buy something that did not require cooking. High tea took the place of the pleasant dinners we enjoyed at Hampstead.

I arrived at Wigan in May, 1899. At first, of course, I had nothing to do except church work. This left me very short of money but gave me time to work for the final examination for Mus.D. at Durham, my 'Exercise', a setting of the psalm, 'By the waters of Babylon' having satisfied the examiners just before I left London. I was so short of money that one day towards the end of the quarter I found I had only a few shillings in my pocket. Then I bethought me of an old cash-box upstairs, opened it and found a ten shilling piece. Looking back it has often occurred to me that I was just as happy in my impecunious state as I was later when things were easier. In fact, my experience has always been that money is the root of all evil, and hard work the panacea for all ills. As regards the examination, again I hurried it too much, for what with moving and settling down I had not really enough time to work hard enough to obtain the facility and speed necessary. To make matters worse, when the time came to go to Durham I had a very heavy cold and was in poor form. So I came down again. Just think of a future professor of the University having two shots at both his bachelor's and doctor's examinations! But I was not discouraged in the least and made sure of the degree the next year.

Things now began to get busy. I was appointed conductor of the Choral Society. It was not a very satisfactory chorus. There were many old ladies with worn-out voices and the repertory consisted of all the old, oft-repeated classics – Messiah, Elijah, St. Paul and Creation. There was a committee meeting at which the conductor humbly suggested something fresh. But whether it was in my time or whether Dr. Moody told me the story I cannot remember. At all events a member jumped up and said, "I propose we 'ave *Judus Mickawbus*". One old lady complained to me of my somewhat blunt manner at rehearsal. "Well," said I, "the members of the last choral society that I conducted were all drawn from the nobility and gentry of the county. If my manners were good enough for them they ought to be good enough for you."

The secretary told me a good story of an orchestral society which existed before my time, and, I believe, worked with the Choral Society. Their efforts were damned by a second trumpet, an amateur who contributed liberally to the upkeep. On one occasion he was unusually noisy and uncertain. The secretary was determined that the concert should not be spoiled by him. The platform in the Drill Hall was put up for each concert. The planks were not quite close together. After the rehearsal the secretary just popped the second trumpet parts between two planks. They were never found until the platform was dismantled. The amateur trumpet never played a note!

In the end we disbanded the Choral Society and formed the Wigan Philharmonic with a fresh young chorus, all of whose powers were tested before admission. There was an inaugural dinner at which the chairman of committee wound up his speech proposing the health of the new Society in these words: "May the Wigan Philharmonic Society prosper for many years in harmony and *euphonium.*" It did. The chorus was keen and efficient. We had a contingent from the great Hallé orchestra to accompany the concerts and to play orchestral music. This was my first experience of conducting professional players. The occasions that are still fresh in my memory are a performance of Messiah with Santley as the bass, and my first meeting with Harry Plunket Greene. What an artist Santley was! Although he must have been about seventy then he sang with marvellous poise, economy, dignity and authority. I was overjoyed because he complimented me on taking the music at the right pace – four beats instead of eight whenever possible. How many times have I quoted my dear old mother to pupils, "If a thing is quick enough done it is well enough done". My introduction to Harry Plunket Greene took place at a concert without orchestra. The programme consisted of part-songs for the choir and a song recital from H.P.G. I had never before heard singing like this; so full of rhythmic vitality, with such wonderful musical and textual insight, and with such perfectly clear, absolutely natural and very significant speech.

After the concert we adjourned to a friend's house. The conversation drifted into the subject of incidents at public concerts. Somebody said, "What was the most terrible moment you have ever experienced?" The accompanist, Theodore Flint, said that he was playing at a gala night at the Albert Hall at which the Prince of Wales and some foreign royalties were present. Clara Butt received a tremendous ovation, and for her recall handed Flint a copy of "The Lost Chord", asking him to transpose it a semitone lower. This, of course was a mere nothing to him, but when he turned over the first leaf he found that the whole of the middle part was missing. However he played it through from memory in an unfamiliar key. H.P.G.'s story was of a west-country festival, where, amongst other things, he had to sing the bass solos in a none too easy Bach cantata. The arias had been rehearsed with the orchestra, but not the recitatives, which were accompanied either on the piano or organ. After the performance had begun he found that two pages of his copy had stuck together. He pulled them apart to discover a very difficult recitative which he had to read at sight! H.P.G. came again soon after that to a similar concert, when he sang Stanford's "Songs of the Sea". This time he brought with him as accompanist Hamilton Harty, then just rising to fame in London. He had been organist to Boyd at All Saints for a short time till he found his feet. There was only one concert grand in Wigan and that was tuned to the old high pitch, impossible for H.P.G. I therefore got a smaller grand as well at low pitch. When we came to rehearse, H.P.G. found that the smaller grand was ineffectual in the long, thin Drill Hall. "Transpose everything a semitone down, Ham," said he, "and play on the big piano." Harty never turned a hair or made a mistake so far as I know. I turned over for him so that I was quite able to detect any slips. The first song on the programme was Schubert's *Litanei*. H.P.G.'s snag was pitch, and the *Litanei* was distinctly flat. But even so he held that vast audience spell-bound through his intense sincerity and personal magnetism. He was so loyal to his friends that he would never lose faith in them until their failings became obvious and unmistakeable. Even then he harboured no ill-will. Early in his career he got into the hands of a German teacher of singing who did not perceive that his vast temperamental energy was a dangerous weapon, but let him force his voice till it lost its freshness. H.P.G. was gullible and curiously at the mercy of cranks and quacks. Many years later he let one of these men give him some sort of electric-ray treatment for a bad throat. He very nearly lost his voice for good and all. His friends wanted him to prosecute the man. But not he. "Poor chap, he meant well," said H.P.G., or words to that effect. The disease which killed him might have been prevented if he had been operated on earlier. But again he was relying on a man who said no operation was necessary.

The Wigan Parish Church was a joy to me. I had never before been connected with a church which was fully alive, where all the clergy were such sincere Christians that they would work themselves to the bone. There were four curates, three of whom, Henry Gunning, W.E.Kingsbury and Edgar Rogers, were exceptional men, each capable of running a big parish, and all full of love for their neighbour. The consequence was that the church was full. The inspiration of the clergy affected everyone. There was no lack of church workers and no lack of work for them to do. The sermons may not always have been free from platitudes, but they were full of simple, gospel truth and were delivered with burning sincerity. The choir was the same. Some of the men were rough and needed a lot of taming, but all were full of zeal. For instance, it was the custom on Sunday morning after service for the choir to come back to rehearse for Sunday evensong. When there was a plain celebration of Holy Communion an adjournment was made to the Parish School, but if the Communion service had been choral then the choir came back to their stalls to practise. One Easter Day there were so many communicants that it was nearly one o'clock before service was over. I said nothing but waited to see what would happen. Every single man and boy came back without any fuss, though it must have meant that the Sunday dinner would spoil.

The Rector of Wigan in those days was Canon Matthew. He was an intellectual type of parson, very unemotional but a sincere Christian. Unfortunately for him and for us he was tone-deaf and could not distinguish between 'God save the King' and 'Rule Britannia'; in fact, music was pain and grief to him. During the Anthems and Services he stood first on one leg and then on the other and peered over the choirboy's shoulder in front of him to see how much longer he had to endure. His wife was fond of music and used to ask me in to dinner to play to her afterwards. But the Rector would say, "I have a confirmation class in about half an hour; you can play when I go out." The custom at Wigan was that services were sung to the canticles on alternate Sundays, Te Deum and Benedictus one Sunday and Magnificat and Nunc Dimittis the next. There was an anthem at Evensong every Sunday and a Choral Eucharist once a month and on festivals. The Rector would very much have liked to cut this down, and we had some fairly heated arguments about it. Last of all I said, "Well, Rector, if you wanted some advice on stained glass windows you would not go to a man who was colour-blind for it." After I left Wigan a friend of mine, calling at the Hall which was the Rectory, asked the Rector what sort of a man the new organist was. "At any rate he is not another Bairstow," said he thankfully.

The church was the only dignified and beautiful building in the town. It was perpendicular gothic with a more ancient square tower protruding from the north-east end of the nave, the lowest storey being open to the nave. Before I went to Wigan the Rector and Wardens had conceived a wild notion to stuff the organ under this tower. Old Father Willis, the great organ builder was consulted. He arrived one day at 2 p.m. and inspected the proposed organ chamber. He then asked the Rector and Wardens whether they had made up their minds to move the organ. They said they were determined. "Will no persuasion alter your decision?" said Willis. "Nothing," said they. So off went Willis back to London on the 2.30 train. Another less scrupulous firm was called in; the organ was moved. In a short time it had to be put back to its previous position on the north side of the choir, for, as Willis had told them, it was smothered and cramped under the tower.

The Rector's Warden in my time was a certain Colonel ffarington, a very kindly soul who stood about five feet nothing in his shoes, but was as straight as a die. Just after I arrived was the Wigan general holiday on which for many years the Colonel had given the choirmen a treat. It began in a saloon on Wigan station about 7 a.m. Into one end of this was packed a mighty hamper. The saloon was tacked on to the end of the Windermere train and we started our day. Meat pies and champagne at that early hour were a novelty to me. Penny nap was then indulged in till we arrived at Windermere, where we had a colossal breakfast at Rigg's Hotel. Then a coach and four drew up to take us to Grasmere or Coniston.

Half way there the hamper was again broached. This time bread and cheese and whiskies and sodas were dealt round. Having arrived at their destination the men would go for a walk, or go fishing on the lake. Then we had tea and drove back to Windermere for a table d'hôte dinner at Rigg's, each man being given a half-bottle of claret. On the way home the hamper was again requisitioned to drink the colonel's health in the champagne that was left. After a year or two the clergy stepped in, and the amount of liquor consumed was considerably cut down. Most of the men were great big strong fellows who could stow away an amazing lot without showing anything. But there were others to whom drink was a temptation and who were half-seas-over before the day was out.

The organ at Wigan was a large, three-manual Hill. Before I arrived it had got into a bad state of repair, and Moody, my predecessor, had got schemes and estimates for its restoration from a few firms of organ builders. I felt that the longer it was left the more money would have to be spent, and was allowed to meet the Rector and Wardens to talk over the situation. Colonel ffarington said, "I would not dream of having a single pipe of our dear old organ touched," evidently thinking that an organ was like a violin and

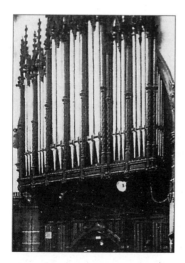

The organ at Wigan Church

Colonel ffarington, V.D.,
Churchwarden

improved with age. "Just a moment, Colonel," said I, and hopping up into the organ I came down with a shapeless pipe, the metal very soft. I believe I squeezed it a little more out of shape on the way down, but, at any rate, it did the trick. The work was put into the hands of Norman and Beard, who made a fine, dignified instrument out of it which satisfied everyone, myself included.*

I used to play after evensong every Sunday during the seven years I was there, and a large number of people used to enjoy these little organ recitals. It was the same later on at Leeds. But lately, at York, people walk about the Minster and make such a noise that the few who want to listen cannot do so in comfort. We have therefore given up the time-honoured Voluntary, for I shall never countenance the degradation of all the great organ music to the status of a restaurant orchestra – a background of music which you cannot help hearing, but cannot listen to. Some clergy and organists cannot bear a silence; they fill every gap with a hymn, or with extemporary organ playing of no musical value. This is done presumably because silences are supposed to lead to distraction. Personally, if I attend a Choral Eucharist, a silence is refreshing, and the following music gets a better chance by reason of the great contrast. The most distracting things to me are the restless movements of the priests, acolytes and servers, accompanied by many genuflexions that to most people are meaningless. The other thing that annoys me at these services is the common habit of many clergy of muttering the words of the service. It certainly can be argued that the congregation have the words before them in the prayer book, or know them so well that they can follow. On the other hand it goes without saying that we should give of our best to God, and that mumble-jumble of telescoped syllables is not by any means our best, but is associated in our minds with careless conversation. The words of the great hymns and canticles of the church are well-known to all, but what would it sound like if the choir adopted the diction of the priest! The commonest place for this murmuring is

---

* E.C.B. related to H.P. Dixon (Yorkshire Evening Post, March 17th 1944) how an old man was heard to say, "Weel, I cannot see that it's made much difference in eawr organ. On Sunday it were so soft you couldn't 'ear it, and as for th' choir, they're getten worse. Why! th'other day they all broke deawn except one chap, and he went on by himsel'!"

at the actual consecration of the elements. Everyone knows that here the priest is performing a function no one else is qualified for. This always suggests to me the magician muttering incantations into a pot. Since I have been at York we have had three great archbishops, Lord Lang, Dr William Temple and Dr Garbett. Not one of them ever whispered, or muttered the end of the prayer of consecration, or any other part of the service. In the far distant organ loft every syllable was audible.

Moody told me that a large part of my work at Wigan would consist of giving solo-singing lessons. I was determined to prepare myself for this, so read a few books and discussed the question with various singers. After some time I felt I had got a grip of the subject and accepted a singing pupil. But she happened to be a freak. She had quite a pleasant head voice which petered out about B flat on the middle line of the treble stave. Below that she used a horrible, forced, rasping chest voice that sounded as if it came from another person – more like a man than a woman. This absolutely dumbfounded me. I did not know of a remedy. Since then in forty years I have only had one or two women with no middle voice, and even they had not the ugly chest notes. It was very bad luck that an exceptional case like this should be my first pupil. But at any rate I could do her no harm even if I did her no good.

Despite my unhappy habit of calling a spade a spade, I seemed to be getting work to do as a choral and orchestral conductor. My first outside job was at a village about four miles from Wigan. The first two miles could be covered in an old steam tramway, very wobbly and rickety, for it was just before the Wigan Town Council took over the line and electrified it. The local doctor ran the Choral Society, and the compensation for the two-mile walk on a wet or snowy night was the excellent dinner awaiting me at his house. He was a connoisseur of drinks. On his sideboard were curiously-shaped bottles of every liqueur you could think of and some you had never heard of. The smoothest burgundy, or claret, or hock was served with dinner. Nothing pleased the doctor better than hauling into the dining-room a collier or farm lad who had called for medicine, and giving him a benedictine. Never having tasted one before, it was tossed off in one gulp. Then came a violent splutteration which convulsed the doctor into fits of laughter. The work for the concert had been chosen before my advent: it was Bennett's 'May Queen'. The chorus make their entry at the end of a rapid upward scale. This was played several times by the accompanist before a sound issued from the chorus, for they were shy of the new conductor. After numerous rehearsals I got it more or less ship-shape and the day of the concert approached. The committee insisted on engaging the singers and the Wigan theatre orchestra. We rehearsed all the afternoon trying to smooth down the rough-nesses. I remember how whenever there was a long note for strings they insisted on playing it with a tremolo. After the rehearsal the band and the male soloists adjourned to an hotel. When they appeared for the concert they were all more or less tipsy, especially the bass soloist, who announced that "he wasn't going to sing with that bloody old cow," referring to the soprano, the May Queen, who was fat and middle-aged. This was certainly the most nerve-racking concert I have ever conducted. My wife (we were engaged in those days) says that this was the only occasion on which she has seen me merry, for, before we went back to Wigan we went to the jolly doctor's who opened some champagne, of which I drank freely.

Edith Harriet Hobson, to whom I was engaged to be married, was the daughter of a widow who had come to Wigan so that her son could be apprenticed to a firm of mining engineers. We were absolutely suited to each other. She was very musical, very athletic, playing hockey and tennis, and she was intensely interested in my work. In 1902 we were married in the Old Parish Church. Looking back over those forty-three years, I marvel at the way she has put up with my idiosyncrasies and worse. A musician is often a diffi-cult person to live with. He is apt to be engrossed in his work, and is therefore not much good in the house. At times he is touchy and moody. At this moment I am recovering very slowly from a bad illness and have been confined to my bed for some weeks. My wife has nursed me much of the time, bringing up all my meals. At the same time she has had all the shopping to do, including waiting in queues. All this at the age of sixty-nine with only one servant in a big house! Naturally I am worrying to be back at work; she calms and cheers me. A wife like this supplies the deficiencies of her husband. Look through the fugues of Bach and note the counter-subjects. A solid, slow moving-subject has a bright, quickly-moving counter-subject, and *vice versa*. Sometimes the counter-subject dominates the whole fugue and the subject is never allowed to appear without her. Sometimes she disappears altogether and a younger and more sprightly counter-theme takes her place. Sometimes both the old *hausfrau* and the new and lively one run in triple harness! Truly J.S.B. gives you many types of married life, good and bad. He had a long experience of it.

One more aspect of our long married life before we go back to Wigan! My time has been so fully occupied that my wife has had far more to do with the upbringing of our three children than I have. One word she never used to them, nor would she allow a nurse to use it. That word was "shy". Their lack of any hint of self-consciousness must have saved them from many a miserable hour, as well as making them much more friendly and useful to all around them.

In the parish magazine of May 1904 the Rector congratulated the Bairstows on the birth of a son and heir and ventured 'to express the hope in musical phrase that their new Vox Humana *will develop into a* Vox Angelica.'

To return to my work outside Wigan: I conducted for a while at Southport, but not with much success. The choir was rather like the old Wigan Choral Society – long in the tooth and not very enterprising. Soon after that, in 1903, I was invited to conduct the Blackburn St. Cecilia and Vocal Union. In some ways this Society has always seemed to me to be the ideal of all the various choirs I have conducted. The Committee was a band of brothers who came from just the right class – the energetic business men of the town (*see letter to Wolstenholme of August 1903, on p.50*). The meetings were held at their houses after rehearsals. Hospitality was provided in the way of excellent Stilton cheese and whiskies and sodas. I remember after one meeting seeing the chairman sitting on the front steps weeping and complaining that the other members had not supported him properly, which was true in more senses than one. The enthusiasm of these men was so great that they had an unwritten law ordaining that the man who obtained the fewest new subscribers in one season should stand the others a dinner at the end of it. Much of the time at the meetings was spent in comparing notes in order to beat up any who did not subscribe. One man would say, "Who are these Sykeses that have come to live in Aspidistra Avenue?" Another would reply, "Oh, I know all about them; I'll go and look them up." The old Corn Exchange at Blackburn was not an ideal place for a concert. The roof leaked, and we were so crowded together on the platform that on one occasion my bâton pierced the bun of hair on the contralto's head. I nipped it out just as the hairpins began to show that it was not her own. But the hall was just the right size for this vigorous committee to fill with subscribers who all paid one rate – one guinea for three seats. The advantage of this system was that as the Committee knew the size of their cloth, they could cut their coat accordingly.

The Hallé orchestra (not all of it) was invariably engaged. At first they were difficult, especially one or two old foreigners who considered me fair game for any leg-pulling. Once, after a rehearsal, they delivered through their leader a round robin signed by all of them, saying that if my language were less strong I should get better results. I had told them that they were careless and would not take the trouble for me that they would for Dr Richter. I pointed out that this was not honest, for they were given the fees they asked for; nor was it the way of the artist, whose love for the music called forth his best efforts. That night they played better for me than ever before, so that after the concert I was able to reply to the round robin to the effect that my talk seemed to have done more good than harm.

Of course such a concert society as the St. Cecilia would have been impossible in a town without a big hall. It became so in Blackburn later on. Nor would it have been right, for it would fail to supply the greatest possible number of the population with good music. But to have a committee who are all good friends to each other and to music, and who will work hard to enlarge the all-important subscribers' list, is not impossible anywhere.

I loved the Blackburn crowd so much that I still kept the conductorship when I went to Leeds, and only gave it up when I became master of the music at York Minster in 1913. The lovely old grandfather clock given me when I left is ticking away in the drawing-room close to me as I write, reminding me of many happy times. I append two press notices which are interesting. The first

is from the Manchester Guardian for December 12, 1907. It is by
F. Bonavia:-

'Brahms' Requiem was the *pièce de résistance* at the concert given
by the Blackburn St. Cecilia and Vocal Union last night. ... In the
bars which conclude the first half of the chorus, "Behold all flesh
is as the grass", the voices blended so beautifully that one had for
the moment the illusion of hearing an organ with human throats
instead of pipes. ... The orchestra played admirably.'

The other is from the Blackburn Weekly Telegraph for April 1,
1911. I cannot recall the name of the dear old man who wrote the
criticisms in this paper. He was a great enthusiast, and head-and-
shoulders above the average local critic:-

'Nearly six years have elapsed since Elgar's 'Dream of
Gerontius' was given by the St. Cecilia and Vocal Union. The
oratorio was then only in the early stage of that widespread appreciation it has since so deservedly won. ... Praise of work done by
the St. Cecilia has a familiar ring in the course of years, and yet to
all that has been said before must be added full and deserved compliments upon last night's performance, which was worthy of its
great theme. ... The chorus has rarely acquitted itself with greater
success. The spiritual solemnity and mystery of that which they
sang was fully expressed in all their work.'

In those days Elgar's orchestral writing for the chorus in the
'Dream' was entirely a novelty, and was felt to be impossible of
achievement by many chorus singers. At Blackburn in 1905 it cost
us a whole season's horse-work, which did not even then result in
a first-rate performance. But, having once broken the ice and
proved that the difficulties were not insoluble, the second performance, recorded above was a delight to audience, chorus and
conductor.

Our first baby, Stephen, was born in 1904. But even before that
I had begun to realise that Wigan was only a stepping-stone. It has
been a good one, and has turned out quite an unusual number of
cathedral organists:- Langdon Colborne (Hereford), Sir Walter
Parratt (St.George's Windsor), Dr Moody (Ripon), Edgar
Robinson (Choirmaster at Liverpool) and myself. By this time
'Bidie's' elder son, George Stuart Robertson, had become a fellow

of New College, Oxford. The organist's post fell vacant and, entirely owing to him, I was put into the short list. I went up to play a service, and afterwards dined in hall. After dinner we adjourned to the fellows' common room. Being winter time we sat in a semi-circle round the fire. A double-inclined plane of mahogany was placed across the hearth; one decanter went up and another slid down. No one needed to get up! I was not to see this piece of furniture again for over forty years, but more of this anon. Afterwards I received a letter from the Warden, the celebrated Dr Spooner, saying that the New College authorities had nothing to choose musically between Dr Hugh Allen, of Ely Cathedral, and myself, but that they naturally preferred a man of their own University. I immediately wrote asking if I could use this letter as a testimonial, and Dr Spooner graciously consented. I then applied for the post Dr Allen was leaving at Ely. I played evensong in the cathedral and spent the night at the deanery. But I don't think the Dean liked me. He asked me if I knew anyone at Cambridge. (Ely being so close, the Cambridge musicians came over and helped at musical functions). I'm afraid I said to the Dean that if a man was a good Christian and efficient at his job it did not seem to me to matter whether he knew people at Cambridge or whether he didn't. Calling a spade a spade again. What a lovely place is Ely! The great church with its wonderful octagonal tower; the green lawns and the old trees. But how quiet! Just a few thousand people and the common name 'Gotobed'.

And so back to Wigan and the 'daily round, the common task'. Nothing happened of moment until 1905. In early August of that year my wife and I and our little Stephen went to London to leave the latter with my parents who now lived at Kennington close to the Oval. We and my old friend Dick Dear and his wife had hired a wherry for a fortnight on the Norfolk Broads. The next day I dropped into the Oval, and, at the tea interval, bought an evening paper. Right at the foot of a column was a small, insignificant paragraph saying that the post of organist at Leeds Parish Church was vacant. My father's cousin, A.W. Bairstow, afterwards Judge Bairstow, lived there. I wrote to him for particulars. Next morning I went up to the Abbey to see Sir Frederick Bridge and met him just coming out of the Cloister into Dean's Yard. He hailed me with, "I know what you've come about. It's Leeds Parish Church. But you wouldn't have a chance. My old pupil Fricker, the Town Hall Organist, will get it." (Bridge, sharp as ever.) "No", I said, "I didn't come for a testimonial, I came to see you. But I did see the little paragraph in the paper last night." Then we set off for the Broads and enjoyed one of the jolliest holidays I ever spent. We were to pick up our letters at Potter Heigham. The Wherry was moored about a mile away. We followed a circuitous path to the post office. Coming back we thought it would be quicker to cut straight across what looked to us like a field to the spot where we could see the mast of the Wherry. We had not seen the dykes which intersected our field. We jumped some, but they got broader, and the last one – close to the Wherry, was more than I could tackle. A boy of about 18 of our party essayed to leap, but I saw his face change expression just as he took off. He went plop into the middle of black stinking mud. We made him strip and bathe in the river. His flannels took a deal of washing.

It is queer how an incident like this remains vividly photographed on the brain. Probably I remember it because I got a letter from A. W. Bairstow giving a rosy picture of Leeds and its music. I therefore applied at once for the post, putting in Dr Spooner's letter. I heard nothing for more than a month and began to despair of getting into the short list. Then Stephen fell ill and there followed a time of anxiety. One wet autumn night I returned from a hard rehearsal at Blackburn, tired out and dispirited, to find smiles on Stephen's little face and a letter from Leeds asking me to go for a week-end to play Saturday evensong followed by a rehearsal of the choir and the full Sunday services. How often the darkest hour precedes the dawn!

In those days H.C.Embleton, a mining engineer, reputed to be a millionaire, took the greatest interest in the Leeds Parish Church music. He was very generous with his money; and one cannot blame him, as he paid the piper, for wanting to call the tune. When the eventful week-end arrived for my trial, I found that he had engaged for me a suite at the Queen's Hotel with sitting-room, bedroom and bathroom. What with the excitement of taking choir practice and the importance to me of the services on the following day, plus the noise of the trams crashing over the junctions just outside, I got very little sleep in my sumptuous quarters. I was much impressed with the choir. The principal tenor and bass, Henry Brearley and John Browning, were well-known professional singers, and some of the other men were semi-professional. There were thirty boys and thirty men in the choir. Wesley's 'Wilderness' was the anthem at evensong and, having carefully rehearsed it, it went very well. Afterwards I played a few pieces and then had to walk out of the church between two lines of curious people. What an interest everyone took in the prospective new organist! In those days I paid a press-cutting company to send my mother anything that concerned me. She pasted these in two old scrap-books which I still keep. The number of interviews and accounts of my career which appeared in the Leeds papers at the time of the trial, and later when I was appointed, is remarkable. In 1906 there was, of course, no wireless and only a primitive phonograph. The only first-rate performances of music to be heard were at the Leeds Festivals, or at infrequent concerts given by touring orchestras, and at the concerts of the Leeds Philharmonic Society. There was some excuse for organists playing arrangements of orchestral music in those days, for that was the only chance people got of hearing the music. The average amateur had not discovered the limitations of an organ – its lack of expression – its insensitive touch – and they were still carried away by the effects only to be obtained on it – its extreme dynamic range from the most ethereal pianissimo to a thunderous fortissimo, and, if it were an organ of large resources, by its varied colours. In these days, when the radio and the gramophone have brought all the greatest orchestral works into the home, people have discovered that the organ cannot hold a candle to the orchestra. I suppose this is the reason why in 1905 crowds of people listened to the voluntaries on Sunday evenings, but in 1945 only a few enthusiasts stay for them.

I had three months' notice to give at Wigan and went to Leeds in January 1906. Years later the Precentor, the Revd. Morris Hodson, told me that the Leeds Committee found two men for their short list without much difficulty. *(There were 320 aspirants)*. In looking through the applications to find a third, they accidentally came across Dr Spooner's letter to me. Dr Bickersteth, the Vicar, knew him well and wrote to him. Finding that all was

H. Bacon Smith, Henry Brearley,
Murray Lambert, E.C.B., Elsie Suddaby

SPECIFICATION OF THE ORGAN AS RE-BUILT
BY MESSRS. NORMAN AND BEARD, 1902.

GREAT ORGAN.	SWELL ORGAN.	CHOIR AND SOLO ORGANS.	PEDAL ORGAN.
*1. Double Diapason 16ft.	19. Bourdon ... ... 16ft.		*34. Sub Bass... ... 32ft.
2. Open „ ... 8ft.	†20. Open Diapason ... 8ft.	(In Swell Box, except Tuba.)	35. Open Diapason
3. Open „ ... 8ft.	*21. Salicional... ... 8ft.	*11. Tuba (on 7in. wind) 8ft.	(Wood) ... ... 16ft.
*4. Holt Flute ... 8ft.	*22. Rohe Flute ... 8ft.	12. Dulciana ... ... 8ft.	36. Open Diapason
5. Harmonic Flute ... 4ft.	23. Voix Angelica ... 8ft.	13. Harmonic Flute ... 8ft.	(Metal) ... ... 16ft.
6. Principle ... 4ft.	*24. Leiblich Flute ... 4ft.	*14. Leiblich Gedact ... 8ft.	37. Bourdon ... ... 16ft.
7. Twelth.	†25. Principle ... ... 4ft.	*15. Gamba ... ... 8ft.	38. Principle ... ... 8ft.
8. Fifteenth ... ... 2ft.	26. Fifteenth ... 2ft.	*16. Suabe Flute ... 4ft.	*39. Bass Flute ... 8ft.
9. Mixture ... 3 ranks.	27. Mixture ... 3 ranks.	17. Clarionet ... ... 8ft.	†40. Contra Posaune 16ft.
*10. Trumpet ... ... 8ft.	*28. Oboe ... ... 8ft.	18. Orchestral Oboe ... 8ft.	
	†*29. Horn ... ... 8ft.		
	†*30. Contra Fagotto ... 16ft.	* New Stops. † On heavy wind.	
	*31. Vox Humana ... 8ft.		
	†*32. Clarion ... ... 4ft.		
	33. Tremulant.		

Specification of the Wigan organ as re-built by Messrs. Norman
& Beard, 1902

satisfactory I was put into the last three – *along with Dr. C.H.Kitson, later to become organist of Christ Church Cathedral in Dublin and Professor of Music in the university; and J.E.Atkins of Preston Parish Church.*

There was at Wigan a worthy man who kept a small music shop. He died and left a large family of sons. He had been an ardent freemason, and the masons offered to apprentice one of the sons. The youngest, Ernest Bullock, was very gifted musically. He came to me as a choir boy of nine years. The masons articled him to me just as I left Wigan for Leeds. As he was only fifteen, the only thing to do was to take him into our house. My wife became a mother to him. We never regretted the decision; on the contrary we were thankful for it. Ernest and I played together on the few evenings I had at liberty. Little Stephen had some elaborate toys – perhaps a little too old for him. Ernest and I could be seen scrambling about the drawing-room floor which was covered with railway lines with many points. The three clock-work engines were wound up and let loose, and the game was to fly round and work the switches so that no engines collided, until the clock-work ran down. All Stephen did was to stand by and shriek "accent" when a collision took place.

There remains one other Wigan activity to record – composition. I blush when I see some of these early efforts now-a-days, for my taste in music and my means of expression have changed much in forty years. Several of them have proved themselves best sellers, but in every case I got a pittance in payment for them from the publishers who bought them outright. I was only too glad in those days to see them in print, after numerous experiences of having them returned over the post with fresh creases in them.

In my mother's scrap-book is an account of a public farewell from Wigan in which Canon Matthew paid a great tribute to me. This was indeed magnanimous, seeing that all music was pain and grief to him.

This account has not survived, but in the parish magazine of December 1905 the Rector expressed his pride and satisfaction at his organist's translation to one of the leading positions in the profession and that his ability and merit had been recognised. His departure would be a heavy loss to music in Wigan. 'In the church and in the Orchestral

*Society he has set a very high standard of music. All know the energy
and success with which he has done his work as Organist, and the
perfection to which he has brought his choir. In this work he has shown,
not only musical ability, but great tact and judgment; there has been little
or no friction and he has not only controlled his choir, but won their
confidence and affection. We shall all miss him ...'*

*Two letters from this period are of some interest as showing Bairstow's
relationship with William Wolstenholme, the blind organist and composer who had succeeded him at Norfolk Square. His music was of the
kind that was acceptable during the Edwardian era but out of date later
and out of favour with ECB who only occasionally played Wolstenholme's
Sonata in the Style of Handel and the Cantilène in A flat. The first two
letters are on writing paper headed 'High View. Wigan', but the second
has, added in his handwriting, '3, St. Boniface Gardens, Ventnor,
I.O.W.'*

*'?2.viii.03 Your kind congratulations arrived just as I was packing
up to come down here: but, as we stayed near London for the best part
of a week before we finally arrived at our destination, this is really the
first opportunity I have had of writing to thank you. I hope I may be of
some use to the St Cecilia. The Committee certainly seem a thoroughly
good, hard working and enthusiastic set of men, and this is the most
important thing with a musical society.*

*We are doing "Unto Thee O God" for the next Festival at Wigan.
The Festival of Parish Choirs I mean. It wont be worth coming to hear,
I fear; they are very rough for the most part, and it takes me all my time
to keep them together and get a fairly correct rendering, without much
finish or expression.*

Many thanks for the Fantasie-Rustique which is truly charming.

*I was sorry to hear of your church difficulties, but I should think that
you wont have much trouble in getting another post. If I hear of anything I will let you know.*

*I do not return until September 4th so I fear by then you will have
returned to town.*

With kindest thoughts, Ever your sincere Ed. C. Bairstow.

I wish you would write a big Communion Service. <u>Modern.</u>

Please send me some double chants when you have a minute or two.'

'24.ix.03. My dear Wolstenholme, ... Glad to hear of the piano work. We started at Blackburn on Tuesday and had a good turn up, and after I had got myself and the chorus warmed up we got on well together. I spent the night at Duckworths, and inspected some harmonies to the Tonus Peregrinus also brought away another chant both by a well known composer. Yours ever Ed. C. Bairstow.'

A third letter, written nearly 28 years later, from York, dated July 26.1931, expresses condolences to Wolstenholme's sister on the death of William three days earlier.

'Dear Mrs. Furrell, Although I expected it, the news makes me sad. The older the friendship the more one feels the loss. It will be an ever-lasting joy to you to think of the years of unselfish devotion that you gave him. I have often thought what a lot he owed to you. I am playing a funeral march this afternoon and his own Romance in his memory. I remember the impression the Romance made on me when I first heard it

E.C.B., parents and family

– I was at a more romantic age then! My wife joins me in deep sympathy. Yours sincerely E.C.Bairstow

I wish I could come up to the funeral, but it is quite impossible.'

(FJ: A small wall cabinet was given to me by the mother of one of the Minster choristers during my tenure of the organistship. She was a dealer in antiques and had come by it, with its two tiny brass plates with minute writing of several different type faces. ("Who was this Mr. Bairstow?" she asked me.) The cabinet was designed to hold smoking materials and is solidly made of oak, its doors with bevelled glass windows. The inscription on the left door-plate reads: WIGAN & DISTRICT/Philharmonic Society/1st Season 1901-2/April 8th 1902. That on the right plate runs: This Cabinet along with cheque was presented to/Dr. E.C.Bairstow F.R.C.O./By the Committee and Members/as a small mark of their appreciation of his gratuitous Services to the Society with/Good wishes for his approaching marriage.)

Leeds

WE MOVED TO LEEDS in January 1906 and took up our residence in a charming but jerry-built house overlooking the
Headingley cricket ground. After living in it some time a crack
developed in the plaster of the wall of one of the bedrooms and it
extended through the brickwork so that if you put your eye to it
you could see into the street. The landlord, who was also the builder,
was summoned with strong protests against such rotten work. But
his response was, "Well! Nobody can say that one of my houses has
ever tumbled down." No door or window quite fitted, but the house
was pleasantly situated and was close to the abode of my cousin,
the barrister. He and his wife and his three girls were very good
friends to us in those days. Before leaving Wigan my brother-in-
law had taken up bee-keeping as a hobby, and I joined him to the
extent of one hive. It was safely transported to Leeds, and planted
in my cousin's garden. My hope was that the girls would get interested in it, as we were too far out of Leeds for me to teach at home
and I was away all day. Moreover I was in Lancashire on the first
two days of each week. However the girls did not love bees. The
end came the following June or July, when, arriving home in the
evening I found a message to say that the bees had swarmed. I
rushed round to my cousin's to find the swarm in a most awkward
position on the slender bough of a laburnum tree hanging over a
sunken tennis lawn. I had no skep in which to take the swarm, for,
having cut out several queen-cells the previous Sunday afternoon
and put plenty of supers on, I never expected them to do it.
However, I had a spare hive and borrowed a large cardboard hat
box. The next problem was how to get at them. I put on a bee-veil

and gloves and tied up the feet of my trousers. Then we got a ladder, the foot of which was held by my cousin and his gardener. Gingerly I crawled up with my hat-box, got it beneath the swarm and gently shook the bough of the laburnum tree. The swarm dropped into the box, the bottom of the box fell out and down went the bees on to the heads of the two men. The gardener fled, but my cousin stuck to his post nobly until I got down. Luckily bees fill themselves with honey before swarming and are not inclined to sting. We picked bees from one another for about twenty minutes, then went into the house to play bridge. Bees still kept emerging until we took off our coats and found the back of our waistcoats black with them. Last of all we sat down to finish our rubber. My cousin had a fine victory in one and slapped his thigh in self-congratulation. Unfortunately a bee had wandered up there and he was stung – the only sting of the evening.

The Leeds Parish Church was built at the worst period – it is in every way a sham. It is sham Gothic. What purports to be carved oak is either painted iron or painted plaster. It has galleries all round. It has no resonance. On Sunday evenings, when it was full with people sitting on what were known as the 'altar flats', a level space between two series of steps leading up to the sanctuary, with others filling the aisles north and south of the choir, and with the galleries full, the mighty choir of thirty boys and thirty men had to work like Trojans. They used to say that it was as if your voice came back and hit you in the face. The organ console was on the floor of the church. It was surrounded by clumsy Gothic unglazed windows. The spaces were filled with parallel metal rods with red baize curtains behind them which people used to try to poke to one side to get a sight of the organist. The organ had five manuals. The foundation of it was by Schulze and had great dignity. Hill's had made an effort to Anglicise it by adding the swell organ and, I believe, the choir. Schulze's choir was called the 'Echo' organ, but as all the pipes were placed at the very top of the structure, it sang out merrily and was anything but mystical and remote. Finally a local firm, Abbot and Smith, added a solo organ. The amazing thing was that, with all these additions by different firms in totally different styles, the Leeds organ had character and dignity. One got to love it as one got to love the ugly church. When I went to Leeds the only residential population in the parish inhabited slum-like dwellings; the more well-to-do folks had moved out to pleasanter and healthier surroundings. Naturally this exodus has continued, but in my time the old church was very well attended and was a live church. The vicar, Dr. Bickersteth, was a very kindly soul with a family of grand sons. Mrs. Bickersteth was a wonderful woman. I believe she is still alive as I write (1946). The curates were fine men, sincere and full of vitality. Most of them were scholars and thinkers also. One dislikes picking out only a few for mention when all were so good, but Morris Hodson, the precentor, was a great help to me. He was very musical and gave me assistance in improving the repertory, casting out worthless music and introducing stronger and better things. He backed me up when there were difficulties and gave me great encouragement. He was succeeded by Arnold Sullivan. He had only been with us a short time when the time came for the annual cricket match of Decani v. Cantoris. This was played behind a little coaching inn at Walshford Bridge. The cricket was by no means first-class. The wicket was mown but the out-field was not. When our new precentor arrived to bat he dispatched about half-a-dozen 'donkey drops' over the inn into the road beyond. "Hallo!" said I, "you've been at this game before". "Well, I used to keep wicket for Sussex in the days of Fry and Ranjitsinhji", he replied.

Then there was George Bell – now the Lord Bishop of Chichester – who started the Church of England Men's Society with an attendance of 25 and left it with an attendance of 500. I'm sure his lordship will forgive the following story. When he first came to Leeds his reading of the lessons was, to say the least of it, dull. He pitched his voice at the beginning of a sentence and then, towards the end, it sank into inaudibility. The other curates besought me to give him some lessons. I told them that it was not my job, and I had no inclination to teach elocution. However, they were so sure that I could do him some good, and were so persuasive, that I agreed to try. After careful instruction in breathing and consonants I began to talk about the imagination which pictures the subject, stimulates the breath and thus puts vitality into the voice. I intimated that, when listening to his reading, it did not sound to be more than a careful enunciation of consonants and vowel sounds. The first lesson the following Sunday morning was the story of Jacob and Esau. Jacob had a high falsetto-ish voice whilst Esau rolled out resonant and deep bass sounds. Next time I entered the Clergy House I was greeted with shouts of: "What have you been teaching George Bell?" "Well", I said, "at any rate he has ideas now, even if they are not always the right ones, and that's more than one can say of some of you!"

William Whitehead, the choir treasurer, and one of the numerous churchwardens, was a great ally. As Embleton's generosity began to diminish and finally ceased when he found he could not always have his own way, money had to be raised by choir concerts and "choir Sundays" and in any other way possible. Whitehead organised these efforts despite the opposition of unmusical churchwardens. The Precentor, he and I formed a triumvirate which ran the choir and the music with very little interference the whole time I was there.

The men of the choir were grand material vocally and they were fair readers. But they were pampered. There was a story before my time of the principal bass coming down on a Saturday afternoon with a few friends and asking the Precentor to change the anthem to one which had a bass solo in it! The two principals had many engagements which took them away. They were certainly underpaid but that did not make it easier for the organist. The congregation worshipped them. This made it difficult for me to deal with them, as will be seen later on. They and five other men had to turn up each day for evensong at four-thirty. This had been started by the great Hook, who was not musical but thought that the Leeds Parish Church should worship God in a more cathedral-like service than the ordinary small parish church. This was in 1839, when S S Wesley was engaged as organist. The daily evensong is still sung, so that it has been going on for 107 years. A few of the Sunday men were paid; the rest were amateurs. Two of the boys, Jack and Jim Park, were identical twins. They were keen musicians, very mischievous, but very merry. Ernest Bullock caught one of them blazing away on the full organ one afternoon just before evensong, and fined him half-a-crown. "Never mind, Sir," said Park, "it was well worth it." Very few could distinguish between Jack and Jim. They could slip into each other's shoes with impunity. During the 1914-18 war they were for some time at Catterick. One of them got into trouble and was confined to barracks at a week-end when he had got leave and had a date with a girl friend in Leeds. His brother did the C.B. and he kept his appointment. One of them ran a string orchestra of amateurs who were quite good. The other brother got a job in South Africa. He came home on leave. The orchestra were playing at the University. The real con-ductor and the brother from South Africa conducted alternate items throughout the concert.

Sartorial consciousness

Then they both appeared to take the vociferous applause. No one in the audience knew of the return of the wanderer and did not discover it until the dénouement.

Leeds had a tradition – not at the Parish Church only – of employing local talent. My predecessor was a purely local product. There was in 1906 scarcely an important organ in Leeds that had not been built by local firms. The result was pretty much what you would expect. The Leeds folk were quite content with – in fact proud of – things which were by no means first-rate. I think, also, that their industrial, materialistic outlook, which they had inher-ited from the Victorian era, was partly responsible for this. The local man would come for less money: the local firm would do the work cheaper. Being proud of their city they did not trouble them-selves as to what was happening elsewhere.

The Leeds choir in 1906 would prolong the second chord of an amen very nearly through the next prayer. Admittedly they did it beautifully, dying away to a perfect treble pianissimo. But one felt that it was sheer effect, probably done to imitate the lofty and resonant cathedral. Being proud of it, it took a long time to wean them from it, for I am all against any kind of forcible directions which only rouse up a more or less equal and opposite force to resist them. There is nothing in the world that teaches this so clearly as music. Stiffness, rigidity, a determination to accomplish by force what should be done with suppleness and ease, account for ugly voices, slow and heavy players, untunefulness of vocalists and string players, rigid conducting and much ugliness in composition. All coldness, continuous muscular tension and the rest of the gang come from fear. I have had a long musical life and yet I have never come across anything but love that can cast out fear. If you love the transmission of emotion through musical sounds sufficiently, if you love your neighbour as yourself, there is nothing to stop you from doing things in the easiest and pleasantest way. Music is just that – a transmission of beautiful sounds to create feeling. If that were not the case, if you could not apply adjectives to music such as joyous, solemn, tender, stern, sardonic, humorous, and the like, no one would listen to it; and the more you love to do this, and the more art conceals art, so it looks and sounds easy, the more successful will you be as performer, composer, conductor or teacher. We are now talking of choir-training. As I have said, it is love that will in the end conquer, but there is another side to the question. You must have discipline. Obviously a choir, or any concerted body of musicians, must all of them do the thing they have been told to do at the right moment, and they must have one mind and one spirit. This takes time. At Leeds they had been told that they were the finest Parish Church choir in England. They had been driven on a loose rein; their absences had been overlooked. They were a little spoiled. But some of them very soon became enthusiastic; some gradually caught fire; a very few, mostly the older men, did not fall for the new choirmaster. Henry Brearley, the principal tenor, did his best to help me from the beginning. He was a loveable man, full of a pawky humour, and at his best in old English songs of a light and humorous character. Not so the bass, John Browning. He held aloof: Jack was as good as his master. This is as clear a description as I can give of the state of things in January, 1906, when I was put in charge.

There is one other person on the staff who should be mentioned, and that is Alf Manley, the verger. He, like everything and everybody else at the Parish Church, never looked quite clean.

There was a coal-tip on the canal, just at the back of the Clergy House which occupied the south side of the churchyard. The curates had to be careful about their bedroom windows or, before you could say 'knife', everything was covered with a thick layer of coal dust. So we can forgive Alf. He was a shrewd judge of men and things, and generally put his money on the right horse where the music was concerned. I had a nervous organ pupil; the perspiration dropped off the end of the man's nose whilst he was playing. He was allowed half-an-hour's practice before his lesson just to settle him down. One day, in the middle of this, Alf comes along with his heavy bunch of keys, rattled them suddenly across the metal rods of the organ 'loft', and in loud tones said, "If the doctor hears you playing like that he'll kick you off the seat." After I had left the Parish Church and gone to York I found myself in Leeds with an hour to spare, and strolled down to the Parish Church. I found Alf in his usual grimy corner and, after a little general conversation, asked him how the new organist was getting on. "Ow, 'ee's nowt but a button-pusher", says Alf, meaning that he confined himself to the stop-combinations obtainable from the pistons, or 'buttons' and did not do any hand registration.

There was a six months' interim between my predecessor leaving and my own advent. During this time the assistant organist, John Groves, had charge of the choir, and very well he did his work. He is still doing good things for music in Leeds. The probationers, of course had not received much instruction, and when I examined them I found that a few were so old that by the time they were fit for the choir their voices would be nearly gone. The Precentor and I determined to give a few of the older ones their congé and get some younger ones at once. Unfortunately the oldest boy was the son of a protégé of Embleton's who demanded that he should be kept on. I pointed out that I and not he was ultimately responsible for the state of the choir, and that to keep the boy who was the least use to us, and to sack several younger ones, was not fair. The Precentor backed me up, and so the rift in the lute began. The next widening of the breach was over the question of free accompaniments. It is curious how few people are aware of the history of organ accompaniment. To give a short sketch of it will be useful. The first attempts to make the accompaniment different from the voice parts were not for organ, but for viols. Many transitional compositions were written round about the beginning of the seventeenth century, which were said to be 'apt for voices or viols'. If our Elizabethan ancestors could not sing they could play their part on the viol, and *vice versa*. The earliest anthems with accompaniment were descended from these, but they had portions for viols alone. The solos, duets, trios, etc., were merely strands from the contrapuntal texture, the viols filling in the missing parts. These compositions were also played on the organ. As the seventeenth century progressed, the Italian Renaissance, opera, recitative and measured tunes all influenced Church music; and counterpoint, which before had been supreme, now took its place amongst the other factors, or was neglected for the novelties. It was at this time that the figured bass, or continuo, made its appearance. The composer, instead of writing every note of the organ part as he wished it played, simply wrote the voice part, or parts, plus the bass, under which he sometimes put figures – a sort of shorthand – to indicate what progression of chords he desired: the rest was left to the accompanist. This, of course, was often the composer, but all keyboard musicians had to be proficient in filling in the voice parts and inventing an appropriate continuo. This was all very well in the cathedral. Our musical boys begin to do it even in some cases before they leave the choir, but of course they know the music and hear me doing it practically every day. Early in the nineteenth century the firm of Novello, all honour to them, began to reprint this music with an organ part, and with the vocal parts printed in the treble clef, except the bass; the alto and tenor clefs being eliminated. Before that the choir sang from single parts, folio size, the organist and a few of the principal singers being provided with full scores. The worthy object of this was to bring all this music, some of it finely inspired, within the reach of the ordinary choirs, whose organists had not had the advantage of a cathedral upbringing, and whose choirmen could not read from alto and tenor clefs, and often came unstuck if they sang from a single part. These editions were printed in handy, octavo size, and were very cheap.

The pity of it was that the accompaniments were all the work of one man, the founder of the great firm, Vincent Novello. Henceforth it would be impossible to go from one cathedral to another and compare the imagination of the various organists in playing the continuo – unless they preferred, as many did and a few do still, to go on playing from the old scores – all you would hear would be Vincent Novello. The compass of manuals and pedals was different in those days from what it is at the present time, and this presented notes which the player could not reproduce. But Vincent's greatest weakness was for a chord called 'the dominant seventh.' He popped this in at every available point. Considering the hundreds of anthems and services he operated upon, the work was well done. Now is the time to allow modern musicians to try their hands. A few have done so. It is a difficult job, but it may make a dull anthem much more interesting and moving. Now Embleton knew nothing of all this, and loathed any kind of free accompaniment. One Sunday night we sang Boyce's "O where shall wisdom be found". I played it with freedom, did not alter Boyce's chords, but rejected Novello's arrangement of them. Embleton was infuriated and went straight to the Vicar, indignant that I had 'altered Boyce'. A few minutes' explanation put things straight with the Vicar.

Finally, at an Advent service, at which the choir sang two Bach Cantatas, I played some free accompaniments to the hymn "O come, O come, Emmanuel". They were very free, but were all designed to heighten the meaning of the words. Again Embleton dashed off to the Vicar with a stormy protest. Unfortunately for him the following criticism appeared in the Yorkshire Post the next morning:- "After these was the Advent Hymn, 'Veni Emmanuel', sung to its ancient tune, and affording an equally fine example of what congregational music should be ... and had it been more familiar to the congregation its effect would have been splendid .... Perhaps, too, they were dismayed by the free accompaniment played with really superb effect by Dr. Bairstow, and perfectly in keeping with the tune." This came from the pen of Herbert Thompson who, Sir Hubert Parry used to say, was the best music critic in the country. In later days he became a faithful friend of mine. He was a man of wide education. He never tried to make "good copy". If he did not understand music he was not afraid to say so. He was absolutely genuine and very fair.

S.S. Wesley was succeeded at Leeds by R.S. Burton, who was a really first-rate choir trainer. He might be termed the father of a race of musicians who specialised in teaching choirs. Many were not executants; some of them were rough diamonds; but the one thing they possessed was personal magnetism. They could arouse a surprising enthusiasm among their forces. Some of them, like the late Sir Henry Coward, could produce effects never before heard. To this school belonged the conductors of the great choirs one heard at the big north-country festivals at Blackpool, Morecambe and elsewhere. It was Burton who began the annual performances of the Bach St. Matthew Passion music at the Parish Church in 1877. This was a brave and far-sighted thing to do in those days, when the choral music of Bach was either unknown or unappreciated. This annual Service has been continued ever since. When I was told that it was the custom for the organist to play the organ on these occasions, and for the choir to sing without a conductor, I was sceptical. But the Precentor said, "Don't make up your mind until you have heard the augmented choir". When I did hear them I was surprised at their confidence and attack. I see that Herbert Thompson says of the second performance I was responsible for in 1907:- "The chorus was exceptionally good. The force and precision with which the dramatic choruses of the crowd were sung deserve warm praise, and the smartness of the attack was all the more noteworthy in the absence of a conductor". But the absence of a conductor who could look straight into the eyes of his choir and clearly show exactly what he wanted by his gestures was missed. But I believe it was not until my last year that we had a small orchestra and I conducted. This has been continued ever since. The augmented choir also joined in the annual performances of Brahms's German Requiem.

In 1907 I was appointed conductor of the Preston Choral Society. This was a very different society from the Blackburn St. Cecilia. There was a committee, but the Society was really run and backed by the brothers Norwood, who owned the most important music shop in Preston. The Preston Public Hall was a great asset. It was a first-rate concert hall from all points of view except one. It was satisfactory acoustically, there was ample accommodation for audience, chorus and orchestra, and very comfortable artistes' rooms, chorus rooms and band room. But the organ! It was at the old high pitch. The orchestra could not tune to it. On one occasion there was a misprint in the programme: 'Concerto in X for organ and orchestra: Handel'. The conductor (leader of the Hallé orchestra in those days) Alfred Risegari, said: "Ah! it is zee only key zee organ can play in". It was a poor instrument tonally also. In fact it was very little use. What a pity public bodies so rarely take expert advice in the matter of organs! So often some public-spirited man comes along and says, "I will give you an organ". Then the church or public hall is saddled for many years with some dreadful producer of ugly sounds; for what is there worse than a bad organ?

It was the custom at Preston to make the first concert of the season largely orchestral. The Hallé orchestra and their conductor, Dr. Hans Richter, were engaged. The chorus sang one short work under my conductorship. Richter had never met me before and knew nothing of me. When he had finished his orchestral rehearsal he said, "now you can rehearse your work. It is ver' good thing for you young men to have the chance of conducting a first-rate orchestra, but you must be ver' strict with zem or zay will make a damn fool of you". (I had not time to tell him of the round robin at Blackburn). The work was Brahms's 'Song of Destiny'. The chorus had had some difficulty with the quick movement where, at the words, "Like water from cliff unto cliff ever dropping", the orchestra are playing three beats in a bar whilst they are singing two. I had accordingly practised beating two with the left hand and three with the right. Richter was rather fascinated by this unusual bit of technique. At the concert in the evening, instead of resting in the artists' room, he came into the hall. After it was over he walked on to the platform and shook hands with me in front of the audience. He had a very gruff, German manner, but a kindly heart. We adjourned to the Park Hotel between rehearsal and concert. He always said on these occasions that he never could eat before a concert – "I am too excite". But he invariably plodded through the whole menu, drinking a large bottle of Burgundy with it. We then set off for the concert in a four-wheeled cab. The traffic coming up our side of the street had to go past the hall, turn round, and then discharge its passengers at the main entrance. We were rather late, so that when we were opposite the entrance I was for getting out and crossing the road, but Richter said, "do not get out yet; we have to turn over". After the concert we went back to the Park Hotel. He again told me that the music made him too excited to eat, but he put away a beefsteak and some stewed fruit with another large bottle of Burgundy. It was his custom at Christmas-time to invite the orchestra in batches to his home at Bowdon in Cheshire and give them a good meal. But even the burly brass players said that he could out-eat any of them. He was very kind in giving me tips about the art of conducting. On one occasion he was talking of the necessity of lightning quickness between the thought and the gesture. He said he had been to some scientific society in London where this speed was measured electrically. A number of people sat at a table with right hands raised against a contact. Then all sorts of tests were applied. A light was flashed, a weight was dropped, they were touched on the shoulder. They had to bring the right hand down on to the table as quick as thought. He had won all the tests although he was then nearly 70, and was very much cock-a-hoop about it. That night, when I reached my wife's mother's house at Wigan, my brother-in-law and I were sitting very quietly in front of the fire when a mouse came out. One of us made a slight movement and it dashed underneath the sideboard. There was about a foot between this and the next piece of furniture. "I'll chivvy it out with the poker and you get it with your slipper as it goes across", said my brother-in-law. I did, and squashed it flat. It was a proud moment.

Richter was 'very strict' with his orchestra. Once the fourth horn was a little worse for wear and made some bad mistakes. At the interval Richter marched down into the band room, confronted the man, spat on the floor, and walked away without a word. His conducting and his interpretations were much the same – strong, even rough, but just lacking a subtle tenderness. He had a colossal memory – he conducted the whole of the 'Ring' without a copy. But of course he had been Wagner's amanuensis and had copied out the music.Blackburn being only a few miles from Preston, it was possible to unite the two choruses and do big works, one night at Blackburn and the next at Preston with the same orchestra. I can recall very good performances of Elgar's 'The Kingdom' and Verdi's 'Requiem' under these conditions.

On 14 December 1907 the Manchester Guardian reminded 'Blackburnians' of the splendid quality of the St. Cecilia and Vocal Society and its recent performances of the Dream of Gerontius *and* Brahms' Requiem. *'Dr. Bairstow deserves every eulogium at command, but I think I cannot do better that repeat Richter's words spoken directly to our conductor at the close of the* Song of Destiny *at Preston, given on December 6th. Richter sat in the audience during the performance and at the close led off the applause. Then after securing Dr. Bairstow a recall, followed him to the ante-room, shook hands, and said, among other sweet things, "You are a born conductor". And Hallé's men endorse the compliment.'*

The next year, the reorganised Preston Choral Society sang Purcell's Remember not, Lord, our offences, *the last two numbers of Handel's* Samson, (Let the bright seraphim *being sung by six choristers from Leeds Parish Church) and* the Challenge of Thor *from Elgar's* King Olaf, *'under the enthusiastic but watchful and painstaking conductor, Dr. Bairstow – who has proved himself to be an encyclopaedia of practical advice – the public may look forward to a rich treat when a complete work like* The Kingdom *is presented.' (This was to take place in the near future.) At this concert Richter's contribution was Beethoven's Fifth Symphony – "the mightiest of the nine". 'During the evening Dr. Richter, who, whenever he vacated the conductor's desk, came into the hall to listen to the chorus, exclaiming "Excellent!" several times, and during the interval, addressing the chorus as a body in the Crush Room, he complimented them highly on their work, and added, "For this you have to thank your conductor".'*

A little later, however, on another aspect of his musicianship, the Musical Standard *of 13 February 1909 carried a rather disgruntled account of the Seventh Municipal Orchestral Concert in Leeds. It complained that, due to the large forces required to perform it, only the Prelude from the incidental music to the Pevensey Pageant,* The Coming of Christianity, *was heard. The critic comments: 'Beyond the fact that Dr. Bairstow's orchestration in the Prelude shows a surer sense of proportion than in his degree piece heard here some time ago, there is little to say and his song, "I arise from dreams of thee" ... is but restrainedly sentimental.' (There appears to be no record of which degree piece is referred to).*

We had a daughter born to us on March 6th, 1907: Nancy Elizabeth. The Vicar of Leeds did a typical act of kindness. He gave her a christening party and tucked between her tiny fingers a little bit of paper informing me that my salary was to be raised by £50 per annum.

1907. In this year I was appointed organist of the Leeds Triennial Festival, which Sir Charles Stanford then conducted. Harry Plunket Greene had arranged a visit to London some time previously for me to meet Stanford at the Savile Club. They had been boys together, and Harry was the great interpreter of Stanford's songs. On the journey up, Harry said, "Stanford likes to play bridge in the evenings. Do you play?" I replied, "Yes, a little. What stakes do you play for?" "Oh, five shillings a hundred," said he. Luckily for me Stanford elected to talk, chiefly about the delinquencies of my predecessor at Leeds Parish Church, who had been chorus-master of the previous festival. According to Stanford, when he arrived for a chorus rehearsal they did not know some of the music. Benton, the man in question, had spent all the time over the music he was interested in, and neglected the rest. At all events Stanford insisted on a change of chorus-masters and H.A. Fricker, the Town Hall Organist, was appointed. Benton conducted the Choral Union, which originally sprang from the Parish Church Augmented Choir and was financed by Embleton. Fricker was chorus master of the Leeds Philharmonic, the senior society, conducted by Stanford and by Richter when the latter came for a chiefly orchestral evening. The Festival Chorus contained members of both. Naturally there was much indignation shown by the Choral Unionites at the way Benton was treated. Stanford was difficult. Those who are curious to know more about him should read Plunket Greene's life.* Harry knew him better than anyone else, was sympathetic to his idiosyncracies, and yet was alive to his dangerous side. Stanford was unusually highly gifted musically. I heard him correcting mistakes in rapidly moving inner string parts as he sat in the hall at a rehearsal when the composer was conducting his

---

* Charles Villiers Stanford, by Harry Plunket Greene. Gowin Arnold.

own work. He was first-rate at a rehearsal, giving his forces a perfectly clear description of what he wanted in a few words. But he was not a good conductor. His left hand went into his pocket, and his right, armed with a thick, heavy baton, just gave the tempo, invariably the right one. Music flowed from Stanford like water from a spring. He went into his study for a regular period every day and wrote it. That may have been good enough in Haydn and Mozart's day when music was younger, but in Stanford's case it produced a deal of very ordinary stuff, much of which he ought to have rejected. Now and then he was truly inspired, as in some of the songs, the Stabat Mater, or the Anglican Services.

It was out of the kindness of Harry Greene's heart that he helped to get me – a young and unknown man – this appointment as organist at the great Leeds Festival. I would rather have put up with any inconvenience than disappoint him; therefore I accepted. But there were a few drawbacks. In the first place, although I had cursed many an organist playing to my conductorship, I had never played the organ part in any great work. My actual engagement was for the London rehearsals with the orchestra and the combined rehearsals at Leeds, and the fee only covered these. But I ought to have attended chorus rehearsals to get to know the music intimately and Stanford's intentions. This was impossible because of my two Lancashire Societies, whom I could not neglect. However, I managed to pull through.

This was my first experience of a great Festival. I enjoyed lots of it tremendously, especially when the score had no organ part. But before it was over I began to get musical indigestion, and had to go outside for a cigarette. There was too much of it – morning, afternoon and evening for four days – moreover there was too much for any chorus to learn. After reading again the many encomiums of this celebrated chorus in the London papers from my mother's old scrap book, I recall sitting at the organ and hearing the mistakes and hesitancy of the tenors and basses behind me. There was a tenor, a grand musician, for many years a member of the Philharmonic. He was dead sure. All the men round him were dependent on him and not sure of themselves. But what musician, or body of musicians, would consider themselves ready to go before the public when they were only more or less note-perfect? In those days the public were satisfied with far less than now, as I have said already. The other drawback to orgies of music of this sort is that they bleed the district. Everyone has a certain amount of money to spend on concerts, and no-one wants to miss the Festival, even when the cheapest reserved seat is 8/-. Lastly the local choruses are jaded with festival work and get stale for their own programmes.

Extra music and a few extra men from the Sunday choir were arranged for at the four-thirty Evensong at the Parish Church on the four days of the Festival. It was remarkable how many visiting musicians came to those services. There were only a few hours' rest between the afternoon and evening concerts, but these men were so keen that they sacrificed one hour. Meeting these people, some old friends, some new acquaintances, was one of the pleasantest experiences of the Festival. Bantock had a new work produced on this occasion. It was fiendishly difficult for chorus. We abstracted a single part – tenor – and when we met a visitor we asked him innocently whether he read music at sight. Some just smiled superciliously, others said, "Of course", but nobody read the Bantock part perfectly. A few were hopelessly wrong.

> We interrupt ECB's writing to give an objective view of him at this period which is contained in the fourth of a series of newspaper articles entitled 'Leeds Musicians and Vocalists', a title which, incidentally, might have caused him some amusement. "His pleasant manner and thorough eagerness to do all things well has already made him a great favourite at the church, and those fortunate enough to listen to the result of his labours cannot help but be impressed thereby. Dr. Bairstow is truly proud of his choir, which he contends is 'of the best'. He frankly says that 'few choirs are blest with such a capable lot of singers, the majority of whom are as loyal and hard working as one could wish'. In composition Dr. Bairstow is not widely known, and, to be candid, the art has only been a sort of recreation with him! He has never been too ambitious in this particular line – perhaps confining himself to the smaller forms – but Leeds people have every reason to believe that the future will bring work from his pen. He has, however, been sufficiently fortunate to gain acceptance of nearly all compositions submitted, which items include albums of songs, pieces for the organ, one of which – the *Evening Song* – has been

played by nearly all the leading organists, a few anthems, and an evening service in D, sung at St. Paul's and other cathedrals.

"I do not think that the number of good voices is greater in Leeds than in other parts of Yorkshire and Lancashire", E.C.B. told his interviewer, "but the enthusiasm for choral singing has increased the technical ability here. The Leeds chorus singers are undoubtedly good readers, and the only evil much choral singing has brought in its train is a tendency to perfunctoriness, due perhaps to rehearsals almost every night; but this may be overcome by a chorus master who has the gift of inspiring his singers. This staleness seems to lead to a lot of singing out of tune, a fact which was especially noticeable at the last Musical Festival, where a great many of the softer passages were just sufficiently flat to take the atmosphere out of the music. Voices which are not very well produced will not stand the strain which has to be put on them by a Leeds chorus singer. Many of them have never been trained, whilst others have got into the hands of ignorant teachers, or cranks. The delicate muscles which control the vocal apparatus will not bear an extreme tension for long, though, of course, the possessor of a trained voice will take good care that undue pressure is not applied. This is not by any means the whole art, but it is the first thing to learn – to sing with flexible muscles, always under control, and not with the muscles in a constant state of rigidity and tension, which causes hard quality, and quickly fatigues the singer".

To appreciate what Dr. Bairstow really wants, and gets, in vocal music, can be ascertained by hearing a service by the Leeds Parish Church Choir, which combination was never at a higher state of excellence than it is today. Dr. Bairstow's playing of the church organ has won for him many admirers, and not a few members of the congregation stay after the service to hear his selections.

Speaking to a Sunday Pictorial interviewer in 1911 he said: "Of course the main features of our choir are the daily choral service, with eight men and thirty boys, and the fine Sunday service, in which, in addition to the boys, are included seven altos, eleven tenors, and ten basses. The devotion to it of the two well-known principal singers, who find time from their many concert engagements to be present nearly every Sunday and very often during the daily services, although they are paid a fee much lower than most cathedrals can offer, is an example followed by the other choirmen, who are all hard workers and loyal to a man. Personally I know of no other parish church where a daily choral service is held with a full choir except St. Andrew's, Wells Street, London; though, of course, many churches have them with boys only.

"Another unique feature of our choir is its list of music. The tradition of the church, established by Wesley, is to have only strong and dignified music sung at its services, and to steer clear, as far as possible, of the maudlin, the sentimental, and the merely pretty music, which is so common in many of our churches. The large and capable choir makes possible the adequate performance of anthems and services which are completely out of reach of the average choir as, for instance, those in eight parts for double choirs, rarely heard even in cathedrals."

E.C.B. continues: Those were strenuous days for me. I left Leeds on a Monday morning too early to shave, had to change at Rochdale and wait long enough to walk to a little barber's shop, suffer the shave, and get back to the station in time for the train to Wigan. The barber seemed to have a different dog each week. On enquiry it turned out that the men on the Railway Lorries left the dogs there and presumably the barber carried on illicit sales of stolen goods! He had a son who was preparing for a Trinity College piano examination, and, having seen music amongst my belongings, he requested me to hear him play. We went into a little room behind the shop; the boy divested himself of his coat and rolled up his shirt-sleeves and then proceeded to castigate in the cruelest way a miserable little tinny piano. I never heard how he fared at his examination. I reached Wigan about 10 a.m., did a day's teaching and went on to Preston for the rehearsal of the choral society. Then back to Wigan to sleep at my wife's mother's. The next morning early I set off for Blackburn, taught all day and took the St. Cecilia rehearsal. There was a 9.30 p.m. train which landed me home not long before midnight. Ernest Bullock, who had now become my assistant, carried on at the Parish Church until I got home. Wednesday was spent in teaching and at the Church. On Thursday evening I taught at the short-lived Leeds Municipal School of

Music. This had been established chiefly through the energies of Fricker, T. Hoggett, then Lecturer in Music at Leeds University, and Percy Scholes, afterwards to become famous. This school did quite a lot of good work even during the short time it existed. It gave scholarships to those who could not afford the fees; it gave an all-round musical education to those who needed it. There were students' concerts to give them experience. All the reputable musicians did their best to help. The fees were small, and the amount we received was smaller. I endeavoured to meet the case by making all my singing students come together and listen to each other, and by giving them twenty minutes individual attention instead of half-an-hour. I forget which political party was in power on the City Council when we started, and I forget just how long we carried on. But when this party was kicked out at the next election and their opponents got a majority, there was a great outcry for economy. The first economy was to stop the Municipal School, which saved them a few paltry hundreds a year. You could not get those Leeds Councillors to see that such a school could never pay, for, if it did, its usefulness would be gone. When premises had been provided, and Percy Scholes's salary as secretary had been paid, the meagre fees of the students, much of which went to their professors, could not possibly make a favourable balance. Many gifted students got instruction who would never otherwise have done so. I had a very interesting group, and kept them on at my own house after the school finished. In it, later on, were Elsie Suddaby, George Parker, and Etty Ferguson, who afterwards went to the Royal College and still teaches in Leeds. Elsie was a grand girl. She was an excellent pianist, and could read splendidly both on the piano and in vocal music. She had a wonderful spirit, worked harder than anyone, and would never give in. She had much difficulty with her voice in the early days and with her breathing. The very things which she does with such perfection of art now – soft, very tender high notes, long-drawn-out phrases with no apparent effort – all these presented great difficulties then and for quite a long time to come. So be encouraged, you neophytes with similar troubles!

George Parker was a first-rate musician when he came to me, with a burning enthusiasm and a desire to know all about music. He was a most affectionate pupil. Before he entered the profession he was underground manager at a colliery. He occasionally brought gifts, and sometimes these were hares. "Where did you get this, George?" I would ask him. "Oh, the colliers bring them along, and the less said the better". When George went to London he actually took a song of mine which he liked and went round the publishers with it till he found one willing to take it. The words of this song, "When I heard the learned astronomer", were by Walt Whitman. It was necessary to obtain permission before they could be published. I wrote to the publisher, who said that the copyright was held by Walt Whitman's brother in the U.S.A. His reply to my request arrived on a post-card which, except for the date and signature, consisted of one word, "Sure"!

Both Elsie and George have always been the most loyal people. They both sang at my seventieth birthday concert in 1944. These two are mentioned because they were the first two of my pupils to come to the top.

Friday night was the great full rehearsal of the choir. The boys came at 6.30, evensong was at 7.30 and after that came the full rehearsal. It was a long and strenuous evening, but most thrilling. Saturday was the easiest day of the week. A little teaching, evensong at 4.30 and then no more. Sunday, with its two big services and a few organ pieces played after evensong, was always a strain. It was not the playing, I enjoyed that, but the continual listening to hear if the choir were going to bring it off and put in all the finishing touches that had been so carefully rehearsed.

In 1908 we left our jerry-built Headingley house and went into one of the opposite sort – Victorian, solid, substantial and thick. It was just behind the University in De Grey Road. The University was our landlord. It had bought up the whole road eventually to enlarge its buildings. The authorities warned me that we might be turned out, but I risked that. We never were, and were very comfortable. In the music room there was a bay window. My new grand piano was in the recess. There was a wall about eighteen inches high surrounding the top of the bay and a gutter to carry away the rain water. One night in the autumn we went to bed and left a big fire burning in the grate. In the night there was a great rain-storm. The gutter was choked with leaves. Whilst we were innocently sleeping all the water above the bay came down into the piano. The next morning I sent for the firm which had sold it to me. They found the sound-board warped through the heat. They could only offer me £40 for it. I tried the insurance company and the landlord, but they both said it was an "act of God". There was nothing for it but to get a new piano. Luckily I came across the man who travelled round with the great pianists keeping the concert grand tuned and regulated. He asked to be allowed to choose one for me. When it arrived I pumped him as to what he looked for in choosing it. By the time he had finished I felt I was an ignoramus on the subject. I remember two things. One was the sound board, which should have a fine and perfect graining without the slightest inequality. The other was that in that particular make of piano there was often a wolf-note about F, the fourth line in the bass stave. I still have that lovely piano. Soon after that I went to London to choose one for a girl about to be wed. The manager came round with us whilst I went through a row of about half-a-dozen boudoir grands and thumped them for wolf-notes, finding quite a few. The German manager's face was a study.

In 1909 I foolishly took on the conductorship of the Barnsley St. Cecilia Society. What led me to do so was the fact that it had been hitherto conducted by Dr. Henry Coward, so I expected something good. But it was another of these choirs that are spoiled by old ladies. One in the front row of the contraltos, with a very obvious wig, told me that she had sung at the opening of Leeds Town Hall by Queen Victoria in 1858! How many organisations are spoiled by putting the importance of the individual before that of the institution. In other words, being kind to one or two, and unkind to all the rest. It must have been round about this time that I gave an organ recital at the church of an overgrown village between Leeds and Bradford. The choir were present and we commenced with a processional hymn, "Fight the good fight", sung to my old vicar's tune. One man with a stentorian bass voice was merely singing "oo-bah". He did this consistently all through the service, including "Amens". I said to the organist sitting beside me, "Isn't that man somewhat of a thorn in your side?" He replied that the man was wealthy and gave a lot of money to the Church. He was quite enough to distract the most pious from their devotions.

To return to Barnsley. They had settled to sing Brahms's Requiem at their next concert. Half way through the first rehearsal I could tell that they would never know it in the time available, and had no sort of idea how to sing that kind of music. One night I was trying to get some thrill into their climaxes, particularly at the phrase "joy everlasting" in the chorus "Here on earth". "This is where you forget dirty, smoky old Barnsley, and are lifted up into the heavens" said I. But this was received with low growls of disapproval. I see that H.T. in the Yorkshire Post complimented me on "pulling them through" the performance.

After those two hard days and late nights in Lancashire, to go on Wednesdays to Barnsley with another late night, was really madness. In the end I got paid out for it.

Occasionally I was asked to adjudicate at competition festivals, first in the Leeds district and then further afield. I was never a popular judge. These festivals have done untold good in raising the standard of performance, in helping people to appreciate the best in music, and in roping-in folks who would never otherwise get any music at all. But many of them are solely dependent on the takings at the door and the entrance fees of the competitors. An unpopular judge can play havoc with both. My intense eagerness to teach them as much as I could in the short time available and my unfortunate directness of speech did not help matters, and left little time for words of encouragement and to make funny jokes for the audience. Luckily I was engaged several times as second adjudicator to Dr. W.G. McNaught, who was then the doyen of that branch of the profession. He taught me a lot. On one occasion I was with him at Blackpool. It was customary to wear evening clothes at the night session. But we had to listen to seventeen mixed-voiced choirs singing three pieces in the afternoon, and had just time to swallow a drink and a sandwich and then go back to the judge's box. The first item was a couple of very praiseworthy orchestras. They were to be judged by a well-known conductor, who apparently had had no previous experience of competition festivals. The hall was tightly packed with a typical Lancashire audience when this gentleman ascended the steps leading up to the throne, immaculate in tails and a white waistcoat. He received tumultuous applause. When he delivered his remarks he did not know that the audience wished to hear his criticisms. They were addressed to the orchestras close to him. Then there was a stentorian voice from the cheap seats "Spake oop". He took no notice. Then another, "Aye, coot all that an' gie us t'resoolt". At this he threw his papers on the floor and marched off in high dudgeon, wagging his behind. The steward picked up the papers and quietly gave the award. When he arrived back in the box McNaught gave him a rare dressing-down.

Once at the Summerscales Competition at Keighley on the children's day, they had been rather noisy and difficult. When we got down to lunch with the Committee, the conversation turned to the question of lack of parental control in these days. An old man told the following story. It is truly Yorkshire; that is why I include it.

"One winter when I was a boy on the way to school there was a dangerous slide down a steep hill and round a corner. My father came along and saw me sliding with the other boys. He said, 'If you go on that slide again I'll give you the biggest hiding you've ever had!' In the afternoon I went on it again, tumbled down and broke my wrist. I was too frightened to tell anybody and spent a sleepless night. Next morning it was very swollen and I had to confess. It was set, and I had my arm in a sling for about six weeks. The very day I took it out my father said, 'What did I say I'd do to you if you went on the slide again?' 'Give me a hiding', I said tearfully. With that he took off his belt and fulfilled his word."

For a moment we leave Bairstow's account of life at Leeds and follow him to Edinburgh where, on February 6th 1909 he gave an R.C.O. lecture on Modern English Organ Music. Professor F. Niecks, Mus.D., presided and there was a large gathering of members and friends. This lecture was published with others in one volume but we quote from the Musical News of February 13th whose digest deals with the main points.

'English organ music was, he feared, lagging behind the rest of our native music which had never been in such a flourishing state since the days of Purcell. Very few modern composers had written anything for the organ and their work for the organ was not on the same plane as their choral, orchestral or chamber music. Until recently the organ had been, of all the greater instruments, the least expressive. Its heavy touch and slow-speaking pipes, its clumsy and cumbersome draw-stop action, made

frequent changes of tone-colour and intensity of sound impossible; there-
fore many great composers had passed it by as an unworthy medium for
the expression of their musical thoughts. But the organ had many advan-
tages peculiar to it. It could present several different parts, each in a
different quality of sound. It could sustain sound more evenly than any
other polyphonic instrument. The effect of its deep pedal notes could not
be got by any other instruments, and modern invention had done away
with nearly all its original defects. But, just as Chopin and Liszt had
understood how to get better effects from the pianoforte than other
masters because they were pianists before all else, so it was to the organ-
ist they must look for the music most suitable to the idiom of the organ.
And it was natural to expect that those English organists who were also
composers would have given to the world something which, beyond doubt,
was of the highest inspiration. But ... this was not the case at present.

'Dr. Bairstow then set himself to account for the fact that English
organ music lamentably failed in its mission, which should be to touch
the heart ... the three strongest factors working against inspiration ...
(particularly that composed by organists) were: 1. the British tempera-
ment, 2. the average musical and general education of an organist, 3.
his daily life and duties. The conservative and law-abiding disposition
of the Britisher was often a hindrance to success in musical composition.
It accounted for the production of large quantities of constructed, obvi-
ous music which had never had the breath of life instilled into it . .... he
commented upon the difficulties in the way of the provincial organist,
who was, as a rule, a kind of general practitioner, obliged to teach every
branch of music in order to make a decent living. Most of his work was
pure grind, and much time was spent in rehearsing and performing church
music, so that, not unnaturally, the organ music he wrote was often only
church music without words. He appealed to his hearers to fight the evil
tendencies by cherishing a high artistic ideal, and allowing nothing to
tempt them to deviate from their principles. He felt that there should be
among the rank and file of organists a greater love of music as an art,
and that it should not be regarded only as a means of livelihood. The
control and education of the taste to enable them to choose the pure and
reject the impure was to be got by the study of the works of the great mas-
ters, but not by the miserably formal analysis one found so common. In
an appreciative study of the sister arts of painting, literature, poetry and
drama would be found also enormous inspiration and encouragement on

the art of emotional expression. He was glad that these things were entering more and more into musical life, and that the modern organist was more in touch with them than his forefathers had been.

'Dr. Bairstow then dealt with the works of the best writers of modern English organ music. They might be divided into two schools – the classic and the romantic. The first were disciples of Bach, Mendelssohn and Brahms, the second showed the influence of the French school, as well as that of Grieg, Tchaikowsky and Wagner. There was much to admire in both. Sir C. Stanford's Fantasia and Fugue in D minor (Op. 103) was mentioned as a truly beautiful example of music of the classic school, and Mr. E.H. Lemare was referred to as the pioneer of the romanticists. Dr. Bairstow thought the romantic school were, perhaps more in sympathy with the modern instrument than the other, whose music would have sounded equally well on the organs of twenty or thirty years ago. He would welcome a great art work for the organ from the pen of Sir Edward Elgar in his latest and noblest vein. In conclusion, Dr. Bairstow begged all – performers, teachers, and composers – to remember Beethoven's inscription on the great Mass in D "From the heart it has come, to the heart it shall penetrate". He then played his Prelude in C and pieces by Ernest Walker, Stanford (Opus 101/4), Harwood, Hollins (who was present) and Wolstenholme.'*

The next highlight at Leeds was the 1910 festival. My experience of the previous one was, of course, a help and gave me confidence. During the whole of my time in Leeds we had a Professional Musicians' Association. It met once a month when very interesting and helpful discussions took place. Through it we came to understand one another and it promoted a very friendly spirit amongst us. It was the custom for the Association to invite to dinner all the principal visiting musicians on the night preceding the festival. This year I happened to be chairman. At the dinner on my right sat Rachmaninoff and on my left Kennerley Rumford. Rachmaninoff, who had very little English, was intensely surprised at the bonhomie and friendship of our musicians. In his own country, he said, they quarrelled. He proved himself at that festival to be the greatest all-round living musician – composer, conductor and pianist. For he conducted his own symphony and played his piano concerto. We know the points to admire and the limitations of his compositions; his conducting was first-class and as a pianist he was without a peer amongst his contemporaries. For an encore after his concerto he played his well-known Prelude in C sharp minor with more *rubato* than any of us had ever heard. The quaver chords after the impressive opening were very agitated, but broadened out quite naturally into the following crotchets of the opening theme. Kennerley Rumford had just returned from an Australian tour with his wife, Clara Butt. He told me that the Australians called him "Mr. Butt".

It was at this festival that Vaughan Williams's Sea Symphony was produced. We were all amazed at it, but I did not fully appreciate its great beauties and intense sincerity until I had conducted it myself several times. Stanford sat in the hall at the final orchestral rehearsal, correcting mistakes in the very imperfect manuscript string parts from a vocal score. Vaughan Williams conducted. Stanford's Stabat Mater also received its first performance. In parts it contains some of the most beautiful and deeply moving music he ever wrote. But it is not all on that high plane.

Harry Greene had to sing the Songs of the Fleet by Stanford. He would not come to our dinner. He would have denied himself all the joys of life rather than prejudice the success of Stanford's new song cycle. I'm sure he never thought of his own reputation. But he was unwise, for the dinner and the jolly companionship of his fellow-musicians would have kept his mind clear of forebodings. As it was he sang them very badly compared with the rehearsal. But when the weight was lifted and he came on to do a group of songs he was in rare form. I can still feel the terrible intensity of "By the waters of Babylon" (Somervell's setting to the Welsh tune).

The St. Matthew Passion was also performed at this festival and thereby hangs a tale. Those who have read Plunket Greene's life will appreciate it. When there were difficult negotiations to be carried out with any individual, Stanford would say, "I'll write him a letter, me bhoy". Then fur flew. I received one of these letters marked "Confidential". It was to the effect that no one could be entrusted with the "continuo" in the Passion except himself or Walford Davies. As he was conducting, Walford Davies would play the *continuo*. Fricker had had the hard work of rehearsing the chorus and would feel hurt if he took no part in the performance. Would I, therefore, step down and allow Fricker to play the organ? I replied that his real reason was that Fricker knew exactly how the work was to be sung and I, not having been at the chorus rehearsals, did not. But for the last four years I had played the whole thing at the Parish Church, and what would people think if I was to be debarred from playing it at the festival?

At this, of course, he got angry, and wrote another letter in which he said I had accused him of practically lying. There the matter stood for some time. Fricker and I were the best of friends, and one Sunday afternoon he came to see me on some point or other. I said to him, "Have you heard anything of a row I have been having with Stanford?" "Do you mean with regard to the St.Matthew Passion?" he said. "Yes," said I. Then he told me that Stanford had said that he would be much happier if Fricker played the organ part. "What about Bairstow?" said Fricker. "Oh, I'll write him a letter, me bhoy". Then I got a letter from Stanford asking me to meet him at the next chorus rehearsal he was coming to. Accordingly I steeled myself up to be firm and went to the rehearsal, wondering what was going to happen. To my intense surprise Stanford put his arm round my shoulders and was all honey-sweet kindness. No more was said.

A glimpse of life in the Edwardian age is afforded by an account in the Yorkshire Post, 21 May 1910, of the memorial service at Leeds Parish Church for King Edward VII. "The service so well reflected the national sentiment of sorrow and of hope that it was a pity all who wished could not come in. Ticket holders took their seats more than an hour before the civic and military procession arrived. Clad in deep black, relieved here and there with a spray of white feather in a lady's hat, they filled the deep galleries and the pews in the side aisles and congregated to the east of the choir up to the very steps of the altar.

'Black fabrics were hung about the clergy and choir stalls, and the seats usually occupied by the Judges of Assize and members of the Corporation. The pulpit and lectern were completely swathed in mournful drapery, and the memorial Latin initials "E.R.I." showed conspicuously in letters of white. The monogram also figured in front of the west gallery around a white crown, and to the organ case was affixed the Royal hatchment in neat colours. A subdued light fell upon the choir and nave.

*'Before the service began the Assistant Organist played Reubke's
Sonata on the Psalm "De Profundis" (sic) and other appropriate
compositions, and Dr. Bairstow followed with Chopin's "Funeral
March", and the strains of the bands outside playing their funeral
marches as the procession drew near reached the ears of the worshippers,
intermingling with the organ notes. Besides these, one could hear the
muffled bells sounding their solemn cadence from the church tower.
Beethoven's "Funeral March on the Death of a Hero" then pealed from
the organ in chords of solemn and impressive dignity, with a well-simu-
lated roll of drums, and to this succeeded the "March Solonnelle" (sic)
of Schubert. Now all was silence save for the churchwardens moving
inward from the porch with crepe-tipped wands as they conducted the
public representatives to their places in the western aisle'.*

The 1910 festival confirmed my opinions of these gargantuan
feasts of music. They are a relic of other days when they supplied
the only first-rate music that could be heard in the Provinces. I hear
that the Leeds people are preparing for another one now (1946)!

It was this year when the Vicar of Leeds had a very severe
illness. He was away for some months. His first re-appearance at
Church was on a Friday evening. The choir was singing the Psalms
unaccompanied. When they got to the verse in Psalm 94 "If the
Lord had not helped me it had not failed but my soul had been put
to silence, but when I said 'my foot hath slipt', Thy mercy, O Lord
held me up", Dr Bickersteth was overcome; he sat down and wept.
It struck me that I should like to set these words to music. But,
thought I, the Psalms have been combed out by composers for
many generations, they must have been set already. However, I
looked through Novello's anthem book and not a soul had tackled
them. That is thirty-six years ago and I have still to find another
setting. When I went to York the Revd. G. Surtees Talbot and I
revised the repertory, and he compiled the weekly music list. He
quite rightly hated to put any nonsense on it, such as "I will wash
Wesley". But he was completely stumped by "If the Lord had not
helped me", Bairstow.

The year 1911 was a sad year for me. I was feeling the strain
of overwork. Just after Easter my wife and I and Stephen went to
stay with my parents in London. We had not been in the house five
minutes before my mother had a stroke. She died the same evening.

My father was overwhelmed. I had everything to attend to. It was the greatest shock of my life. She was the most saintly woman I ever came in contact with. A man who had known her for many years wrote the following in the Methodist Recorder:

"She was the greatest living example of entire sanctification within the range of our experience. She suffered long from adverse circumstances, but no anxious worry or sour despair ever furrowed her brow. And she was kind – kind to the poor, to the sick, to domestic animals, to birdlings which came to be fed almost from her hand daily. She would invite into her house poor begging women with their little children and feed them at her table. Some even found a permanent home with her. Her love "vaunted not itself", was not "puffed up", but was the embodiment of gentleness, unselfishness, self-effacement. As for not being "easily provoked", nobody ever saw her angry. Nor did she ever "think evil", for she was ready to forgive the deepest injuries when there were the slightest signs of repentance".

All this is absolutely true. Her last words were, "Have they had a cup of tea?" referring to my wife and myself after our journey to London.

At the end of June I suddenly came to a full stop; I felt I could do no more work. A black cloud of deadly depression settled on me. The doctor said, "Keep still". But that made me liverish and miserable. The whole affair was new to me; I had never felt like that before. My old friend, Dick Dear, cured me. He invited me down to his lovely house at Eastbourne, where he was organist of St. Saviour's. We watched the great tennis tournament at Devonshire Park: we played clock golf in his garden. My mind was taken away from myself. I went back to work at the beginning of October fitter than I had been for years. The Vicar of Leeds insisted on my seeing a Harley Street specialist, Sir John Broadbent, on the way home. He pronounced me "fit but soft". My own doctor had said "plenty of potatoes, but no green vegetables". Sir John said "plenty of green vegetables but no potatoes". There were a few more contradictions of this sort.

It was in 1912 that I first examined for the Royal College of Organists. I had been a member of the Council for some time. In those days the big three, Bridge (Westminster Abbey) Martin (St.

Paul's) and Parratt (St. George's, Windsor) ruled the roost. If a young member of the Council made a remark in any debate every head turned towards him, as if to say "How dare you interrupt!". There was an unseemly scramble to get on to the staff of examiners. After one meeting a certain man said of his next-door neighbour, "I nominated him because I thought if I did he would vote for me. But he voted for someone else." Evidently he had peered surreptitiously over his shoulder at his neighbour's voting paper! I began with A.R.C.O. organ-playing. There were three of us, Dr. Alcock, Dr. Sweeting, and myself. Although we gave minute attention to the playing of the candidates that did not preclude a lot of fun. In those days candidates had to choose one piece from a given list. Most of them chose Bach, so he was barred out from our sweepstake. We all put pennies in the "kitty" for each candidate and chose a piece. There was a fairly long list, so that quite a lot of money would accumulate before a candidate would strike up your selection and you would scoop the winnings with great rejoicing. Sweeting turned up with some funny tricks and catches from Gamage's. Alcock was given a pencil with a waggly rubber point. There was also a circular india-rubber contraption which when sat upon gave forth a high squeak. Sir George Martin was so pleased with it that he took it away, putting it in the tail pocket of his morning coat. He was a most benevolent looking old gentleman with a beard. He went back home on the Underground with two old ladies who were much confounded when Sir George sat down on the squeaker. The climax was reached at a Council Meeting. I had annexed an ostensible petrol-lighter. When you touched the button it sprang apart, and pieces jumped in all directions. I handed it to Dr. Alcock to light his pipe. He was so amused that he fitted it together and handed it to Dr. Alan Gray for a similar purpose. He was sitting immediately opposite the President, Dr. C.H. Lloyd. All the pieces went into Dr. Lloyd's lap who gave us a lecture on the seriousness of our work and said we were behaving like schoolboys!

Ever since 1912 I have been closely connected with the R.C.O. I was President in 1929 and 1930. It has gradually changed its outlook altogether. To begin with, I fear, the thought behind the minds of a certain number of the Council was, "What can I get out of the

College?". Now it is, "What can I do for the College and for the raising of the standard of organ-playing and general musician-ship?". In the old days it was a most inartistic place – it is not beautiful now – but then it was all varnished pitch-pine with very cheap enlarged photographs of previous Presidents and Secretaries disfiguring the walls. The Hall with the organ in it had bare walls and dirty paint. By way of a protest I made a portrait of Sir John Stainer framed with the old large Bryant & May's Matches – a tiny and insignificant thing – and stuck it up on one of the gaunt walls. This had the desired result and now large pictures of some of the Cathedrals mitigate the dullness. The Council still has amongst its members some of the best-known musicians and organists in the country, whose ideas and advice are worth much to the College, but they don't rule the roost as the big three used to do.

I cannot resist a few further stories of the R.C.O. They all concern a very old and dear friend, Dr. H.A. Harding, who was honorary Secretary from 1908 till 1930. He was full of human kind-ness and cheerfulness. He was as humble and innocent as a child; you could pull his leg as much as you pleased. One very hot July I was examining A.R.C.O. paperwork with him and Dr. Bennett, then organist of Lincoln Cathedral. I sneaked out of lunch early, got a piece of the official manuscript music paper from the office and proceeded to harmonise the melody. The first few bars were full of the most elementary errors. The rest was marked "A la Stravinsky" and was as "modern" as I could make it. I labelled it No. 67 and put it in Harding's pile. Bennett was in the know. We proceeded with our long job in the heat with blue-bottles buzzing round. After about an hour, Harding reached Number 67. He made several loud grunts and then said "By jove boys, come and look at this." But Bennett had to look out of the window; he was gurgling with laughter. "Look here", says Harding "the fellow was no fool. I wonder what he was thinking of!" "How many marks are you giving him?" I asked. "I don't know what to do. I don't see how you can mark it, I shall give it a moon", replied Harding, and put a huge naught in blue pencil on it. When we came to enter the marks on the sheet he found, of course, that he had two number sixty-sevens. Then he began to see that someone had hoaxed him. "There's only one man in this building who could have done this" he blustered, and that's Charlie Macpherson." (who was examining organ playing upstairs). "I know what I'll do. I'll wait till a candidate is absent and go and sit on the keys." Unfortunately it occurred to him that the clerk in the office would know who had obtained the music paper. That gave the show away. Harding was a teetotaller. Once, on some special occasion, there was champagne at lunch. Harding drank ginger ale. He was called upstairs for a minute to see someone. During his absence someone filled up his glass with champagne. When he came back he had a long draught and said with intense enthusiasm, "By jove, boys, this is the finest drink I ever tasted!"

The examiners have to choose the pieces for the next examination. Their choices are handed round at the next Council meeting. At one of these meetings there was a characteristic grunt from Harding. "This piece will never do" (It was in the days of hobble skirts) "Why, how will the ladies play this?" What he objected to was a double pedal – top F, the highest note together with F two octaves below.

The summer of 1912 was wet and cold. We took the children as usual to Sandsend, three and a half miles north of Whitby. The bracing weather did me more good than heat. We could play tennis on the hard courts just after rain. Sandsend when we first went there was picturesque and attractive enough with its two valleys and streams, joined by the little front of houses, no two alike. It must have been very beautiful before the building of a few villas and a high red-brick, lodging house type of house with the modern hotel at the northern end. There is an old sea-wall past the hotel with two old cottages on it, at right angles to the front. We stayed in each of these. On stormy nights the spray from breaking waves thundered down on the roof as we lay in bed. Stephen fished diligently from the sea-wall, but had no luck for days. I offered him half-a-crown for each fish and went off to Whitby. When I came back he confronted me with twenty-one mackerel. A shoal had come in. A retired Wesleyan Minister had built the tennis courts – two grass and one hard. They must have cost him a pretty penny levelling the hillside and building the little club-house. One day when we were playing his wife came in desperation. She had got up a concert in the barn – Sandsend's concert room – and could not find an accompanist. "I'll play for you if you can't possibly find anyone" I said. She had not the slightest idea who I was and asked my name. "You can call me what you like" I replied. On the programme I appeared as "Mr King". This sounds like snobbery, but I well knew the type of song and singer I should have to accompany. The first performer was a middle-aged woman in glasses who proffered a song in G flat, whispering in my ear that if I found the six flats too many to cope with I could play it in one sharp.

Sandsend is spoiled now. A mine that had come loose shattered the two old cottages; a straight, broad motor road has ironed out the little curly lane that followed the course of each valley on the way to Whitby. The worst drawback in our time was the villagers themselves, who threw their refuse into the streams and let their children break glass bottles on the beach. August found us there until 1918. That year we had a tall, modern, red-brick house. The drawing room was on the first floor. I was writing letters one afternoon with the window wide open when there was a terrific explosion. Within a mile was a destroyer dropping depth charges assisted by an aeroplane. A German submarine had sunk a small coasting vessel that morning when the weather was dirty. Now, with a spring tide and all clear, the submarine had tried to take refuge close inshore on the flat shale. It was plainly visible to the aeroplane which dropped fizzling lights on the sea surface to show the destroyer where to plant the depth charges, very few of which were needed. Then a patch of oil showed, which eventually extended in a stream all the way to Whitby. Another great excitement took place one Sunday morning. I was just walking home from Whitby where I had purchased the Sunday papers, when I saw approaching the shore what looked like the bow waves of a motor boat, but there was no boat. Presently a huge torpedo nosed its way between two rocks and came to rest. The coast-guard dashed down on his bicycle. Throwing it down he rushed to chivvy the crowd back into their houses. Our two maids ran upstairs to their bedroom to get their money – why, I do not know. Very soon a naval detachment arrived in a motor launch and towed the torpedo out to sea.

Once, Stephen, always a keen fisherman, went out in a small boat with an officer friend on a very foggy afternoon. Out of the fog appeared two ships' boats full of sailors. They enquired as to

their whereabouts and were directed to Whitby harbour, much to
their relief. Little Sandsend has had its share of excitement in both
wars.

It was becoming increasingly evident that the Leeds Parish
Church organ wanted attention. I was determined that the work
should be done by a first-rate firm and recommended Harrison
and Harrison of Durham and London. Arthur Harrison was the
natural successor of Father Willis. Like him he scorned any shoddy
work; like him he had a marvellous ear and a great flair for making
his organ perfectly suitable to the building wherein it was to be
erected. At Leeds Schulze's old echo organ, remodelled and
revoiced, was put in the Lady Chapel and for the first time sounded
ethereal. The rest of the instrument got the same thorough treatment. A worse building acoustically it would be difficult to find,
but Arthur Harrison made the organ powerful and dignified, and
yet the softer tones had spirituality and mystery.

I had begun a "Service" or setting of the canticles, by composing the Magnificat and Nunc Dimittis in 1906. I felt that I should
like to do more of it for the reopening of the organ, so I set to work
on the Communion Service. In those days I think I was more or
less under the spell of Elgar, though of course it was purely
sub-conscious. At all events the Communion Service was written
on the *leit-motiv* principal, the themes recurring wherever they were
appropriate. For a great occasion like the re-opening of that colossal organ I did not hesitate to use fully all the material I had to
hand. Both choir and organ parts were by no means easy.

In the autumn of 1912 Ernest Bullock left us. He had been my
assistant practically all the time at Leeds, and now went to fill a
similar post at Manchester Cathedral. We missed him sorely in the
house, for both the children loved him dearly. He was just beginning to write very attractive music, and it was not long before his
songs and his church music began to be known and enjoyed.

Mr. Tertius Noble, the organist of York Minster, had been over
to play for us, and the Leeds choir had joined with the Minster
choir in a performance of Brahms's Requiem in the Minster, at
which Noble played the organ and I conducted. He and I were very

good friends. It was somewhat of a shock to me to hear that he was seriously thinking of accepting a post in New York. He told me that his income from all sources at York – his salary at the Minster, teaching and adjudication at competitive festivals – was considerably less than I was earning at Leeds; that the Dean was a dear old autocrat who insisted on Noble asking his permission if he wished to be away from the Minster, even for a day. He also said that most of the men in the choir were old and worn-out, but there was no pension fund for them. He then went to New York to spy out the land. He was away some time. When he returned he said that the monetary prospects were so much better at St. Thomas's, Fifth Avenue, New York, than at York Minster, that he had determined to accept the offer of the post. After Noble's dismal and hopeless description of the prospects at York Minster, you may imagine I did not jump for it when he suggested that I should become a candidate for the organistship. I rather dreaded that two Cathedral Services a day would tend to cramp my imagination and turn me into a mere church musician. I had such a glorious choir at Leeds, and very soon I was to have an organ that would be the last word in tonal beauty, resource and up-to-date mechanism. Then there were the two flourishing Lancashire choral societies, both of which I should be obliged to relinquish, and I had as much teaching as I could do. In the other scale was the great Minster, the most spacious, strong and thrilling cathedral in England, a lovely old house close to it and – a point I overlooked until I got to York – the kudos that the position of cathedral organist carried with it.

I entered half-heartedly for the job. I was asked to send three testimonials. I wrote back sending three relating to personal character and saying that the best testimony to my musical ability was the service at Leeds; all others referring to music were given me so many years ago that they were of no present use. There I left it. In a few weeks time I discovered that some of my friends were keener on getting me in to York than I was to go. Dr. Alan Gray, organist of Trinity College, Cambridge, Herbert Thompson, the Yorkshire Post critic, and a few more were quietly acquainting the members of the big Chapter – residentiaries and honorary canons – with my virtues. Miss Violet Argles told me that she had so many letters to copy for her father, Canon Argles, extolling my powers as a church organist and choirmaster, that she was tired of me before she had even seen me! I may say that in after years she was honorary secretary for the York Musical Society, the Minster Augmented choir, and the Diocesan Festival, and did invaluable work for all three. Noble let me know how things were going, and from him I found that dear old Dean Purey Cust was much in favour of Charles Hylton Stewart, then organist of St. Martin's, Scarborough. The Vicar of this church, Archdeacon Mackarness, had been the Dean's curate when he was vicar of Reading. The Dean was greatly beloved; no-one liked to cross him, nor did he like to be thwarted. On the actual day of the great Chapter Meeting, I and a friend went for a long walk up Nidderdale and had a rare good lunch at the Inn at Middlesmoor. I don't believe we gave the all-important Chapter Meeting a thought, so little did I care which way the voting went. When we came back to Leeds in the evening, my wife was waiting for me on the station to say that I had been elected by eleven votes to eight. I went straight to church to take the full rehearsal of the choir. When I got home I found several sanguine press-men still on the doorstep. My wife had told them that the only information she had was a private telephone message from Mr. Noble, and that they must wait for the official announcement from the Chapter Clerk. She was always a rare good diplomatist and would never give the show away. The Pressmen had to go home unrewarded.

Noble accepted the New York appointment in January 1913. The search for his successor came to an end two months later. On Friday the twenty-eighth of March the press reported that 'At a meeting of the Dean and Chapter today Mr. Edward Cuthbert Bairstow, organist of Leeds Parish Church, was appointed organist of York Minster in succession to Mr. T. Tertius Noble who relinquishes the post to take up the duties of organist of St. Thomas' Church, New York next month. There were over fifty applicants for the post, and these were reduced to three by the selection committee, and at today's meeting the testimonials of those three – Mr. Arthur Charles Hylton-Stewart (organist of St. Martin's, Scarborough), Mr. Edward Cuthbert Bairstow ... and Mr. H.W. Hunt (organist of Bristol Cathedral) – were considered.

'The Dean and Chapter sat at twelve o'clock noon, but it was close upon three o'clock before a decision was arrived at. Appended we give details of the career of the new organist of York Minster:- Bairstow,

Edward Cuthbert, Mus. Bac. 1894: Mus. Doc. 1900, Durham: Trained Westminster Abbey: Organist and Choirmaster, All Saints Norfolk Square, W. 1893: Parish Church, Wigan 1899: conductor Wigan and district Philharmonic Society 1901-6: Southport and Birkdale Philharmonic Society 1901-3: Blackburn St. Cecilia and Vocal Union 1903: Preston Choral Society 1907: Barnsley St. Cecilia 1908-11: and Leeds Parish Church to the present time. University examinations (Mus. Bac.) Psalm 84 O how amiable; *(Mus. Doc.)* Psalm 138 *(sic)* By the waters of Babylon. *Published compositions, album of songs, pieces for organ, anthems, services, carols, part songs, hymn tunes, chants, etc. Residence: 10 De Grey Road, Leeds.'*

On the following day, 29 March, interviewed at his residence, ... 'though he had not then received any official confirmation of his appointment, he had been inundated with letters and telegrams from friends congratulating him upon his success. "And", he added, "the very first telegram I received, couched in the warmest terms, was from Mr. Hylton Stewart, who also applied for the appointment." Doctor Bairstow pointed out a remarkable coincidence in connexion with his success. He has only held three appointments during his career, at London, Wigan, and Leeds respectively, and at each place he has stayed seven years. The remarkable thing about it all is that at the time of his departure from each of these places a new organ was about to be installed at this church. At the present moment there is a new organ on order, and will shortly be expected in Leeds Parish Church. The sequence will be broken at York.'

In three months' time my connection with Leeds Parish Church came to an end. The seven years during which I was responsible for its music were very happy ones. The choir at the end of the period was, I think, unique. There were thirty boys, all of whom could sing, and nearly thirty men, strong and well balanced, some of whom were fine soloists. The only man I had lost was the bass, John Browning. We were to give a choir concert and he was to sing a cycle of songs with chorus. He was ill just before the concert and would not say whether he would be able to take part. The second man could learn the songs rather in a hurry, but was in no mind to go to all the extra work involved if he was not sure to sing them. It got very near the date, and still Browning would give me no answer. Last of all I wrote him a note saying that the second man must sing. When he got well and turned up again at daily evensong I greeted

him and said how sorry I was he had been ill. He turned his back
on me before the choir and would not speak. After that I told him
one of us must go, and I did not think it would be me. Dear Dr.
Bickersteth asked us both up to the vicarage after service on the
next Sunday morning. After talking to us for a while he suggested
prayer. We knelt down and he prayed. When the prayer was over
he asked me if I felt differently towards the matter. But I said, "Not
in the slightest degree, Vicar. It would be a very bad thing for the
choir if such conduct as Mr. Browning's were passed over". So
John Browning resigned.

There were two memorable evenings at this time. One was at
the presentation by the Leeds Parish Church congregation of a
silver tea service and salver to my wife and myself. The other was
at Blackburn, where the committee and chorus of the St. Cecilia
Society gave us a fine, dignified old grandfather clock and a silver
salver.

During the whole of my time at Leeds I had been slowly learning and maturing. I can look back now and remember how long it
took to realise things which are now obvious to me. Before I went
to Leeds I simply did my work by following the technical instruction I had acquired. Whilst at Leeds I began to ponder on the more
spiritual side: what put the petrol in the tank? In other words, why
had so many people beautiful voices and yet could not sing? Why
were there so many musical players who never seemed able to
develop a fluent and rapid technique? Why was it that, at competitive festivals, you could divide the choirs into two groups – the
purely conscientious who did all the printed copy asked for but left
you cold, and those who moved you from the first note to the last?
Gradually I began to realize that the vitality, the energy, the moving
quality in satisfying performances came from love. Then I began
to call to mind many who loved music devotedly but could not
either sing or play to any sense. Again it occurred to me that a
burglar who was fascinated with burgling, like the celebrated Raffles
of Hornung, would burgle with far more success than some unimaginative criminal who hated the dangerous side but was keen on
the spoils. Last of all it slowly dawned on me that we are justly
punished for using any of God's good gifts for a wrong and usually
a selfish purpose. Moreover the punishment is inescapable, just as

the reward for using the gift aright is certain. It matters not whether it is the abuse of a good appetite or a healthy thirst, or whether it is singing or playing just for your own selfish enjoyment instead of for your neighbour, or whether it is cultivating a love for something which you know to be wrong, like Raffles, all these sins will certainly bring their own appropriate punishment. What, then, was the use of teaching purely technically when the result would only be like a well-made motor car without any petrol in the tank? Of course some have the spirit born in them, some have it to a slight extent, some have none at all. But even the best can be helped if they are constantly told that every consonant they utter must carry to the man on the back row, or, as Flesch, the great violin teacher, used to say to his pupils, that every demisemiquaver has in itself a message for the audience. There was another question: was not technique to come first and the rest after a while? The answer to that lay in the fact that every technical law is designed with a view to expression, and that everyone learns quicker when they are quite clear as to the use of what they learn. The teacher who is full of the right love explains the purpose of all technique in clear, simple language and radiates enthusiasm unconsciously at all times. Thus the pupil is also enflamed. All the other tenets in the creed that I have slowly become aware of are generated by that all-embracing little phrase of five words: "Perfect love casteth out fear". Like all great truths it is true of all things, from the love of the God who made it to the love of the tiny bird for its eggs and its young. The slightest movement is enough to cause the bird to flutter off if it has no family, but it has the courage to remain in its nest until you are close to it when there are young to defend.

The next fact which it took me a long time to absorb is this: nothing moves with a continued, uninterrrupted motion, although it appears to do so. Movement consists in alternate periods of energy and relaxation. Every syllable we utter has energy on the consonant and freedom on the vowel. Every step we take has energy at the moment of the pressure of the foot on the ground and freedom in the swing from one foot to the other. One good thing kicks you off on to another. You do your work during the day with joy. When you put your head on the pillow you say, "I know it might have been better, but it was the best I could do". Then you sleep the sleep of the just, and next morning you spring out of bed refreshed for another period of energy. The land rests in winter but springs to life in summer. These examples are a few out of many. One would have thought that everyone would learn the lesson from them. But my experience is that relaxation, economy and ease are the most difficult things to teach. The great bugbear is worry. Christ said "Sufficient unto the day is the evil thereof", and "Take no thought for the morrow" and "Come unto me all ye that *labour* and are *heavy laden,* and I will give you *rest*". Yet what happens in the case of an embryo pianist? You put the fingers of your left hand under his wrist and ask him to relax, so that the hand droops from the wrist you are supporting. This takes time to begin with. Then with the right hand you feel the fingers. You will nearly always find a certain amount of resistance. Sometimes, of course, energy is also lacking, but not nearly so often as relaxation. But just think how quickly and easily those alternate stresses and eases succeed each other in a rapid passage! It must, therefore, be easy of accomplishment. Suspicion is the cause of heaps of the trouble, just as it is in the world today. People suspect the various members of their own body. But treat them as your willing servants and they will do wonders for you; suspect them and they will surely fail. Those who have employees working for them know that there are several essential principles which you must follow if you want to get the best work out of them. First of all explain precisely, simply and comprehensibly what you want them to do. Then leave them alone to do it, don't be constantly at their elbows watching suspiciously for failure; give them the impression that you never dreamed of such a thing. Be patient when they are new to the job. Tell them that no-one does a thing perfectly the first time. I knew an old lady who kept the tea caddy locked up. The maids brought it to her and she parcelled out the contents. She was asking for trouble and she got it. Follow these ideas in your treatment of your own body. Say with the Psalmist, "I will praise thee, for I am fearfully and wonderfully made, and that my soul knoweth right well". Some time ago I was rehearsing the choristers. They came to grief at a large and difficult leap from a low sound to a high one. So I made a lightning jump from E, G, C, in the middle of the piano to A sharp, C sharp, F sharp at the top of the piano. Said I: "I know you think I have practised that. As a matter of fact I picked out those two chords because I never remember them occurring in any piece. It was done through faith: I trusted my fingers, hand and arm.' Do not try to understand the mechanism: you never will. But use it thankfully. Be a simplifier, not a complicator.

The next fact is also obvious, but many there are who fail to see it. It is this: the amount of satisfaction and happiness you will get from any undertaking (not material benefit always) is proportionate to the amount of work you have put into it. If it has cost you nothing it will not have any permanent value. My experience with the little composition I have done bears this out. You get a flash of inspiration: you know roughly what you want. Then comes the hard work. What you write does not come up to your inspiration. You tear it up and start again. After a while other and better themes come to your mind and things move easier. But even then there are places where it disappoints you. Finally you get it as right as in you lies, and the satisfaction is great. Or take the Leeds Philharmonic chorus. I have conducted them since 1917, but they have never come so near to my ideal as they have this season (1945-6).

Lastly, "Seek ye first the kingdom of God, and all other things will be added unto you". Music is the most spiritual of all the arts. If used aright it will do more than any other to make God's kingdom come "on earth as it is in heaven". But it may be grossly misused, like love. Therefore do all you can to persuade people to keep to the best and reject the worthless or harmful. Not from any highbrow attitude, but because you know that the great things in music will bring to them a deep happiness nothing else will. It would be a thousand pities if they missed these glorious thrills. Never be afraid and suspicious of the public, they are thirsting for the best in these days when, alas, they get very little from religion. There are so many dead and empty churches and so many uninspired, cold and heartless clergy. "Man cannot live by bread alone", and so people turn to the next best thing – music. Be not afraid that your pocket will suffer: you will have enough, though you will not make a fortune.

Of course, being of a slow, rather conservative type of mind, these basic principles of life inside and outside music did not come upon me in a flash, but over a number of years, some in Leeds, some in York. It was their applicability to all things great and small which convinced me of their truth. Nor do I want you to run away with the idea that I have invariably succeeded in conforming to them; I have suffered the inescapable punishments which come from breaking them. But they have been of the greatest use to me, obvious as they are, both in teaching and in ruling my own spirit. It has been a great source of satisfaction to me when pupils have said, "You have taught me many things outside music".

V

York (1913-1946)

With antique pillars, massy proof,
And storied windows richly dight,
Casting a dim religious light;
There let the pealing organ blow
To the full-voiced choir below
In service high and anthems clear
As may, with sweetness, through mine ear
Dissolve me into ecstasies,
And bring all heaven before mine eyes.

Milton

IN JULY WE MOVED into the old house in Minster Court. We had scarcely got into it when we had a visit from Dean Purey-Cust. Though he had dreaded my coming, he was my first caller. After he was dead his daughter told me that someone had poisoned his mind against me, and told him that I was very difficult to get on with. He was a most picturesque figure, with the kindliest of faces framed in white, mutton-chop whiskers. He wore a long, black Inverness coat and hat with a biggish brim, turned up at the side, surrounded by a ribbon with a rosette in front. He had the perfect manners of an old aristocrat. He never heard of anyone in trouble but that he would set off immediately to comfort them. I never had a wrong word with him. He would take my two young children out with him in the old carriage with coachman and footman. Sometimes these drives had as their objective a bazaar or other charitable meeting. Once Nancy arrived back with a bowl of goldfish. To prevent spilling goldfish and water from the jerking of the carriage, the Dean had put his pocket handkerchief over the bowl and fastened it with an elastic band that normally went round his pocket book. He allowed the children to play in the Deanery garden. It was an ideal place for them, with fine old trees and no flower beds. The Dean never forgave the City Council for allowing the public to walk round the walls between Bootham Bar and Monk Bar because it destroyed the privacy of his garden, for the walls formed two sides of it. So he let his garden run to seed except for having the grass cut. This made it an ideally wild and beautiful place for our children's games and adventures. By now the trees and shrubs have grown thicker and shelter the garden from prying eyes to a certain extent. But little boys can still get over the barbed wire in some miraculous way and steal apples and break glass.

The Dean was certainly an autocrat, but a very kindly one. Moreover he was 85 when I was appointed and often entirely forgot some command that he had given. For instance, he called me in one morning and showed me an enormous pile of hymn-books. The tunes had been composed by the Maclagan family, father and daughter (*the Archbishop, and Theodora Georgina Jane*). I forget whether he had bought the hymn-books or whether they had been given to him. At all events he thought it would be very nice if we sang one of the hymns every Thursday morning instead of an anthem. Now the most difficult thing in the world is to write a hymn-tune; for what with the restrictions imposed by the fact that the congregation must be able to join in, and the fact that thousands upon thousands have been written for hundreds of years, it is almost impossible to create one that has any individuality or *raison d'être*. There is only one that I know, written during my time, which has really done its duty by turning out a bad tune that had great popularity, and reigning in its stead. This is Vaughan Williams's tune to "For all the saints". This tune will live. The mere stringing together of well-worn phrases which are not your own has no value, and consequently such tunes have but a very short existence. So you can imagine I was determined, if possible, to avoid sacrificing some of our beautiful short morning anthems for tunes of this sort. The Dean was very deaf, and I don't think he heard what

I said to him about 'thinking it over' or words to that effect. To my great relief he never mentioned the hymn-books again.

When the first consecration of a bishop came along I was told that the Dean had ordered Dykes in F to be sung at every one of these great services "because it was so short and the service was so long". I took the risk, tabooed Dykes in F for evermore, and put on some really fine and suitable music. Nothing was said.

Dean Purey-Cust had a great sense of quiet humour. He it was who told me the following story. In the early days of the last century there was a certain Dean Cockburn at York. He loved the pleasures of this world, particularly eating and drinking, and kept open house. Unfortunately he did not pay his bills. Amongst these was a large one for wines and spirits from the firm of Oldfields, still in existence in York. In those days when a living in the gift of the Dean and Chapter fell vacant, the Dean and the residentiary Canons appointed a new incumbent in turn. Nowadays there are nominations and these are voted on by the Chapter. It was Dean Cockburn's turn to appoint. A living had just fallen vacant, and a young Oldfield had just taken holy orders. The Dean popped him into the living; the bill for liquor was squared. Thereupon Archbishop Harcourt, father of Sir William, threatened to inhibit him for simony. There was a deadlock. The Archbishop would not come to the Minster. Then appeared on the scene a general officer to the Northern Command, of which York is the headquarters, who knew both the Archbishop and the Dean very well. He determined to make peace, and persuaded the Archbishop to allow him to take the Dean to Bishopthorpe. There, after numerous bottles of port, they wept on one another's shoulders. Dean Purey-Cust's dear old eyes used to twinkle in a delightful way when he reached the end of this story. He also had another. The old Duke of Cambridge came to service. He had a deep, cavalry voice which carried far. When the collection plate came to him the coin dropped on the floor. Numerous vergers and sidesmen immediately started to hunt for it. When the deep voice which could be heard all over the choir boomed forth, "Oh, don't you trouble, it's of no consequence at all", this proved to be true, for when the coin was eventually found it turned out to be a sixpence.

The house in Minster Court which we took on from the Nobles is unique in my experience. Never did I see a house so long for its breadth. On the ground floor the spacious and dignified dining-room, facing south, has a large kitchen to the north of it. These two rooms are flanked by the hall and staircase on the east side. At the end of the hall, still further north, is a little room which the children used as a nursery when they were young. In these days of fuel shortage my wife and I have our meals in it. This ends the ancient part of the house. North of the kitchen is a small yard and then the music room begins. This was built by a clergyman named Singleton who was a friend and admirer of Monk, organist from 1859-1883. It was built for an organ, and had a well-made two manual with quite a lot of spotted metal in it. The legend goes that at Singleton's death it was given to the City Council for the Exhibition Hall, and that it was eventually sold by them for £5. I could not vouch for the truth of this story, but it must have been far too small for that hall. After that the old house was used for the Song School during a short period when the Dean and Chapter tried the experiment of a boarding school. The music room was the boys' dormitory. Then one of the Vicars Choral had it until the Nobles went into it. The Nobles let the music room to a lady with a physical culture class. As there was a shortage of bedrooms we got the Chapter to cut it in halves and made the southern half into two bedrooms, one above the other. The rest of the room will com-fortably seat 60 people. It has an entrance reached from the back lane, so that pupils need not come through the house. It has been a godsend to me; its only drawback being the difficulty of keeping it warm in the winter. The glory of the house is the drawingroom, on the first floor, over the dining room, nobly proportioned and with the most beautiful hand-moulded ceiling I ever saw. The prob-able period of the older part of the house is Queen Anne. There are evidences that the three houses in Minster Court, which cover three sides of a square, were originally one. The middle house has Tudor beams with carved bosses in its upper rooms. They seem to have been designed to form the roof of a common room or hall.

The first time I heard the Minster choir I was somewhat depressed. Noble, what with his first visit to New York to see what things were like, and then his final departure, had given no attention to it for months. The assistant was one of those 'nice' people who cut no ice. I made the boys sing a scale, walking round to look inside their mouths. As I suspected, many of them had their tongues rolled up like a sausage at the back. I remember giving them a realistic imitation of Canon Watson's cat. He lived at No. 3. It was a very similar noise. The men were a mixed lot. There were two very good altos and one dear old man who died only a few years ago. (*see airgraph letter 22 December 1942, page 203*). If he had lived a few more months he would have been a songman for fifty years. He never made a mistake, had very little rhythm, but for some mysterious reason blended well in a quartet. There was one really musical tenor and one who had absolute pitch and perfect time, but a thin voice. The other two were very little good. The principal bass and senior songman, Andrew McColl, had in his prime been an ideal lay clerk. He followed every prayer in his prayer book as an example to the rest. He was also librarian and put all my marks into the copies with meticulous care. At almost the first full rehearsal there came along an anthem "Hear my crying" by Weldon. "This is supposed to contain the first known example of the use of a certain chord" said I. "Yes, the last inversion of the augmented sixth on the last page", said McColl. The other three basses were what the Leeds singers called "lamb basses". In those days the principal singers were paid only £100 per annum: the rest got £75. If one grumbled to the Canons the reply was always, "Well, you see, the Minster is so poor". Why do Cathedral Chapters never issue a financial statement? The public run away with the idea that they are wealthy corporations and put pence in the collection plates and boxes. The majority of the public love these wonderful old buildings. They would never allow them to suffer if they knew just how much it costs to keep the fabric in order, pay organist and choir and run a school for the choristers. The Societies known as 'Friends' of the various cathedrals have extracted a certain amount of information from the Chapters, but I have never seen a plain statement of income and expenditure. All the best young singers at York moved on to Durham, St. Pauls or Westminster Abbey. (*See page 103*)

It struck me that nine good singers would be better than eleven mixed ones. Also that the three worst might resign if they were given a substantial present for long and faithful service. Accordingly I had a letter printed and sent round to the Minster congregation. I forget how much I got, but it seemed to satisfy the men. We gave them a parting dinner. After that not one of them was ever seen in the Minster again. The rest got an increase of between £20 and £30 a year. We managed to get an extra amateur tenor and bass for Sundays who were quite useful.

There was a vicar choral at the Minster at that time whose name was George Surtees Talbot. He was the most delightful 'naughty boy' I ever met. When anything upset him – usually something in the music that he disliked – he would bang the door of his stall when he came back from reading a lesson: then he would gabble through the final prayers at an incredible speed. If anyone essayed to join in the psalms or responses he would dash down to the south transept door, intercept them as they went out and tell them in plain language what he thought of them for spoiling the service. The first time he banged his door and gabbled during my early days at the Minster I went down into the vicars' vestry and asked him how he thought I was going to persuade the men to behave themselves if he went on like that. He put out his hand and said "Shake. Most people would have gone to the Dean and complained to him, but you come straight to me". We were firm friends from then on to the end of his short life in 1918. His enthusiasm for the Minster music and all good church music was intense. He gave me invaluable help in converting an ill-balanced and ill-chosen repertory into one which no cathedral would have been ashamed of. There is an article by him in the old scrap book. In it he gives two lists of anthems; there are fifty-one new ones that had not been sung before and forty-two revivals of anthems that had been allowed to drop out of the rota. He had irreproachable taste, so that I could always trust him. His experience of the working of a cathedral choir helped him. He never put down more new music than it was possible to learn, but he kept us all hard at work. I did not object to the new anthems being sung even if they were not very finished, for once the choir had sung them at service, the finish could be much more easily achieved at their next appearance. In 1916 I determined to re-edit the Minster chant book which had far too few chants in it, and some of them dull and lifeless efforts. One day Talbot came along with five chants, and in the most shy and apologetic way asked me if I would look at them. They were remarkable, for in those few bars he had written five of the most distinguished and beautiful chants I know. The one for Psalm CL which we sing as a recessional after the choral eucharist is a great moment in the service. Dozens of people have written to me for copies of it. But the Minster chant book is not on sale to the public. Thus we avoid having to pay copyright on many chants.

(The new chant book was printed with the help of private donations in memory of former choristers who had died during the war. A revised edition was made in 1930 and a further, slightly expanded version in 1974 but with very few amendments, which is testimony to the excellence of the original choice that stood the test of 58 years of daily use. As well as those composed by Talbot, the book contained 15 of Bairstow's own as well as modern ones by W.G.Alcock, Ivor Atkins, Alan Gray, J.R.Dear and Cyril Musgrove (1887-1920), Assistant Organist at the Minster.)

Thus began in 1913 the long and arduous journey to make York Minster music as worthy of York Minster as was possible. Talbot deserves all the credit for the remodelling of the music list. He had in those days a wider knowledge of English church music than I had. He spent "many years of patient toil" to quote from his article, over it. Probably this is the first time his unselfish work has received due recognition. His was a sunny soul. He often came in from Huntington, a village four miles from York of which he was vicar, with stories which have stuck in my head ever since. They were usually about his old Parish Clerk. Here is one:- Talbot to Parish Clerk. "Well John, how's your son getting on in Mesopotamia?"

P.C. "Ay, he's been in t'Garden of Eden, parson".

T. " What did he think of it?"

P.C. "Ay, not mooch. I don't think they're keeping it oop like these days".

Talbot died in May 1918. The Minster choir went out to sing at his funeral. His own little choir of boys and girls sung the first part of the service in the church, whilst we sung at the grave. I shall never forget the effect of Psalm XC, 'Lord, thou hast been our refuge' sung by the choir on which he had spent so much time and trouble. The tone was sweet and free and in perfect tune; every syllable was audible; there was not a single false accentuation. Most remarkable of all, it was perfectly sincere and very moving. I have missed Talbot ever since.

AT THIS POINT SIR EDWARD'S WRITING WAS
PREMATURELY CUT SHORT BY HIS DEATH
ON 1 MAY 1946

VI

York II

"PERHAPS E.C.B., WHEN HE wrote that last sentence about
Talbot, had resolved already that his own last resting place
should be Huntington churchyard. At all events his devotion to
Talbot is obvious, and this is the place to indicate more precisely
what Talbot achieved for the Minster repertoire." Thus wrote
H.Percy Dixon, pupil of Sir Edward, organist (of Bossall church),
poet, journalist, sub-editor and leader-writer for the Yorkshire
Evening Post, whose hopes of completing Bairstow's autobiography were to remain unfulfilled through his untimely death not
long after Sir Edward's. He claimed to have had the last lesson given
by E.C.B., in the Purey-Cust Nursing Home a few days before his
death.

In a short article sometime in 1916 Talbot lists 92 anthems
newly taken into the repertoire of which about half were entirely
new and the other half 'which have been "dug out" after remaining for years on the shelves of the library'. Byrd, Gibbons, Purcell,
Greene, Wesley and Bach were all well to the fore numerically, Bach
being represented by nine items and Purcell by eight. All, of course,
had English words, the eleven foreign composers having their
contributions furnished with suitable translations.

Talbot pleads poverty as the reason for not being able to keep
songmen of high quality. "Our rich northern neighbour (*Durham*)
can take any good young voice away from us, if it so wishes, by a
very legitimate process of gentle bribery. Then again, the boys have
to be recruited from a district which has the double disadvantage
of an enervating climate and also distinct racial characteristics of
Danish origin which never make for naturally robust voices, as in

the case of the West Riding singers who come from a totally different stock." All the more glory, then, to "a most capable choir-master.... whose share in the 'revival' it is quite impossible to over-estimate".

Foreshadowing this in the previous year Bairstow had made known his feelings on the standard of taste in church music: a spirit of triviality and sentimentality had crept into it. It should first of all be dignified and strong and not merely pretty. However, people in the congregation had shown good taste by expressing their approval of the right kind of music – the kind that was written 'long before the days of publishers and when music was written with one aim – to be the very best and most appropriate for the purpose for which it was written'. The music list should contain the very best music, for a place like York Minster should be an example to every other church in the diocese.

The Minster Choir which, as he confessed many years later, was always a worry, fared better under wartime conditions than might have been expected. At the Song School speech day in April 1917 he was "very thankful that, while certain cathedrals were reduced to a choir of two men or none at all, they still went on and the services were kept up to a certain state of efficiency". It was much the same in the second world war: whenever a songman was obliged to leave, his place was providentially filled.

Shortly before Easter each year the choristers' prize-giving took place. This was a great day in the life of the boys and included, as well as speeches and an address by some notability, a short programme of solos and part-songs. E.C.B. was always one of the speakers and could be relied on to deliver one of his characteristically trenchant utterances. These were usually about the attitude of parents and the training of boys, but sometimes on musical subjects of more general interest. At his first appearance at one of these gatherings he was introduced by the archbishop, Cosmo Gordon Lang, as one who had brought 'great and singular gifts to the Minster'. The archbishop commented on the improved singing of the choir and looked forward to hearing some of Bach's music and Brahms' Requiem. E.C.B. was warmly received. In his speech he referred to the extreme kindness he had been shewn since he came to the Minster. The choir had done their level best, and he encouraged the congregation to help by letting the choir know of any appreciation they might feel. But they must be careful in that, 'because every choir is prone to swelled heads'.

He made innovations in the running of the Minster music and the boys' musical education. Previously during the holidays the choir had been halved – part men and part boys – but this Easter (1914) the men and the boys each sang for a week by themselves, which he considered a better arrangement.

As to Bairstow's extra-Minster activites during these early years at York, records are scanty. The scrap-book is silent. The minute books of the Symphony Orchestra and Musical Society record that he had accepted the conductorship of both bodies, but his association with the former was not to last. Editha Knocker was appointed co-conductor and was allotted the lighter pieces while the doctor took the serious works – Beethoven's second symphony and Schumann's piano concerto in which the soloist was Herr Padel, then resident in the city. Bairstow expressed the opinion that the poor attendance by the public was thought to be due to the presence of a symphony in the second concert of the season. The next two concerts had to be abandoned, but a performance of Brahms' Requiem was planned for the Minster, the only available venue. This was given jointly by both societies with soloists Agnes Nicholls and George Parker. Herbert Thompson wrote in the Yorkshire Post that it was to Bairstow's "able direction, that the high level of the performance may be in great measure attributed". Schubert's unfinished symphony also figured in the programme, which was on December 15th 1915.

At a meeting of the Y.S.O. committee two months earlier, Bairstow introduced a discussion on the amalgamation of the Y.S.O. with the Y.M.S. on certain conditions which he presented. Nothing more, however, was heard of the project until the next meeting nearly four years later, when it was decided to try to resuscitate the orchestra (there being 'still about 15 to 20 experienced playing members in York and district') and not to amalgamate with the Musical Society. Doctor Bairstow was willing to help but could not 'undertake the detailed rehearsing, technical drill work, etc.'; and his connexion with the orchestra ceased.

These two societies had grown out of a music club which was founded in 1765. The York Musical Society became a mixed chorus of something like a hundred members, while the York Symphony Orchestra was founded in 1898 by T.T. Noble, its personnel being provided mostly from the Musical Society. Therefore, if Bairstow's efforts to join the two had succeeded, it would have been a re-uniting and a return to the former state of affairs.

His acceptance of the conductorship of the Musical Society was reported by Miss Knocker to its committee on 23 May 1913, his fee for the season being twenty guineas. The works submitted to him were 'The Bride of Dunkerron' by Henry Smart with, in the second part, two part-songs by Dr. Bairstow, and solos. The second concert was to consist of Elgar's 'The Kingdom'. Another meeting was called two months later because the conductor "had expressed the opinion that 'The Bride of Dunkerron' was not quite up to the standard of the Y.M.S." (*Poor Smart! And Grove 5 unequivocally rates it his best work*). It was decided to include Parry's 'Pied Piper' and Dear's 'Songs of the Open Air' in the first concert. Later still, Bairstow asked for the substitution of the St. Matthew Passion for The Kingdom which he considered too difficult at that juncture. Considering Bairstow's extremely high standards as regards the quality of music (chapter X), one recalls, in parenthesis, his opinion of Smart in the 1916 edition of the Minster chant book: "a composer of the highest ideals, whose music wears well"...

Of the war years and after, and of the Passion performances, Alice Knight wrote:- "For me, E.C.B. was a great opener of doors, and this began long before I had, or ever dreamed of having, any personal contact with him. I grew up in York, in the world before and during the First World War, a world without radio, without effective gramophones, and long before the rash of local music festivals which have enlivened one's later years. Music was what one made oneself, or heard in church or through the rare visits of touring celebrities or opera companies. In common with most of my generation, my home-made music was anything my fingers could encompass on the piano, the accompaniment of the indifferent ballads of domestic songsters, part-songs around the piano, Gilbert and Sullivan, and Hymns A. & M. The first opening of a door out of this restricted world occurred in 1916 when I began to attend the organ recitals which E.C.B. gave in the Minster during the war years. The programmes would scarcely pass muster in these purist days, but were memorable to a music-hungry fourteen-year-old. There was always a Bach prelude and fugue, usually an orchestral transcription (the Andantino from Tchaikowsky's fourth symphony, the Larghetto from Beethoven's second) Schumann's Sketches for the Pedal Piano, pieces by Vierne, MacDowell, Alan Gray, E.C.B. himself, Harvey Grace and Widor (the now so popular Toccata, of which E.C.B. wrote in 1917 "it gives great effect to the new 'Tuba' stop on the Minster Organ"). It did indeed, and also to another item which appeared more than once in these programmes – Rachmaninoff's Prelude in C sharp minor!

"One of the greatest events in those early years was the performance in the Minster in Advent of the Brahms Requiem. To hear an orchestra at all was a virtual impossibility except on such occasions; to hear one in such surroundings and in such music was an experience almost as vivid now in memory as when E.C.B. and Brahms together first bowled me over completely with the throbbing drums and soaring violins of 'Behold, all flesh is as the grass'.

"The greatest of all doors opened, in 1917 or 1918, on to an event which was to become for me not so much a performance, more a part of life – the annual Bach St. Matthew Passion. E.C.B. used a shortened version, without interfering with the course of the narrative, enabling the performance to be contained within the span of one afternoon. At my first hearing of it, I remember standing throughout the whole performance, too absorbed to feel fatigue, consumed with envy of the piano continuo player, and having only a rear view of the soloists. Of these I thought the women good, the tenor divine, the baritone slightly disappointing. From the next morning's paper I learnt that they were Agnes Nicholls, Dilys Jones, Gervase Elwes and Plunket Greene. These, incidentally, were typical of the fine artists of the time who came year after year, often for nominal fees, to sing for E.C.B. at these performances. And I came too, every year, an anonymous fraction of the great congregation, absorbing the work almost into my bones, perhaps unconsciously preparing for the day when I should be drawn into the performing of it."

From their beginnings in 1914 these York Passions became an important feature of the musical life of the north of England. Outside the largest cities it was rarely possible to hear them, and some of the audience travelled great distances, this before the days of motor-ways and reliable motor-cars. Their undoubted artistic success was, unfortunately, not always matched by financial solvency. In 1916 the collection amounted to £26.10s. whereas that for Messiah was £42. As there was no charge for admission, the performance relied almost solely on the collection as well as upon the services, freely given, of most of the participants. According to the Yorkshire Herald report, Bairstow was outraged to see among the coins "farthings, Belgian coins, pebbles and lozenges". A further irritation was caused by the levying of entertainment tax on what were regarded by the Dean and Chapter as religious services, as witnessed by the fact that the event would begin with the lesser litany and Lord's prayer and end with the blessing. The Herald report continued: "When we were approached by the revenue authorities and told that these special services would be regarded as entertainments, we wrote to the subscribers explaining the circumstances. They responded well to the appeal made to them. I am afraid one or two people are saying they are tired of passion music, but I am of the opinion that there is no work which can take its place. There is no questioning that the story of the passion can be told more beautifully in musical form than any other. I have done passion music three or four times a year since 1906 and am still looking for new points of beauty in it. With regard to the special musical services, speaking logically I do not think they could be regarded as entertainments."

In 1917 he expressed the wish that money could be given as easily for the 'oratorial services' as for the Minster chant book which he had edited. If more money was not forthcoming they would have to be given up. York Minster was the place where such things should take place, and if done at all they should be done in a way worthy of the building. In 1920 the situation was somewhat improved: "If we do not come through with a balance on the right side we shall not be more than a pound or two short". It was an endless tussle until eventually tax on concerts in churches and cathedrals was abolished which was not, however, until some years after the second world war.

Around this time George Gray (later organist of Leicester cathedral) was studying with E.C.B. "One's overwhelming impression of his interpretation of choral singing" he wrote, "both in the Minster services and his choral societies, was that they were always live, sincerely felt and full of atmosphere. His Matthew Passion performances were most moving. Not everything he did would be approved in detail today, but the memory of them has guided me all my life. They set a standard of a most moving and tremendous musical experience, which one has always tried to convey in one's own performances of this work." Gray also mentions some of the works performed by the Y.M.S.: Vaughan Williams' Sea Symphony, his Sancta Civitas and Benedicite, Holst's Hymn of Jesus, Elgar's King Olaf, Music Makers and Gerontius, Stanford's Stabat Mater and Songs of the Fleet, Dyson's Canterbury Pilgrims, Handel's Semele, and many smaller pieces.

Herbert Thompson praised the performance of the Hymn of Jesus in the Yorkshire Post, commending the daring of the York Musical Society: "When one goes back to the earlier doings of the Society, it makes one rub one's eyes to find its chorus achieving a notable success in music as exacting as this, and in an idiom very different from that which has passed current. The trying intervals and the harsh discords were approached with something approaching ease, and there was hardly a single dubious phrase in the whole work. ... Dr. Bairstow must have devoted much pains to training his chorus, for his conducting was broad and expressive, but singularly effortless, and he secured what he desired with the minimum of fuss".

"These performances", observed Alice Knight, " necessitated an orchestra, usually an *ad hoc* collection of players from the Hallé and Leeds Symphony Orchestras, and E.C.B. occasionally included an orchestral item in the programmes. Thus I heard the Schubert Tragic Symphony, Mozart's E flat K 543 and Tchaikowsky's No.4, Elgar's Enigma Variations, Mozart's B flat Piano Concerto, Vaughan Williams' The Lark Ascending and Wasps overture in live performances otherwise impossible to hear in the city. Among the soloists...were pianists Myra Hess, Harold

Samuel, Eileen Joyce, Irene Kohler, Cyril Smith; violinists Jelly d'Aranyi, Sybil Eaton, and a constellation of singers, Agnes Nicholls, Elsie Suddaby, Isobel Baillie, Dorothy Silk, Astra Desmond, Gervase Elwes, Arthur Jordan, Steuart Wilson, George Parker, Harold Williams, Robert Redford, Plunket Greene, Keith Falkner. Add to this the daily music of the Minster, and one had, of E.C.B's providing, the basis of a sound appreciation of good music. True, compared with the riches now available every moment, the fare was thinly spread, but one had at least the time to digest each meal before the next was due – no bad thing."

"His thoroughness and attention to detail particularly fit him for the conductorship of a choir, and though he is often severe with the members of choral societies he leads, yet the admirable results he obtains reveal him to be a man of unusual qualifications". Thus an article in a series on people in the public eye in the York Gazette in March 1923. "It is an inspiration to sing under him. It is, too, an inspiration to see him conduct. His decisive, expressive beat, his intense enthusiasm for his work, and a keen, artistic understanding of the capacity of the forces under him, all mark him as a conductor of outstanding ability. An oratorio conducted by Dr. Bairstow is worth going miles to hear – and it is not uncommon for noted musicians to travel long distances to attend an oratorio service led by him in the Minster. ... He has the subtle art of getting the most out of a choir and orchestra..."

In June 1919, the war having ended, Bairstow announced his intention of starting a new choir to be known as the York Minster Augmented Choir for works for which the Minster Choir was too small. This, he declared, was in no way in rivalry to the York Musical Society. Indeed, its life appears to have been short, and in no way did it affect the pre-eminence of the venerable Y.M.S.

Alice Knight continued: "Perhaps I may be forgiven for mentioning two more doors opened for me by E.C.B. – one very small but indescribably precious – when he gave me the opportunity of hearing my own music, a short introit and kyrie, sung in the services of the Minster. The other door, a magnificent one, opened quite by chance. Some twenty-three years after first hearing the St. Matthew Passion I at last found myself at the piano as continuo player, when through the accident of war the previous incumbent,

Dr. and Mrs. Bairstow with Nancy and Peter

Francis Jackson, was called up for military service. My 'invitation' was typical. Being asked by his secretary who would be playing, E.C.B. replied, "Oh, Alice will have to do it – tell her to get hold of Frank's copy and mark up her own". That was all. Thereafter I 'did it', for him and for the same F.J., his successor, for twenty-four years, to my unfailing delight and satisfaction. If the 'invitation' was laconic, however, there was no lack of warmth in E.C.B.'s appreciation. After one performance, in 1945, he wrote to me, in a letter I shall always treasure, "I feel I cannot let this Sunday pass without telling you how much I appreciate all you did to make the Passion a success. Thank you for all of it; for your help in the organisation, which ran so smoothly, for trying voices – a trying job – and above all for your sterling accompaniments, so artistic and so sure". I was well rewarded.

"In these days when musicology and scholarship flourish, it is the custom to decry the use of the piano as continuo, and the singing of the chorales by unaccompanied choir, both practices of which E.C.B. was guilty throughout (in common, one may add, with Vaughan Williams). He was, of course, as well aware as anyone else of the anachronisms, but, pragmatist as ever, he knew that his ideas *worked*, in the circumstances of the Minster. As Dr. Herbert Thompson wrote, the performances were ' in complete harmony with the work and the occasion'.

"My tribute has perforce been entirely a personal one but I think it will be shared by many pupils, whose eyes were opened by him to wide vistas of musical beauty, and by countless music-lovers to whom he communicated worlds of delight, E.C.B. was in many ways a 'difficult' personality and in all the years I rarely felt entirely at ease with him. But one had to learn to take him as he was. I have so many reasons to be grateful to him and there was so much to like, admire and respect. Above all he imparted his own unwaveringly high musical standards and integrity. I did not always agree with his methods – the abrasion could sometimes be too severe – but it is with pride, gratitude and affection that I can subscribe myself, to an extent and in ways of which he was quite unaware, a Bairstow pupil."

VII

Philosophies

A LL THIS TIME BAIRSTOW WAS becoming more and more firmly established as a leader in his profession and a power to be reckoned with, especially in the north, but soon as a national figure whose ideas and opinions were widely noticed and taken seriously. In 1920 an interview with Percy Scholes was published, anonymously, under the title "What the Organist said". Bairstow's identity was disclosed later. As always it is packed full of sound sense. Scholes relates that it came about by reason of a meeting between deans and cathedral organists to discuss the effects of the financial situation. The war had depleted the funds of cathedrals, several of which had found it necessary in consequence to drop choral matins. He questioned Bairstow over lunch. *"To my surprise he said never a word about the present discontents, but came down to something so much more fundamental and before he had done he had, whilst talking all the time of church music, provided me with a criterion by which I could test any artistic product whatever – the pictures at Burlington House, or the Cavell monument, the Russian Ballet, as much as the music of Westminster Abbey or a village church. There are some superior musical people about, who, neglectful of all we owe to organists, would consider that "what the organist said is not evidence". But everything this one said was common sense; there was nothing really new about any of it, but it was all so clearly put that it seems to me to be well worth repeating – for the guidance especially of some of our younger and more thoughtless singers and players and composers.*

"The first point made was that in church music two essentials have to be looked for – beauty and expression. And here, of course, is the trite old truism that applies to every form of art. Applied to church music it

113

would abolish at least fifty per cent. (and more likely seventy-five per cent.) of the music in use."

After developing this theme he continues with veiled references to some singers of the day, one of whom is probably not difficult to identify. *"There is a famous woman singer whose voice and presence and ability would enable her to popularise any fine song she wished, but who frequently sings music that has no real depth or meaning. And there are three men singers to whom nature has given very imperfect voices, but who choose nothing but stuff that has beauty and meaning and who sing it with brains. Honour to the second type rather than the first. If we cannot have both beauty of voice and expressive force the latter is the more important of the two".* (Two of the singers he refers to are likely to be Clara Butt and Plunket Greene.)

The second principle concerned interpretation. *"There are cathedrals famous for their music that give us merely the product of rehearsal room drill. Brains have been used, but spirit is stifled. .... And connected with those must be also the old admitted principle that art must conceal art. But this, I imagine, when the former principles have been applied, comes about of itself ... For the art of self-expression covers up the evidence of the art that has been employed to secure beauty.*

"Another requirement (this time especially of the conductor and choir-master) is that of being able to control oneself in order that one may then control others. The man who could keep his head during an air raid ought to be able to come into church on a depressing November Sunday morning, pull himself together and carry things through. His choir boys will respond to him more quickly than his choir men, but both will feel his influence coming down from the organ loft. The player or singer or conductor who can only do well when conditions are perfect will have few opportunities of doing well. When Frangçon-Davies was to sing Elijah and the conductor insisted on starting amid the hubbub of late-comers arriving and programme sellers taking money, he had such self-control that his first few notes controlled the audience and the hubbub ceased. Another man would have been disturbed, made a bad beginning, and perhaps never emerged into the glow of self-expression to the very end of the oratorio. The ability to concentrate on one's work, to control one's own mood, is of even more value to the pianist than the ability to play scales at lightning speed. 'Greater is he that ruleth his own spirit than he that taketh a city'.

"*Lastly (and here is something which elaborated would become a sermon) – it is no good undertaking any artistic work whatever unless you have a 'sense of message'*". Bairstow himself was a potent example of the choirmaster's 'influence coming down from the organ loft'. His choristers were intensely aware of it, as they were also of its absence when he was not present.

An Anglo-American conference which took place in Lausanne during the first week of August 1929 was attended by some 400 people – 225 from Great Britain. Bairstow gave a lecture on the training of church choirs 'from a devotional, and also from a common-sense point of view, using no technical language, but giving simple hints'. The following notes were taken by a Miss Sayers and were approved by the lecturer.

The training of a church choir differs mainly from an ordinary choir in three respects:

1. The choir sings often without a conductor, therefore the ensemble must be better.

2. Boys' voices are needed (though boys' singing does not differ from that of women).

3. A different class of music is dealt with. There is also the chanting part and free rhythm.

Singing is speech beautified; but it is still speech. Therefore singers have a message to impart to those who hear.

Singing is not only beautiful tone.

Stereotyped methods produce failure and monotony.

Boys are easy to teach because, unlike grown-ups, they have not many preconceived ideas, self-consciousness, self-importance etc.

Here the lecturer got part of the audience to act as choir and to sing 'ah' with varying expression – in surprise, in anger, in despair, etc., also the phrase 'Man is like a thing of naught'. From their efforts, which were not wholly successful, he drew the lesson that it is hard for sophisticated people to throw themselves easily into the meaning of what they sing. "*There is more nonsensical bosh talked about the voice than about anything else in music*". *It is only necessary to know that the voice has three essentials – a motor; a vibrator; a resonator. The breath is the motor. As it goes in, so it comes out. If easily, then beautiful tone issues, and vice versa. Breathe as if you are thrilled. If you are not thrilled, why aren't you? It is the business of the choir master to make you so.*

People can or cannot do things in proportion as they like them. In other words you must have love. There are four loves which singers need:

1. LOVE OF THE ACT OF SINGING. It is difficult when one has two daily services as at York, when words and tunes are very familiar, to teach the choir to put meaning into wonderful words and beautiful music, and really sing to the glory of God.

2. LOVE OF VERSE. This is lacking in most people. Leave them alone in a room with some volumes of poetry, you will find they would never think of opening one. Force is no use. Don't say as I used to, "Now boys sing your words clearly"; the effect only lasts a few minutes. Teach them the meaning, make them love them, and then they will themselves want to make them clear, they will come clear naturally.

3. LOVE OF MUSIC. Singers are notoriously bad musicians. They don't work at their art as a whole and study intelligently what they are meant to sing. They think it is enough to let their voices 'go', to sing heartily as we say. Such singing is very limited in effect. If you love music you are in deadly earnest over it. Make your choir constantly feel that it is sharing something gloriously immortal.

The motor is of most importance in singing, then the vibrator and the resonator.

Love opens one out – warmth. Fear closes one up – coldness – shyness – selfconsciousness.

"Perfect love casteth out fear". If you do not love you cannot be a success as a singer.

All curious vocal sounds are due to stiffness, closing, fear, selfconsciousness. Also, the singer must use the whole of himself, one hundred per cent.

Everything done well is done with a swing; with rhythm; with metre.

What is good tone? It is nature's method. Perfect freedom. The singer's voice must be free as his speaking voice.

4. LOVE OF YOUR NEIGHBOUR. We must make our singers want to share their joy with others. Get rid of any inferiority complex. Know what it all stands for. Help others to feel it too.

Consonants are the drums of the vocal orchestra. Vowels play the actual tune. Consonants are fences separating the fields of vowels. Vowels are unimpeded tone. Resonators are big insides with small openings, e.g. the mouth. Bad vowels are too much like consonants, and bad consonants like vowels. Phrasing is the effect of the imagination upon the music. The musical phrase governs everything. If there are four lines to a hymn and four phrases, keep your musical phrases intact. Never cut them up because of the words. Unless you become as little children you can never enter the kingdom of music.

The following year, at Speech Day, he explained some of the methods he used in training the Minster choir. "Force is no earthly use whatsoever. It might be necessary to force a boy to learn his three Rs, but you could never force him to learn to sing, because singing depends upon his breath, and the moment you do anything to interfere with his breath it is useless. You have got to get a boy to learn to possess a desire to sing". He went on to say that, although he had thrashed only three or four boys all the seventeen years he had been in York, they certainly ought not to be thrashed. Neither should one suspect any choirboy. "There is trouble and evil in this world through suspicion, which comes from fear. We should always trust people to do things. Thirdly, we must understand human nature". He contended that the most mischievous boy was the best one of the lot. A little quiet mouse was not the boy who would do much good so far as singing was concerned. Success was due not so much to marvellous technical knowledge as to the three things – doing things for love, not distrusting anyone, and knowing a little about human nature.

He was emphatic that people should love their work, but it was difficult sometimes to cast out fear when he was present. He did not appear to be aware of the devastating effect his personality could have. To perform in front of him was not something to be undertaken lightly, and called forth plenty of courage, preceded of course by adequate preparation.

"He was a hard task master, one not given to suffering fools gladly. One felt praise from him was worth having. He had great integrity and devotion to work, sincerity, vitality and utter devotion to music. He was a strange mixture of toughness and sensitivity, with a greatness of mind and heart, perhaps unusual in his day". These are the words of Elsie Suddaby, his pupil from 1911. She went to him on an assisted scholarship at the Leeds School of Music. 'You will have to know your work if you go to him' was the warning given by those who knew him as a teacher. They were all afraid of him. Elsie Suddaby confesses that she was an introvert forced by E.C.B. to be an extrovert. 'You must not apologise to your audience' he would say. His advice to boy competitors at the 1929 West Lindsey music festival at Gainsborough was 'Always go on to the stage as though you meant to do something worthwhile. Stick your chest out, deliver your message, and say – (*he surely meant 'as if to say'*) – Put that in your pipe and smoke it'. He later told Elsie Suddaby that at one time he nearly despaired of her, with her nerves and stiff jaw. Perhaps it is not to be wondered at that she encountered such difficulties since, before her very first lesson, she was witness to the precipitate ejection of the pupil who had had the lesson immediately preceding hers, followed closely by her copy of the music which was flung out after her. Balanced on a knife-edge it was not easy to feel relaxed and at ease. It was only later, when master and pupil knew each other better that an easier relationship would develop and ripen into a friendship based on a mutual love of music.

Elsie Suddaby continued, "He had many friends who thought of him with affection, and many disciples who admired him but stood in awe of him. He loved friends and his friends loved him. He was impressive in rather an eagle-like way with a commanding voice. He was given to humorous and sardonic remarks and did not mind telling stories against himself. He was generous to young musicians in time, money and advice. I was grateful to him for setting a high standard of work and understanding of the poetic word, which enabled me to use the technique and sing for fifty years".

His thoughts about rhythm were expressed at the Song School speech day of April 7 1923 and they led into hints of his conception of psalm singing which culminated in the English Psalter two years later. "Rhythm is the heart-beat and the life and soul of all music; without rhythm there can be no music. The speech accent is important, for all good music carries with it the accentuation and the syllabication of the words in which the song comes out much more like speech by going straight to the point and expressing the meaning of the words. That is why we have been making changes in the singing of the psalms; we want to get away from the false accentuation and wrong length of syllables. There are those who would prefer to go on in the old way, but if we have people getting at the right spirit of the words through their right and natural inflexion, then we are improving. When we are approaching the stage when music is as natural as writing, and when the mind is riveted on expressing feeling without any apparent effort, then it can be said that music is improving."

The association of the Master of the Music and the Dean, Dr. W. Foxley Norris, was evidently at that time a happy one. At the 1923 school speech day the Dean declared that in the course of a long experience extending over 40 years he had never been so happy as he was with the choir, the organist and all with whom he came in contact at York Minster; in fact he did not think there was a dean in England who enjoyed such happy relations with his church as he did at the Minster. A few years later, when the Dean was translated to Westminster Abbey and Sir Sydney Nicholson had resigned the post of organist and choirmaster in order to found and run the School of English Church Music (later the Royal School of Church Music) it was natural to speculate on who might follow him. If Bairstow were to be chosen, one newspaper suggested that the 'Bridge tradition' would be re-established, because he was pupil and assistant to Sir Frederick Bridge for six years. 'The Minster, under his care, has achieved distinction by wireless, and the musical scheme for the recent 1300th anniversary shewed English Church music at its most virile. ... He has composed much church and chamber music and has the requisite scholarship for such a post as Mr. Nicholson is now laying down at about the same age as his most probable successor. If he goes to Westminster he will only be following his former dean.'

This happy relationship with his dean did not obtain throughout Bairstow's tenure at York, as we shall see. But for the moment we note that York Minster Choir was the second choir to be affiliated to the new venture, the School of English Church Music, the first being the village church of Childe Okeford in Dorset. The School was registered at Somerset House on August 8 1930. That same year Bairstow conducted a summer school in choir training at the college (then at Chislehurst) and wrote as follows:

'The choir was a very welcome surprise. It was not merely efficient, it was expressive and moving. The boys had a free and beautiful tone; the men – students of the college – were musicianly and intelligent. All had perfectly clear and significant speech, and all had just the right spirit of spontaneous reverence and great enthusiasm. ... It will, I hope, be possible to maintain a band of men from the college who will visit many a country district to help with advice, instruction and encouragement to those who hitherto have had no one to help them'.

As for music apart from the church, the uncertainty of its future, as he saw it, was much in Bairstow's mind as the B.B.C. was emerging inexorably as a power in the land. In a letter to the Yorkshire Post of 3 November 1931 he called attention to the dwindling audiences at his concerts with the Leeds Philharmonic Society which by then he had been conducting for fourteen years, and states that

'the advent of wireless, the gramophone and the cinema, bad times in trade and various other factors, have caused the demise of hundreds of choral and orchestral societies in this country. In fact there is a danger of England losing its undoubted supremacy in the art of choral singing'.

An earlier letter, to the Morning Post about 1926, testifies to his concern in much the same way. In it he dealt with the "Mechanisation of Music", being of the opinion that music was at a critical stage.

'The most musical nation is obviously the one in which the greatest number of people are making music for themselves, not the nation where the greatest number of people are listening to music. For instance, the United States has a large number of magnificent orchestras, but these are almost entirely composed of foreigners, and there is very little music of the higher class put forth by American-born composers or performers'.

This statement makes it fairly clear that Bairstow was unaware of the not inconsiderable achievements of such composers as George Whitefield Chadwick, Amy Beach or John Knowles Paine whose first symphony has been said to be worthy to stand beside that of Brahms which was composed at about the same time; or of

Horatio Parker whose cantata 'Hora Novissima' was favourably received at the Three Choirs Festival of 1899. The popular salon pieces of Edward Macdowell, well known in this country, had no doubt overshadowed his more important works and given the impression of an inferior talent. This did not prevent ECB's including some of his piano pieces in his earlier organ recitals. (See chapter XI). It was not only England, however, that stood in ignorance of America's music. Much cold-shouldering of it took place among its own people.

> 'In this country since we began to make music for ourselves without the aid of foreigners, things have been going ahead in a most gratifying way. Competitive festivals have brought small country choirs to a splendid state of efficiency and have increased the number of such choirs by leaps and bounds. There has been a wonderful output of highly-inspired music, which could only have been written by Englishmen. But now we are getting prosperous, and therefore slack, and now that gramophones and the wireless have reached such an astonishing state of efficiency, there is a danger that listening will take the place of doing. If that is the case, then the standard will inevitably fall, as it has always done in the past. It is up to the professional musicians in this country to see that this does not happen. We can never blame the amateur; we must blame ourselves.
>
> 'The comparison you make between mechanised music and photography is hardly a fair one, because a photograph is not an expression of emotion. Both the wireless and the gramophone have now become most expressive'.

He went further when he addressed the I.S.M. conference in January 1932.

> 'The love of music should rank alongside religion in our lives, and music should be regarded as the greatest antidote to the poisonous materialism that is so prevalent today. ... It is no use grousing about the British public and their ignorance of music. After all, we are responsible – and the man who says he would not do half so much teaching if he could afford to lose the money, is not the man who would get us very far. ... Our musical future depends on whether we can get people "bitten" with the love of music. You know the glut of mechanised music today, and how

easy it is to get it. But the more a thing costs the more it is generally regarded as worthwhile, and so long as music is accepted merely as a background, what good can it be to anyone? It is for this reason that I am going to suggest that opera is not and cannot be the highest form of music because so many other things in opera go with the music, which cannot therefore be regarded as 'pure'.

'What are we to do to get people in love with music? The teacher who believes that music should rank alongside a man's religion has gone a long way to becoming a successful instructor. Motive and intention are far more important than achievement, and I think we are far too much taken up with technique, which alone will not give us an intimate knowledge of music as a language. The teacher must stir up the imagination of his pupil. He must not say "you must not". Enthusiasm is positive, not negative, and it is sure to be infectious, but if we are going to bring about the state of things we desire, we teachers must have the faith in our pupils that removes mountains'.

The Yorkshire Post account adds "In a reference to the foreign musicians question, Dr. Bairstow recalled that he used to keep bees, and that robber bees came to sneak honey only from poor hives". It also reported that "The President, winding up the debate, said Dr. Bairstow's remarks about the possibility of overstressing technique filled him with joy, because there was a real danger of making a mere fetish of correctness and technique at the expense of interpretation. He would rather hear a few wrong notes struck so long as the musician was getting at the heart of the message than any amount of mechanical correctness". With regard to these sentiments, recurring as they do over and over again from 1910 onwards, and probably from earlier still, it could be said that the situation remains, six decades later, exactly as it was, and that it will probably remain in the same state for ever. ... One cannot but be continually impressed by his insistence on the main purpose of music as he saw it – to touch the heart . His devotion and love for it was his life's sole purpose and unending joy.

At Buxton between the last day of 1934 and the fourth of January he attended the annual conference of the Incorporated Society of Musicians. His presidential address provided him with a platform to discuss the present position of the musical world and the part that must be played by musicians in bringing about a better future. The Musical Times reported Sir Edward as pointing out that:

> To a large extent, musicians are powerless against certain factors that have in a short time done so much damage to the art. (*And here he employed one of his favourite themes*) Moreover, being artists, musicians do not believe in force. We cannot force the B.B.C. to stop encouraging people merely to hear music and not to listen to it, or to cease putting over so much trash. ... All this does not mean that we are to sit still and watch English music go to the dogs".

What then could musicians do to defend their art? The report continues:

> He dwelt chiefly on the responsibilities of the individual artist: his admirable address was, in short, a plea for self-examination – is our work for music the best we can make it? He drew a picture of the ideal musician as he saw it: "he has not only a great belief and faith in his own work, but also faith in those with whom he comes in contact. He is a confirmed optimist and believes that very slowly but surely the world is becoming a better place to live in. He knows nothing of fear, self-consciousness or worry, and goes the shortest and simplest way to accomplish his object. He is not unduly elated by success, and is never daunted by failure. Having no care, he can 'switch off' – that is, he can relax or sleep the moment his work is ended, nor will he proceed to defeat the Spanish Armada until his game of bowls is completed. He can laugh and enjoy life, and can focus things to find their relative importance. He is as straight and honest as the day and loathes cant, bunk, humbug, flattery, boasting, and self-advertisement. He is an excellent showman, but it is his art he shows to its best advantage, not himself." And he ended with a stirring appeal to musicians to make their chief aim in life the stimulation of a love for music-making.

We may regard these last lines as a self-portrait, though he himself would not have intended them as such. It is as good an assessment of himself as one could hope to find. These were his ideals and he spent a lifetime living up to them with fierce determination.

VIII

The Teacher

"A S A TEACHER" WROTE Doctor F.H. Wood, "he was alive and compelling. Harry Plunket Greene said he was one of the best teachers of singing in this country". Alice Knight applied to him for lessons. "Thus one April day", she relates, "in time snatched from my lunch hour, I found myself facing the penetrating stare, the wolfish smile and the rasping voice that I was to get to know so well in the succeeding years. The piece I had nerved myself to play to him was Liszt's transcription of Bach's A minor organ prelude and fugue, one of the items I had heard in the early organ recitals I have mentioned, though I had forgotten the fact. My obvious technical faults were immediately tackled, I was set on a course of Bach Partitas and Schumann's Kreisleriana, told that I was 'musical enough' to warrant going ahead with my studies, and I left my first lesson braced and stimulated, even then conscious that there would be no softness, no short cuts or easy ways, but that hard and sincere effort would be recognised. And so it proved throughout my studies with E.C.B. He never succeeded in making me a first-rate pianist .... but he greatly increased my ease and pleasure in playing and enlarged my capacities, both technical and musical. I was soon given the opportunity to put my playing to further use, becoming, on his suggestion, deputy accompanist to the Musical Society, an association which was to last, in various capacities, for nearly thirty years. In the course of my early lessons a point of interpretation arose which involved some principle of harmony, and my admitted ignorance of the subject set him talking, to a completely fascinated listener. For several weeks, after my stint of playing, I would ask some leading question on musical form or harmony, to set him off again, he as ready to expound as I to listen.

"Realising that my interest was serious, he said one day, 'You'd better work through my book'. This was his *Counterpoint and Harmony*, at that time still in manuscript – one collected one's required chapter from whoever had finished with it. This was the start of several years of hard study, in evenings, weekends and holidays. ... As a beginner, I found E.C.B.'s teaching eminently practical and clear to follow. Each step was fully explained, the theory being always firmly related to practice. This, I believe, was characteristic of all his teaching and possibly of his whole attitude to music. He was essentially a pragmatist, the worth of a theory depending on the value of its practical application. One's studies, in consequence, were not with dry rules alone but with living music, through which the application of sound principles was discerned. Thus, if one's efforts were greeted with a harsh "No, you can't do that", there followed an explanation, not only of what rule one had transgressed, but *why* the transgression led to musical disaster."

In one of his presidential addresses to the Royal College of Organists he bade us remember:

> That every rule of technique has its foundation in some great principle – probably one of Nature's laws, and that these rules were made for children in the art of music in order that they might appreciate the great fundamental principle which under-lies them. If you cannot find out what natural law underlies every rule, you are not fit to teach.

> Children or beginners must be led – you must hold their hands to cross the busy road. But in your heart of hearts you love the spirited youngster who wants to dash off on his own better than the tame and nervous child who cries the moment you release his hand from yours. So also you admire the pupil who has the urge in him for adventure. It is your difficult task to know just when you can safely loosen your grasp or when a firm hand is necessary. Certainly you never allow rules to be broken through ignorance of them, nor do you permit the youngster to break away out of sheer bravado. It is when the spirit of the rule has been thoroughly learnt that sometimes it may be broken or dis-regarded because the fundamental law at the back of it has been

kept. To give only one instance – consecutives. Clearly they are forbidden, to avoid monotony, so that every part shall have independence and a shape of its own. You do not permit people to write them from ignorance any more than you would allow the child to run across the road because it was so young that it did not appreciate the danger. Nor would you allow your pupils to put them in to show off. You would not let the child run away and make a grimace at you; this would be disobedience and cheek. But if a pupil brings along music in which he points out the consecutives, and shows you that they sound well and do not interfere with independence, then you can commend his enterprise.

Alice Knight continues: "The next step was totally unexpected; at one lesson E.C.B. suddenly said, 'I'd like you to have a go at the Durham Mus. B. – you could do it'. He knew I had no intention of entering the profession of music, but he realised, and wished to encourage, my interest in music rather than my performance as a pianist. 'I want you to be an all-rounder', he said on another occasion. So I had a go, and am happy to think that I justified his faith, receiving my degree in 1937. Indeed I unwittingly became a kind of shining example, E.C.B. telling me that to some full-time music student complaining that he couldn't get through the required work, his reply was 'I've got a girl who does it in her spare time!' But to me, the journey rather than the destination was the reward, those years of study with E.C.B. being the most musically enriching of my life and the effect, in deepening musical appreciation, still remaining after more than thirty years, though I hardly even remember that I am what an aunt of mine would refer to as a 'Musical Bachelor'.

"I learnt, too, that E.C.B. had no use for timidity. One had to be prepared to have a go at whatever he demanded, showing no sign of the panic one might feel. It had a bracing effect on one naturally nervous, as I found when called on by him, at a moment's notice, to conduct the Musical Society in a folk-song arrangement of my own, at the final rehearsal and the following evening's concert, never having attempted such a thing before. I managed to do it, on the strength of knowing that I should be damned for ever in his eyes if I funked it, and he believed I could do it, and that my mother had spent the final afternoon sewing on very securely the many buttons fastening the back of my regulation white dress."

George Gray remembers his first piano lesson. "I played a Beethoven Sonata, very imperfectly, and was quite prepared to be told that I would not make the grade. E.C.B. stood with his back to the fire, and gave me a talk of some length. He first enumerated some of my deficiencies, and my heart sank. He hesitated a moment and said, 'but you show signs of being a good pianist. You did several things which show artistic feeling and musicianship'. (He then enumerated these). I was surprised and delighted to know this, and my fears diminished. I was also unprepared by his quick discernment and also to hear of virtues which I didn't know I possessed.

"I owe a tremendous debt to E.C.B. for what he taught me, a great proportion of which was from his own personal example, particularly in service playing. He was incapable of being unmusical or inartistic in his own playing though he was human and did very occasionally make a slip. I soon learnt from him that technique (however good) was only a means to an end, and that interpretation and beauty of phrase, appreciation of climaxes and all other interpretive virtues, were essential. I never remember E.C.B. being annoyed about the occasional wrong note, though a series of them, if due to lack of preparation, would be condemned. But he could not stand insensitivity, or spineless playing or singing, or insincerity of any kind.

"He gave me great encouragement to believe more in myself. Fortunately, with an early examination success (the F.R.C.O.), I was able to show him some result of his early tuition. I well remember that when I returned to him with the news that I had won the Lafontaine prize (*for the highest marks in organ playing*) he said ,'Well done. Now we'll get on with some organ playing'. No more, but how one appreciated it. He was genuinely pleased, but the warning was clear. He had no intention (*a*) of letting me think I could rest on my laurels; (*b*) of allowing me to think too much of myself. And it is true that this was just the beginning for me. I learned much more from him after that, and he gave me unmistakably the idea that one never should stop learning."

During the same period, Gerald Finzi was studying with
Bairstow, and he and George Gray had most of their lessons
together. More than once ECB included a piece of Finzi's in his
choral concerts. After a few years Finzi left ECB to study with R.O.
Morris. It appears that he could have been rather disenchanted
with the strict methods employed by Bairstow, or at any rate felt
the need of some sort of change. He was scarcely ever mentioned
by ECB, and none of his works were in the repertoire of the Minster
choir.

In January 1929 Bairstow gave his first address as President of
the Royal College of Organists. At the distribution of diplomas, as
it was then called, he was, according to the Musical Times, received
with 'rapturous and prolonged applause'. His four presidential
addresses, all well worth reading, are of serious purpose and filled
with weighty matter and valuable ideas. He used these opportunities to project a message to his audiences which would be a help to
them in their pursuit of music and in their lives generally. They are
lengthier than usual on such occasions and give evidence of careful thought and preparation. The first, entitled 'Retrospect and an
Ideal', was another chance to make known his concern for the future
of music which, at this time, was a subject never very far from his
mind. He began by stating his ideal: "We look forward to a musical millennium in which musicians, professional and amateur, will
so love their art that they will play and teach only the best music
in the best way. We look forward to a time when children will be
taught music as a language – will be taught to understand its true
message in such a way that, as they grow up with it, through
familiarity with the language they will easily distinguish good from
bad. They will, in fact, see behind the notes to the heart of the
composer. Just as we, by a man's speech and by his written word,
can judge pretty shrewdly of his sincerity, of his power of imagination and instinct for form, so we look forward to a time when
people will be able to sum up the value of music as easily as we do
literature or speech."

His second address, on 20 July 1929, had as its title 'Music in
Relationship to Life'. Far from being a talk exclusively for organists it was helpful to any kind of musician. One of his perpetual
cares was to prevent the organist from confining himself to one

small corner of music's wide field. He began: "It may be said that mine is a slow-moving mind, but the fact remains that for many years music was to me no more than a series of sounds which in some mysterious way stimulated me more or less. Why some music moved me whilst other music left me cold I neither knew nor cared. The mystery to some extent still remains, but it is no longer quite so unfathomable, for at last I am beginning to find that what I dislike in music I also dislike outside music. It was when I came to see how closely life and art are related that music became a more living thing to me; it helped me to a fairer criticism of music and the performance of it, and it made it easier to get to the root of the difficulties of those whom I taught. It was through rhythm that these ideas dawned on me. I began to see that love and fear stir up very different kinds of emotion, the first orderly but not stiff and mechanical, the second a disorderly hash of jerky, tiring movements alternating with a complete hold-up of motion of any kind."

He took his examples from nature – trees, clouds, sunrise and sunset – from architecture and from human beings. 'We all have the same bodies and minds, yet none of us are alike': it is when builders have been stimulated by some spiritual vision that the dull and obvious constructional elements are cloaked in beauty and variety: a tree retains its trunk and branches but its leaves, blossom and fruit are continually changing. ... Choir boys taught 'on some stupid system, such as the vowel OO... by a man whose one idea was to unify them and make them as like as two peas in a pod' turned out each with a different voice 'when he has done his worst'. Equally one must refrain from impressing too strongly on a pupil one's own ideas of interpretation, but find out whether he has ideas which conform to sound principles and encourage him to use his own imagination. The composer who is technically faultless but can think of nothing worth putting on paper has never perceived the relationship between music and the experiences of life.

The spirituality of Byrd's music is contrasted with "plodding through Boyce in A or Cooke in G which, though these have vitality and strength, have nothing like the power of detaching one from earthly things as have Byrd's masses..." and they in their turn are likened to the stained glass windows of the 13th and 18th centuries.

One of Bairstow's favourite guiding principles concerned the economical use of both effort and resources. His third presidential address to the Royal College of Organists develops this theme, pointing out that the virtuoso, a first-rate motor car and a race-horse equally can thrill by the ease with which they can achieve their purpose, because the "friction caused by their movements is reduced to a minimum, nor is the effort prolonged for an instant beyond what is absolutely necessary for the attainment of their end." He would illustrate this on the gleaming stainless steel composition pedals of the Minster organ by pressing them only far enough for contact to be made, rather than insensitively stamping hard and forcing them to the fullest extent.

He then applies this principle to the doing of dull but necessary jobs, and speaks, in terms of sporting activities, of "swing and follow through" as applied to teaching a dull pupil or working at counterpoint exercises. The pianist's fingers, the singer's breath, the economy of Schubert's accompaniment writing, the unnecessary duplication of tone colours in organ design and in organ registration, and finally, words of advice to contenders for the fellowship diploma as to how to achieve their goal with less expenditure of effort; all these are touched upon to illustrate this attitude which, with him, became a way of life and entered into every aspect of his activity.

His last R.C.O. address, delivered in July 1930, rather amusingly took the negative title "Inappropriateness" rather than the positive one, perhaps denoting his exasperation with too many experiences of it. The composer, the candidate for Fellowship and Mus. Bac. had furnished him with things to complain of, which he attributes to 'faithless teaching'. "If we, as teachers, are constantly giving our pupils the impression that we have more faith in them than they have in themselves, we shall spur them on to achieve what to them seems at first to be far beyond them."

The overdoing of climaxes, the excessive use of the tremulant and the *glissando*, badly chosen *tempi* in performance, and "mere busy and fussy movement for its own sake" in composition, are all inappropriate, and this is due to ignorance of the emotions of music and the language of these emotions. Technique is everything to some musicians, who "do not in the least understand what result their efforts are likely to have on the emotions of their audience. We cannot hope to interpret emotion to others unless we understand it, not so much in ourselves as in others, and perhaps not so much in others as in the things of the imagination. ... It is the over-conscientious, introspective people who can never do the fitting thing in music, for they never give their imagination a free hand. They are continually arguing with themselves as to whether they are doing the right thing technically or materially, whilst all the time they are doing the wrong thing imaginatively or spiritually. This side of music has improved tremendously since my school days. It is our duty as teachers to see that the other and far more important side receives more attention."

The Musical Times reported that the address "was followed with delighted interest by the large audience". Professor P.C.Buck proposed a vote of thanks in which he said "I do not think there is a man in England who works harder", and Professor Kitson (of Dublin) seconded the motion which was 'carried with enthusiasm'. On another occasion, on the subject of what is appropriate, he is quoted as saying that "there is nothing more ridiculous than to see a woman, perhaps stout, wearing a light dress, standing on a concert platform and singing 'I know that my Redeemer liveth'. It is fearfully inartistic and irreverent".

Incidentally, it is interesting to note his stricture on overdone climaxes, when one is fully aware of his own propensity for drowning the choir in full organ at moments of special power and magnificence. No doubt he expected the well-adjusted musician to be aware of the borderline between magnificence and vulgarity. In such situations he certainly did not like punches pulled and would have preferred to err on the vulgar side rather than the timid. He did not like 'white-livered' musicians – or people, for that matter: this was one of his epithets which any timid chorister might have to stomach.

Perhaps his greatest and most lasting achievement as a teacher is in his writings, and most of all in his splendid book *Counterpoint and Harmony*, published in 1937. Up to that time it had been considered the proper thing to learn harmony first and, having done so, then to tackle counterpoint. His own pupils were allowed to use the precious typescript of any chapter which they needed to be studying, a concession which, before the days of easy copying, was extremely generous and trusting of the author.

A detailed review by R.H. Walthew is largely appreciative. He quotes paragraph 271 which deals with a kind of music Bairstow disliked. "Of Chromatic Passing Notes we are told that they are very easy to write, and like all things which cost little, they are not worth much; and if used for long together and without an admixture of diatonic passing notes, may sound very cheap and give the impression of much ado about nothing. A shining example of this type of music is the Prologue to Sullivan's *Golden Legend*" – and the reviewer remarks that this remark might well have been omitted. But it is the only criticism in the article. Edmund Rubbra's review in *Music and Letters* stated firmly that 'Emancipation cannot commence until species counterpoint, given prominence in Sir Edward's book, is thrown over as useless academic lumber.' Opinions have certainly differed on this subject, but Bairstow's book treats it with every respect and obviously believes in its worth as a discipline. The book was revolutionary and unique in its day, and there is little doubt that over the years it has fulfilled its purpose handsomely in the hands of many of the right kind of students.

Mrs. Bairstow outside Minster Court

I X

The Thirteen-Hundredth Anniversary
Celebrations

ONE OF BAIRSTOW'S GREATEST achievements at York was the
week-long festival of music celebrating the thirteenth centenary of the founding of the Minster in 627 A.D. He had been in
office fourteen years, so had had sufficient time to mould the music
of the Minster to his liking. In his fifty-third year he was in the
prime of life and at the high point of his achievement.

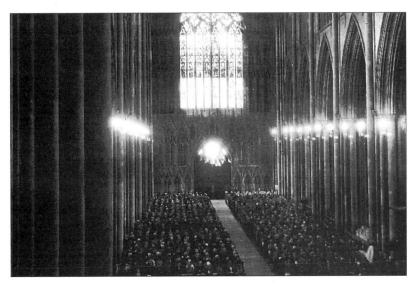

'From the Screen, 1300th anniversary, July 1927'

133

At that time festivals were few and infrequent. The programme was an extremely concentrated one, beginning on Tuesday, June 28, the eve of the patronal festival of Saint Peter and continuing throughout the octave. The choirs of twelve northern cathedrals and Leeds Parish Church came to take part on various days, and the central musical event was Bach's Mass in B Minor in which the Minster choir was joined by the York Musical Society and the Leeds Philharmonic Society, forming a choir of more than 400 voices. This was the first time the mass had been heard in York and, like the annual Passion music performances, was a rare event for music lovers of those days. It received ample coverage in the national press, and the second half, in fact, was broadcast. The Times critic thought that the event was "worthy of the time and the place. Dr. Bairstow has shown us in occasional visits to London that he views the work in the big and as a whole, and cares very much for the architecture of the performance. It is partly a question of *tempi* but still more of climax. As an example of the care for climax may be mentioned some sudden sweeps of tone from the sopranos in some of the earlier choruses, which showed an unusual and dramatic use of choral phrasing that seemed entirely right. ... Honours in the matter of tone were with the women. For even in Yorkshire the tenors were weak. The sopranos sang brilliantly throughout, and the contraltos, being genuine contraltos and not debased sopranos, sang strongly and with the right vocal colour. Consequently, many moments were thrilling for their sheer beauty of tone. ... The acoustics of the Minster are a help to this effect, though the effects sound very different in different parts of the nave.

"The orchestra, which was composed of players from the Hallé and Leeds orchestras, further added to the great tonal beauty of the performance, by a keener edge to the string tone than our more lethargic London orchestras are apt to give us." The *obbligato* instruments, particularly the flute ("exceptional sweetness, almost like a dove's note, gave a light and beautifully airy effect after the great waves of sound of the preceding chorus") and the four soloists all received praise. Elsie Suddaby and George Parker were Bairstow's pupils; Muriel Brunskill was the contralto and Steuart Wilson the tenor, who was also a frequent participator in the annual Saint Matthew Passions. Surrounded thus by friends and familiar forces

E.C.B. must have felt a warm gratification, a sense which surely helped him to make this a notable and unique musical event in the musical life of the north of England. Reginald Rose in his review expressed the feelings of those who were present: British writers from all periods, he says, were represented during the festival, so there was, therefore "a special appropriateness in the fact that this should find its culmination in the performance of the crowning consummation of the creative genius of the greatest of all musicians, who soars above nationality and frontiers. To Dr. Bairstow... we can only pay our tribute of respectful admiration and congratulation. By his genius alone was it possible for such results to be obtained, and the musical history of York Minster can chronicle nothing finer than this. We have written eulogistically, but in our opinion truthfully, of a service difficult to describe but impossible to forget."

Herbert Thompson, too, praised the performance in the Yorkshire Post, but with this reservation: "save that the tenors did their best to wreck the first Kyrie by anticipating their lead, the performance realised admirably the majesty of the work, and rarely, if ever, has one heard it given so impressive an interpretation."

E.C.B. came to the rescue of the tenors (for once!) in a letter to the Yorkshire Post:

> I feel that I cannot allow the tenors to take responsibility for a mistake which was not theirs. It was I who gave them a cue half a bar too soon. It was extraordinary that I should have done this in a work the notes of which I know so well, having conducted it four times recently, and taken innumerable rehearsals of it. I do not want to excuse myself, but perhaps the strain of the previous week and the long orchestral rehearsal on the hot afternoon of Tuesday may have accounted for it. It was impossible to erect the platform for the chorus until Monday night, and the chorus had never rehearsed on it. The tenors were a long distance from me and the light was not very good. It is quite likely, therefore, that both the tenors and myself were a little over anxious at their first lead. The way the chorus backed me up and the orchestra covered my mistake by skipping half a bar was beyond praise.

A further letter (from the Reverend H.G. Potter of Halifax) says that this letter "taking upon himself the blame for the mistake will enhance him even more in the eyes of those who were present. An Englishman always admires courage and honesty. Dr. Bairstow's letter is full of both."

One of the tenors "could not recall any circumstances which imposed a more difficult task ... for conductor and chorus. ... The structure of the orchestra gallery placed two rows of singers on each step, thus the second rows of singers on each tier stood behind the front rows on the same level, and could not see through or over the persons in front. The very narrow oblong space which the orchestra gallery occupied, with its straight rows of seats (instead of the usually radiated orchestra), made the very large chorus a mere strip of singers, stretching to a distance far away from Dr. Bairstow, and there was no lighting over the heads of the tenors and basses. It was a position to invite disaster, more especially in a work like Bach's great Mass, and Dr. Bairstow has to thank the nerve and confidence of a large majority of his chorus, and their knowledge and experience of Bach's music; and the chorus have to thank the splendid regularity of Dr. Bairstow's beat, in that the performance was so faultless."

Of the opening service of the celebrations The Times gave a colourful account: "The 12 bells of York Minster were making a cheerful noise this morning while the people collected in hundreds for the great service of the Festival day. Holy Communion had already been twice celebrated in the early morning, but the special Festival service began at half past ten with the solemn Eucharist and Procession.

"The congregation was very much larger than that at yesterday's Evensong, and it was credibly reported that every seat in the Minster, in nave, aisles, transepts and choir, was occupied; outside, moreover, in the seats in the Dean's Park, there were many people sharing in the great service, and those that were there found that they could hear distinctly every word of the Archbishop of York's sermon in the midday special service, and the music which was sung within the Minster. In all there must have been some 80 of the clergy in the temporary stalls, on either side of the altar that had been put, for the Festival services, at the east end of the nave, just west of the choir screen.

"The procession, therefore, which preceded that solemn Eucharist was very long and very stately, and the hymn 'Hail festal day', sung to the tune by Philip Armes, which is known as York prose, sounded magnificent. ... The service sung was Macpherson in E flat, and the final hymn was 'City of God, how broad and fair' (sic)." Bairstow's descant was sung to the last verse. "It is no reflection on the York Minster choir to say that the descant was inaudible except to those in the front rows. The choir was simply outsung by the tremendous volume of sound which rose from the huge congregation. ... It is not likely that in all its long history York Minster has been filled from end to end, from ground to topmost height, with so huge a volume of congregational singing, perfectly led by the choir and controlled by the Minster organist, Dr Bairstow, from the organ above the screen."

And the Yorkshire Weekly Post provided a post-script to this memorable chapter in Bairstow's life: "Upon nobody can the strain of the week's constant and elaborate musical service at York have rested more heavily than on the Minster Master of Music, Dr. E.C. Bairstow. We in Leeds have long known him to be an indefatigable and ever-inspiring leader.

"In the capacities of conductor, composer, organist and choir trainer, Dr.Bairstow has still further enhanced his already high reputation. Musical people competent to judge tell me that Yorkshire has every reason to be proud of him. It is generally agreed that the festival music has maintained an exceptional level, and down to the smallest details one can find the influence of his brilliant directive mind."

Afterwards, Archbishop Lang wrote in the Diocesan Gazette: "I have long and special knowledge of ecclesiastical functions and ceremonies in all parts of the country; but it is no exaggeration to say that none of them has equalled – I had almost said approached – this great anniversary. None of us can ever forget the vast congregations, varying from 2,000 to 5,000 or even 6,000, assembling thrice a day for seven days from all parts of the Diocese, the Province, and indeed the whole country with many visitors from overseas, or the most impressive spirit of reverence which evidently filled them."

The Archbishop thanked the Dean and Chapter, Dr. Bairstow and his choir, the Reverend F. Harrison and the Chamberlain, the Reverend Horace Spence; and continued: "As to the music, I have no words with which to express my admiration and gratitude. The spirit and quality and reverence of the singing, passing into the choir from the genius of the choirmaster, were sustained throughout all those exacting days. I doubt whether any nobler offering of music has ever been made in any English cathedral or church."

Musical Times, August 1927

And some years later, and translated now to Canterbury, at the luncheon of the Royal College of Organists on June 2nd 1934, Archbishop Lang referred to the "great delight and inspiration of being within the genius – for I can call it nothing else – of Sir Edward Bairstow. I shall always say to the end of my life, that there was one moment when I realised what the Church of England might give in the way of dignity of worship and beauty of music, and that was during the celebrations of the thirteen hundredth anniversary of the Minster. I am glad to have lived to have once, at least, seen and heard what this Church of England can be and do in its worship."

In his 1928 Speech Day address E.C.B. himself spoke of "the magnificence of the music during the week of the celebrations," and claimed that "no other cathedral city had ever heard a selection of music like that in one week. All the rehearsal was done previously, and during the week there was no rehearsal and no choir practice of any sort."

At the end of Herbert Thompson's Musical Times account of the celebrations, an editorial postscript says "apropos of the Festival reported above, we present a reproduction of a recent photograph of Mr. Bairstow, to whose fine, all-round work, English music both in and out of the Church, owes so much."

The nine days of sung services, from the eve of St. Peter's day, up to and including the octave, contained exclusively English music, and the best the repertoire could furnish. It covered a wide range of period, beginning with Henry Smart's Magnificat and Nunc Dimittis in B flat and Gibbons' setting of the collect for St. Peter, 'Almighty God, who by thy son Jesus Christ'. The organ music was by Purcell – Toccata in A and Chaconne in F. Every day after that saw Sung Eucharist at 10.30, Matins at 12.0 and Evensong at 4.0, except for Tuesday 5 July when the Eucharist was sung at 7.45 in the morning by the old choristers to Bairstow's unison setting in E flat, then fairly new, published four years earlier. What was then considered the grandest communion service setting – Macpherson in E flat – was chosen for the patronal festival, replete with trumpets and drums. Next day there followed Stanford in G, then Byrd à 5, Ireland in C, Vaughan Williams in G minor, Batten in the Dorian Mode, and finally, Bairstow's own 1913 setting in D, quite as imposing as Macpherson's.

The canticles at Matins began with Stanford in C and continued with the Tallis dorian service, Farrant "in G minor", Alcock in B flat, Dyson in D (for the Sunday morning civic service), Purcell in B flat and Wesley in E. The second evensong of St. Peter was sung to Stanford in A, the next day Byrd's Great Service, then Alan Gray's splendid Magnificat and Nunc Dimittis in F minor, (the composer, a native of York, being then organist of Trinity College, Cambridge), Walmisley in D minor, Wesley in E, Gibbons "in F" and Bevin in the Dorian Mode.

The anthems were; Boyce: *I have surely built thee an house to dwell in;* Bairstow: *Blessed City;* Tallis: *O Lord, give thy holy spirit;* Greene: *Lord, let me know mine end;* Stanford: *The Lord is my shepherd;* Blow: *O Saviour of the World;* Battishill: *O Lord, look down from Heaven;* Gibbons: *God is gone up;* White: *O praise God in his holiness;* Wesley: *Let us lift up our heart;* Parry: *I was glad;* Holst: *Lord, who hast made us for thine own;* Boyce: *O praise the Lord, ye that fear him;* Purcell: *O Lord Jehovah;* Weelkes: *Hosanna to the Son of David;* Tye: *I will exalt thee;* Croft: *Sing praises to the Lord;* and S.

Wesley: *When Israel came out of Egypt*. This last was an English version of *In exitu Israel de Aegypto*: Latin anthems were a rarity at this time.

The following voluntaries were played at the end of each even-song; Stanford: *Sonata in F;* Parry: *Fantasia on the Old Hundredth; Croft's 136th; Martyrdom; The 'Wanderer' Fantasia and Fugue;* Wesley: *Choral Song and Fugue; Andante Cantabile;* Gibbons: *Voluntary in D minor;* Vaughan Williams: two of the *Three Preludes on Welsh Hymn Tunes;* Stanley: *Adagio and Finale from an organ concerto;* Smart: *Postlude in E flat*.

The Musical Times reported that the voluntaries met with the usual indifference: "the shuffling of retreating footsteps, combined with the murmur of voices, made it difficult to appreciate their efforts". However, the recital by the previous Minster organist, T.T. Noble, fared better. His programme included works by Thomas Adams, Basil Harwood, Vaughan Williams, Veaco, T. Frederick H. Candlyn, and himself.

Each day, except on the Sunday, other cathedral choirs aug-mented the home team: Manchester, Liverpool, Durham, Ripon, Wakefield, Sheffield, Bradford, Carlisle, Newcastle, Southwell, Chester and Lincoln, as well as Leeds Parish Church, the last for a special and obvious reason. The organisation of the whole event would have been a herculean task, but it all appears to have gone with no perceptible hitches, and to the evident satisfaction of all the participants, leaving them, to be sure, with a glow of satisfac-tion and a feeling of real achievement.

At the 1928 Song School Speech Day Lionel Ford, who had succeeded to the deanery in 1926, declared his belief that there was a higher ideal now, greater care, greater pride in the music of the Church than there had been at any previous time in the long history of the Church, and he liked to think of the boys of the choir continuing that great and inspiring tradition. He did not think it ever reached, ever could have reached in the history of the Minster – and he doubted whether it ever reached in the history of music in the whole Church of England – a higher point than it reached in the great services of last year. About the music of those services, there was something which could only be described as inspiration

– the inflow of a spirit – which moved and touched those vast congregations. He had no doubt whence that spirit came. They in their generation had really passed through a time when that noble tradition of English cathedral music reached what they thought to be its highest position. They knew what they owed to Dr. Bairstow even in that, and though he personally had had many anxieties during the past year, one of the greatest was on the question whether or not York Minster was to keep its Bairstow. Knowing that Dr. Bairstow was at present safe had given him great relief.

To digress for a moment: it should be explained that the Dean's veiled remark was occasioned by the situation which had arisen soon after his predecessor, Dean Foxley-Norris, had left York to become Dean of Westminster and was faced with the task of appointing a new organist following the resignation of Dr. Sydney Nicholson. The post was offered to Bairstow by the man who had been his Dean for some ten years at York, a fact which speaks well for their relationship. Such a translation, no doubt, was thought by some to be a step up the ladder, and Bairstow's reputation at that time was among the very highest in the hierarchy of cathedral organists. He had been at York for fifteen years and was surely due for a change. But he did not think so. His early connection with the Abbey as a student must have given him a clear insight into the life of its organist. He was well settled in York and saw no need to move. He had been dubbed the uncrowned king of the musical north, and is reported as saying that he would rather reign in hell than serve in heaven.

Nancy, his daughter, writing in 1973, said that "he felt he had made his name in the North and he would lose his pupils and have to compete with so many other musicians in London and probably lose his source of income". He himself, in a broadcast talk in April 1933, gave these reasons:

> "Thirty years' work in the North has given me an insight into musical life here which is valuable to me and also, I believe, to those with whom I come in contact. I was born in the West Riding, and I know the Yorkshireman, with his fearlessness, his energy, his rather material outlook, and his straightness which sometimes develops into rudeness.

That is the main reason why I stayed – because I believe I am more useful here than in London. But, naturally, there was also the pull of the Minster and the beautiful city of York. Usefulness and a life amidst beautiful surroundings are of far more importance to one's happiness than notoriety and a large income."

ECB continued his talk with a fascinating glance at an aspect of music in the last years of the century:

"I well remember in the old days how we London men sniffed at the provincial musicians. We met them at Durham University when we went there to be examined. They, too, had come for what they called their *Moos Bock* degree. Certainly they were rather an uncouth lot. In those days there were very few men in the provinces who were known outside their own district. But all that has changed now.

"Then the musical societies in the big provincial cities used the local man to do the spade work of teaching the orchestra and choir the notes, and got a big gun from London to conduct the concerts. Today this is the exception rather than the rule, as indeed it should be, for the standard has risen all round. The provincial musician is more cultured and more efficient than was the case when I was a young man, and meets his London confrères on equal terms.

"When the public are educated enough to understand a man's musical message, apart from his mere technical skill: when they can judge of his sincerity and of its selflessness; when they can enjoy listening to singers with brains and musical insight, even when their voices are not very large or very rich; in fact, when they will listen for more than the mere sound, then the provincial musician will come fully into his own. His job, therefore, is to do all he can to bring about the millennium by every means in his power."

The 13th centenary celebrations left two legacies, one being the Diocesan Musical Festival, to which, each year, every choir in the diocese was invited to take its part in the singing of evensong in the mother church during the octave of Saint Peter, the Minster's patron saint. The Church Times called it a "noble invitation (which) in view of the great area of the diocese ... has had a grateful and eager response. ... As in former years, the afternoon was devoted to rehearsal of the whole service. ... Sir Edward Bairstow is a great genius, who yet (or, maybe, consequently) understands how to teach very simple people. He knows intuitively how to elicit the very best that they are capable of giving. The one unpardonable sin is not to care and not to try. ... The much-prized privilege of an hour and a half's teaching from Sir Edward was over all too soon, and the choirs dispersed till Evensong at six o'clock... The choirs had mastered the singing of Psalm 148 to the English Psalter pointing. There was a joy and abandon about it that could never be with the old tortured pointing. And so the company departed home again, mostly to remote country villages. Year by year they carry back with them the same impression from Sir Edward's teaching, and the example of all at the Minster including the choirboys, who gave up a fine Saturday afternoon to help with the rehearsal, that it is the meaning of the words they say and sing that matters, even more than a perfect performance of the music; although the two are interdependent, even as a picture depends upon both drawing and colour. ... a heterogeneous collection sitting in no special order. ... What a task, to unify and weld such a company! But the slight, graceful figure on the high rostrum was equal to it. Encouraging, rebuking, sometimes with humour, sometimes with gentle sarcasm, but mostly by the fire of his own enthusiasm, he got his way with them. One of the choirmen remarked as we broke up for tea at 4.30, 'I could sit a week at a practice like that'." This festival has continued annually without break ever since.

The other legacy took the form of gramophone recordings, and on April the seventh 1927, just over two months before the celebrations were to begin, the Gramophone Company's recording van was in position to make records of the Minster choir, presumably intended as mementos for the crowds of music lovers who would be visiting the city for the festival. Two discs were made and published, of music which meant so much to ECB: 'Christe qui lux es et dies' and 'This day Christ was born' by Byrd; and Gibbons' 'O Lord, increase my faith' and 'O clap your hands'. They appeared on the twelve-inch plum label, numbered respectively C 1334 and C 1337. The second side of Gibbons contained the latter part of

'O clap your hands', beginning at 'God is gone up' and was recorded on the following day along with two other anthems. These were 'O praise God in his holiness' by Robert Whyte, and Blow's 'Salvator mundi', but they were never, for some reason, issued. Both sides of each record were recorded twice. In the record catalogue at the time the choir's discs were preceded by a ten-inch record of the Minster bells. This item came after *Yodel Songs* and *Yon assassin is my equal* from Rigoletto, and following the choir, available for purchase was 'You and a canoe' played by Emile Grimshaw's Banjo Quartet.

At this time technology was progressing. Just over a month after this session, Charles Lindbergh made an early crossing of the Atlantic, landing his plane *Spirit of St. Louis* in Paris after a flight lasting thirty-three and a half hours. In the field of sound recording, the new electrical system supplanted the acoustical method in 1923. Among early examples of this, excerpts from Bach's Mass in B minor were issued. These were sung by the Royal Choral Society with the Royal Albert Hall Orchestra, conducted by Dr. E.C.Bairstow and were recorded at a public performance in the Albert Hall on Saturday afternoon, April 24, 1926. This was in commemoration of the first performance in England, which had been given by the same chorus fifty years before, on 26 April 1876. The four records issued contained only choruses. The soloists, Dorothy Silk, Muriel Brunskill, Archibald Winter and Herbert Heyner were left out of the picture. This, of course, was long before the days of complete works on records, which only began to blossom fully with the emergence of the Long Playing Record in the nineteen-fifties. The marvellous invention, which enabled sounds to be captured on wax seems, to later generations familiar with the C.D. and the cassette, to be a cumbersome affair. Hence, what amounted to selections or tasters were perforce only representatives of the large work on 78 r.p.m. discs. Later, when automatic changing devices came into being, a few of the more popular works appeared in albums, somewhat heavily, and sometimes in what were termed automatic couplings which facilitated the record changes but did not avoid a break in continuity every four minutes or so.

These Bach discs were on the H.M.V. black label. *Crucifixus* and *Patrem Omnipotentem* were back to back on the record numbered D 1113; *Qui tollis* and *Hosanna in excelsis* on Dlll4. These were on sale in September 1926, and in November followed the *Sanctus* (in two parts) on D1123; and finally, on D 1127, the *Gloria in Excelsis* (parts 1 and 2) in the mid-November catalogue.

The rest of Bairstow's recording consisted of two solo discs of Bach on the Minster organ, the Prelude and Fugue in B minor and the chorale prelude *Nun komm der Heiden Heiland* now designated BWV 659. These were on the twelve-inch plum label, numbered C 1534/5. But in the previous month he was at St. Margaret's, Westminster, recording his own Prelude in C and Scherzo in A flat as well as Mendelssohn's second sonata. Unfortunately, they never saw the light of day. The composer's own account of his compositions would have been, to say the least, instructive. The Prelude, however, does exist in acetate, taken probably from a broadcast, and a player roll at Blenheim Palace contains the Scherzo as played by William Wolstenholme, but with defects in the registration mechanism, which by now have probably been rectified. Bairstow is known to have grumbled, quite justifiably, that his financial reward for these efforts at St. Margaret's on 3 January 1928 (which consisted of one take each of the four Mendelssohn sides, two takes of the Prelude, and three of the Scherzo) was nil.

There is also an acetate recording of the first section of the Fantasia in E minor by Edouard Silas (a piece he enjoyed to play) which perforce ends inconclusively on a chord of the dominant, the fugue, which should follow, being missing. It is unfortunate that he did not make more recordings, but those that remain give a fair idea of his approach. It is pleasant also to be able to hear the very sounds that he heard and to speculate on his reaction as he listened to them. The technique in all his recordings is faultless, as is only to be expected of a musician bent always on perfection: not a slip or a wrong note, and, with the Royal Choral Society, perfect discipline with complete clarity and unanimity, even in the vast spaces of the then over-resonant Albert Hall; surely quite an achievement in those pioneering days.

The Morning Post declared that the old-established Royal Choral Society had never done anything better, commending its vitality and alertness 'which, to be frank, we have not always associated with these concerts'. The Daily Mail thought that the immense choir was nimbler than might have been expected. The Telegraph expressed the opinion that, rather than aiming for superficial effects by sheer weight of numbers, which on some past occasions was all the singers seemed qualified to give, 'a very real and often very successful attempt was being made to produce something more than the outward shape'. Naturally the style of performance has changed since those times – *Sabaoth* comes out as *Sabayoth,* for instance – but purpose and drive are there in good measure, as well as the nimbleness already mentioned.

Before the revival of the classical organ in Britain, weight was inclined to take precedence over brilliance (a notable exception being the York organ with its fine, bright quint mixture on the Great organ, voiced to Bairstow's requirements: but there was weight aplenty too). The Bach B minor fugue, which in Bairstow's recording begins on eight-foot tone, increases in volume as far as the final entry of the subject, and appears to change hardly at all as stops are added, the eight-foot line predominating throughout. Even the quint mixture makes little headway against the massively smooth trombas, with which it fails to cohere completely.

All these recordings were gratefully received by reviewers on behalf of the music lover eager to take advantage of the emergent sound-reproducer. 'Very fine are the records made actually in York Minster' (Telegraph). 'The echo of great spaces and the whole majesty of trained voices are caught miraculously' (Sunday Chronicle). 'I admired the boys particularly ... really splendid in the ease and certainty of their attack, the clear, pure quality of their tone and the general sense of conviction with which they express their music...' (Glasgow Herald).

His performance of the Prelude in C is much as might be expected, with the addition of some unmarked swell-pedal *sforzandi* on the second and fourth beats of bars 30-32 and 35-37 which provide an intriguing point of interest. He takes it at exactly the tempo indicated in the copy, allowing a slight relaxing in the central section. The neapolitan fanfare at the end is, however, treated *rubato,* the dotted minim being considerably shortened. This is strange, considering how particular he was in observing strictly what was written. Now and again he was asked to broadcast an organ recital, and one of these included his sonata. How wonderful it would have been to have had it recorded.

As a conductor, also, he occasionally appeared in broadcasts. On 10 April 1927 (two days after his recording sessions with the Minster choir) he directed the first part of Bach's St. Matthew Passion which was broadcast, as was part two of the Mass in B minor on 5 July. Taking into account his regular, daily commitment to the Minster services, these extras would provide him with an intensive period of exacting work to do. Other broadcasts included, on 6 October 1931, a Bach Cantata Club concert from St. Margaret's, Westminster. This was a small choir of 26 voices and an orchestra numbering 13, including the well-known oboist Léon Goossens. Herbert Dawson, organist of the church, played the organ. The soloists were Dora Stevens, Jessie King, Steuart Wilson and Arthur Cranmer. The programme consisted of three cantatas, *104 Du Hirte Israel Höre, 26 Ach wie flüchtig*, and *140 Wachet Auf*. The Universe critic declared that 'Dr. Bairstow conducted with an authority and vitality which gripped the choir and orchestra from the very first note'. The Daily Chronicle considered that his rare appearances in London have stamped him as a choral conductor of the front rank'. (*But compare this with Neville Cardus, three paragraphs further on. Which is right?*)

On 14 December 1931, part two of Messiah was broadcast by the Leeds Philharmonic Chorus in Leeds Town Hall, the soloists being Isobel Baillie, Muriel Brunskill, Frank Titterton and Harold Williams. Part one of the Bach St. Matthew Passion came from York Minster on 20 March 1932, and on 12 March 1937, Stanford's *Stabat Mater* also from Leeds Town Hall, with the Leeds Philharmonic Chorus, the Northern Philharmonic Orchestra and Kate Winter, Gladys Ripley, Henry Wendon and Keith Falkner as soloists.

Twice he conducted the Hallé Choir and Orchestra in *Messiah* in successive years. The first of these occasions (on December 21, 1933) drew the Manchester Guardian critic's commendation of the unity of style in the first part of the oratorio, and the opinion that the interpretation was 'the cleanest we have heard in recent years. The chorus singing was brilliant, and not for a long time have we heard such firm articulation of words as well as notes. There were

Some impressions of Dr. E. C. Bairstow
(The Yorkshire Evening Post, 20 November 1924)

no loose ends, no wasted tone, and no let or hindrance to a delivery that happily combined fluency and vehemence. Yet, though the reading gave us many splendours, it was not one that expressed the full geniality of the composer. We felt that in Sir Edward's strongly disciplined treatment much of the festal music in the oratorio came through without the heart-easing effect that makes us sure of the composer as a dear companion, even though he has a giant's stature. Still, a clean, forthright reading that allows due weight to, and no exaggeration of, details is something to be thankful for.' This write-up was concluded with the initials GAH.

Neville Cardus, the following year, was not so happy. 'An inspired conductor', he thought, 'was wanted to get the best out of the forces which were by no means born to the manner. The chorus sang well; a metronomic beat did not assist transition. To give one characteristic instance – in the "Hallelujah" chorus, at the marvellous change with the words "The kingdom of this world", were given merely a change of tone, an external affair of softening volume; we were not taken into another world. It was the same in "All we like sheep, have gone astray"; nothing happened to fire the imagination at the sublime "And the Lord hath laid on him". The conducting was earnest; it played no tricks. But a competent reading of the *Messiah* is not enough at a Hallé Concert. The orchestra played accurately; it was urged to do no more than that.' At this distance in time it is impossible to refute any of these sentiments. They have a slight feeling of superiority and, maybe, of exaggeration, but it would appear that they were heeded by the concert organisers, for Sir Edward was not asked again to conduct for them.

The soprano and bass solists on both occasions were Isobel Baillie and Keith Falkner. In the earlier performance Margaret Balfour and Walter Widdop were the contralto and tenor respectively. At the second (on December 20) the contralto was Vera de Villiers, and Steuart Wilson the tenor.

X

What is Good Church Music?

S UCH WAS THE HEADING to a write-up in the Yorkshire Post of
6 November 1908 reporting a lecture given by E.C.B. in connection with the City of Leeds School on a subject "which is still,
unhappily, of a controversial nature. For the present state of affairs
the clergy are greatly to blame. They tolerate in their churches no
architecture, sculpture, painting or literature quite so bad as the
worst of the music in common use there. Congregations, too, by
the glib way in which they pronounce the solemn words of psalm
and hymn show a very unsatisfactory attitude of mind."

Bairstow was always worried about standards and was constantly referring to "good" music – and of course its antithesis "bad"
music, otherwise "tosh" or "tripe" ; or (if he had gone to America)
"trash" or "garbage", a word he must surely have enjoyed enunci-
ating with all the requisite scorn in that nasal voice of his. At the
annual congress of the Incorporated Association of Organists in
Glasgow in 1938, of which he was President, he chaired the Annual
General Meeting. Running his eye down the agenda until he came
to 'Crooning', in evident disapproval he commented: 'There is no
need to discuss crooning. It's a damn ugly thing'.

Many years earlier, in 1909, at a dinner of the Royal College
of Organists, he was entrusted with the toast to the ladies in which
he somewhat unexpectedly and rather curiously included a criticism:

> It is no news to you all that the ladies are a source of great inspi-
> ration, but I do wish they would inspire us with something else
> beside love – we get such a lot of it! Look at the songs that are
> written nowadays. They are absolutely full of love of the most

mediocre type. I am sure you will all agree that the ladies are capable of inspiring us with something stronger, something healthier. I embrace all the ladies – in the toast, of course – not only those who are favouring us with their presence tonight, but the fair sex as a whole, and I ask you to drink their health.

As to the standard of music at Leeds Parish Church, he told a Sunday Pictorial interviewer, back in 1911, "The tradition of the church, established by Wesley, is to have only strong and dignified music sung at its services, and to steer clear, as far as possible, of the maudlin, the sentimental, and the merely pretty music, which is so common in many of our churches."

The critic of the Bradford Telegraph (some time in 1909) was "afraid that Dr. Bairstow's comments upon the worth of Wallace's song *She comes in all her loveliness* would come as a rude shock to those bass singers who have long regarded the song in the light of a 'classic'. Dr. Bairstow said he could not understand such worthless songs being imposed as tests of musical competitions at this day."

In the Mrs. Sunderland competitions he "entered a humorous but needed protest against choirboys being asked to sing songs informing some person unknown that 'My heart is all for you' at an age when they were not out of reach of parental control.' There was a touch of comedy "in the assumption by the choirboys of the role of ardent lovers calling to their 'dearest dear' to come out and greet the sun. ... They should be kept off that sort of thing until they got a little older ... and he hoped the lads as they sang 'You are all the world to me' were thinking of their mothers."

At an organ lesson I ventured to play John Ireland's 'Villanella', a piece with a distinctly popular flavour, perhaps a youthful work, but by a composer I knew he respected. Immediately I began to play I became aware that I had made an error and that this piece did not meet with his approval. He fidgeted and was ill at ease, but I did not dare stop. All the while I wondered what terrors would be unleashed when eventually I came to the end. All that he needed, however, was one of his favourite epithets; "That's tripe". I was left in no doubt, and was more careful after that to choose music that he was certain to find acceptable. So I became acutely aware that there must be a dividing line of some kind between what he approved of and what he considered sub-standard, and I was not yet fully confident of where it was drawn.

Even in the case of Chopin I could not be sure that he might consider some pieces merely pretty ear-ticklers without depth. He once told me that he preferred Chopin when he was a Pole rather than a polite and fashionable Parisian; but I never found out from him which of the works fell into either category. He was inclined to be disparaging, too, about Ravel's 'Valses Nobles et Sentimentales' because, I suspect, he probably thought them light and slightly frivolous. I was encouraged, though, by H.K.Andrews, then at Beverley Minster and a friend of E.C.B's, who had a high regard for them.

Yet he liked the Brahms 'Liebeslieder' waltzes. Having got the Ravel bug rather badly, I lent him my records of the quartet (which he took a long time to return to me). His comment was "I played that quartet of Ravel's" (pronouncing it as rhyming with gravels): "it's all in four-bar phrases". I did not at the time think of countering this with the fact that the same can be said of Grieg's piano concerto and that this does not worry the listening public in the least. The harmonies, which so attracted me with their colour, he regarded as "just a trick" which anyone could learn. ... He was more interested in soundness of construction, but I wonder sometimes if he had come across Ravel's dictum on the subject; that "The one and only test of good form is continuity of interest". (Bairstow was not quite six months older than Ravel, so was very much of the same generation). His opinion of Delius, as related by Whiteley Singleton of Brighouse, ECB's pupil, that 'he could paint but he couldn't draw', denoted his preference for music with a readily recognised form of construction rather than with highly coloured harmonies.

As to colour, Bairstow's own works do not eschew the use of it at appropriate moments. There is a stunning example near the end of the anthem 'Lord, I call upon thee' where the orchestral oboe, accompanied by Debussyan chords, magically ushers in the words "I will lay me down in peace and take my rest, for it is thou, Lord, only that makest me dwell in safety" conveying exactly the feeling of deep relaxation when the eyes swivel as sleep approaches.

At some time in the thirties, Bairstow expressed to me his belief that the symphonies of Elgar had 'had their vogue'. This seemed to be a gesture of dismissal to these works which, admittedly, were, at that period, suffering neglect but which, in later years, have had their greatness fully realised. It is an example of the hyper-critical attitude which was then abroad and which prevented composers who were not well known from gaining a hearing, in competition with Beethoven and Brahms who were the staple fare at the time. And it is a fact that snobbism was not slow to castigate Elgar for his lighter pieces. This feeling probably spilled over into the assessing of his larger, serious works, on the principle that a composer who can write a melodious, popular piece such as *Salut d'Amour* was not worth consideration among the great masters.

An incident with Elgar may also have played a part in his thinking. Elgar was using the Station Hotel at York as a staging post and, having some time to spare, thought he would get on with some fairly hack work for his publisher – perhaps some rearrangement of part-songs – but was without music paper, and the shops were shut. The situation was saved by the dispatching of Elgar's valet or chauffeur to ask Bairstow for some. ECB complied, but thought that Elgar could have had the courtesy to come round himself in person, however briefly.

As far as the music for the Minster services was concerned, it appears that there was a good deal of interest taken by the congregation, at any rate those members of it who wrote him letters telling him they were "bored stiff" with some of it. He told his choir school prize-giving audience in 1928 that there were people to whom music was unintelligible and who tried to impose their wishes on those who had a greater knowledge of music. There were also people who resented being told what was good music and what was not. (One wonders darkly whether this might have been a dig at a vociferous member of the clergy staff perhaps). Quite recently, he said, he had made certain justifiable observations regarding the suitability of Sullivan's compositions which had brought him many amusing letters. But it all rolled 'like water off a duck's back'. Why people should think he had a sort of grudge against Sullivan he could not say. But surely, anyone reading these remarks of his could hardly be blamed for arriving at that kind of conclusion. This he appeared not to be able to realise; or, if he did, it did not bother him. He had participated, as we have seen already, in productions of Sullivan's operas during his days at the Grocers' School.

The episode which sparked the controversy is an example of Sir Edward's habit of saying exactly what was in his mind in order to direct people's attention to something which needed to be looked at afresh. An even more notable instance follows this one.

It was in March, 1928, that he openly criticised some of Sullivan's music and his "feeble anthem *O love the Lord*" which had been a test piece at the Carlisle Musical Festival. The anthem had been written when Sullivan was 22 and still immature. ECB perhaps went a bit far in asserting that, although he was a great composer of comic opera, in church music he "never wrote anything worth a cuss". He went further: "This particular effusion is the feeblest type of Victorian music. Stupid, nonsensical music has driven thousands of people out of church. No intelligent person is going to listen complacently to such music. Today we do not get such music in the concert hall. Even jazz has more life in it than that stuff. Yet there is no lack of beautiful anthems".

Strong stuff. And he had a supporter in Martin Shaw who, writing in the Church of England Newspaper (23 March 1928), said: "I must admit that the doctor is quite right to say it when he did. ... I wish all adjudicators would follow his example whenever they come across any unworthy music."

Several letters appeared in the newspapers from supporters of Sullivan, most of them, while expressing astonishment and indignation, agreeing that Sullivan was a great composer of comic opera; which is anyway what Bairstow had said. One correspondent declared that his church music had "soothed myriad millions of people all over the world; who is Dr. Bairstow that he should criticise so great a musician?" Another wished to register a strong protest "against the narrowness of this condemnation and the vulgarity with which it was expressed". Another wrote of "this elegant judgement of Dr.Bairstow", while a Morning Post editorial thought he had expressed himself a little crudely, perhaps, and went on to reason that Sullivan's genius "was such that we can afford to neglect the manifestations of it in its minor aspects, and concentrate our attention on the fields wherein it achieved supreme and abiding success".

ECB enlarged on the subject in the London Evening News (26.3.28) He began by saying that, when he criticised Sullivan, he had had no idea he was stirring up a hornet's nest. He went on:

> The use of bad church music is due to three I's – Ignorance, Indifference and Inertia. Probably the last two are a result of the first. It goes without saying that we should offer our best in religious music, and that our best is the music we feel most deeply, whether we compose it or perform it. Music which scarcely ruffles the surface of the emotions, like the anthem quoted above, is bad enough in church, for the spirit of the music and the spirit of the text to which it is set are in antagonism.

> But still worse is the flippant type like the opening of Sullivan's anthem 'Sing, O heavens'. Tunes like this would have been welcomed in one of his lightest operas. The melodic and rhythmic attractiveness of Sullivan's music, taken apart from the words to which it is set, must account for the long reign of such hymn tunes as 'Onward, Christian Soldiers'. The jolly march rhythm of this may suggest a band of children with paper helmets and wooden swords, but it certainly does not bring forcibly to one's mind the Church of God marching against the forces of evil.

> Sullivan was a very gifted man who found his *métier* in comic opera, and wisely devoted most of his time to it. He has left us an inimitable group of these operas for which we are eternally grateful. Naturally he would have liked also to be remembered by works which touch a deeper note, but who can imagine what an oratorio by Offenbach would be like, or a mass by, say, Johann Strauss.

What would he have thought of Rossini's Petite Messe Solennel, unknown during his lifetime and rediscovered in the nineteen-fifties? An early modern performance of it, incidentally, was given by York Musical Society on Saint Cecilia's Day, 22 November 1957, shortly before the one in London under Sir Malcolm Sargent.

> Thus, when Sullivan attempted serious works, although the clever touch was still there, his long and close association with the comic opera stage must have influenced him subconsciously,

for he was evidently obsessed with the thought of what effect his music would have upon the public. He got what he asked for – popularity amongst ignorant people.

He flourished at a time when English church music was at its worst; when it was the musical counterpart of comfortable satisfaction, of cushioned seats and of bad imitations of Gothic architecture; when there was plenty of money, a sure hope of Heaven and when Hell was remote. His contemporaries had neither his cleverness nor his flippancy; they were merely smug and dull. Thank goodness their music is gradually disappearing. Never has there been such a strong desire to eliminate everything unworthy from our services as there is today. No wonder that the Tudor composers have lately come into their own.

If there are ulterior considerations at the back of the composer's mind, his music may have a merry life, but it will be a short one. It matters not what those considerations are, whether a desire to please, to make money, or to be proper and correct, or to be modern and up-to-date; they will prevent the man from putting forth the best that is in him, and his music will soon grow stale. Those who disagree with this should rehearse music and perform it repeatedly, as we cathedral organists have to do. They would soon perceive the type of music which wears well and understand why it does so.

No better proof of the truth of these words could be found than in the way Bairstow's own music has held its place and has become increasingly better known and appreciated for its worth, its depth and sincerity, all of which conspires towards its undoubted durability.

Herbert Thompson of the Yorkshire Post followed up the controversy on 9 April 1928:

I must take leave to differ from Doctor Bairstow's assertion that in church music Sullivan 'never wrote anything worth a cuss'. He did write a good deal of music which was worth a cuss, not the least striking example being this anthem. ... But when one remembers the output of English musicians in the (*eighteen-*)sixties ... one can understand why Sullivan's little anthem could not be expected to have any marked distinction. Probably in some places of worship where music of a sweet and sugary type is cultivated it may still have a certain vogue.

Wesley was a different matter: "he has given us music that stands by itself in these days" wrote Bairstow:

> and at the time when it was written it was as a mountain in the middle of a plain. By reason of his impelling inspiration and child-like sincerity Wesley had the instinct of a Beethoven for great moments. Much modern music impresses us with the cleverness of its texture, but leaves us disappointed because of the lack of those wonderful flashes of inspiration found in the works of all great men – moments when, with the simplest technical mater-ial, they could suddenly lift us into the very heavens, or make us hold our breath.

During his years of training he found the services and anthems at the Abbey:

> mostly rather dull and uninspired, but eminently dignified and respectable. Now and then works of real genius would come along, such as the works of the Elizabethans and Purcell, with here and there an odd thing by Croft, Greene or Boyce, which thrilled the more musical amongst us to the marrow. ... We love Wesley because he was sincere when many musicians were shal-low and smug, because he was bold when his fellows were timid and conventional, and because he was English at a time when it was considered the right thing tamely to copy Mendelssohn and other foreigners.

This article, with the title "The Anthems of Samuel Sebastian Wesley", in the Musical Times of April 1926, is of especial inter-est as showing ECB's perception and his sensitivity to the atmos-phere of great music in its moments of extra-special expressiveness. The same feelings can be engendered by some of his own music, such as *Let all mortal flesh keep silence: If the Lord had not helped me: I sat down under his shadow:* or the Variations for violin and piano. He was profoundly susceptible to the effect of music when he was listening to or performing it and, judging by such moments as these in his own works, he must have been equally moved in the act of creating them. Music, to him, was the essence, the distillation of all that was beautiful and which meant most to him; never a thing of mere notes (however accurately played) or of sterile velocity, brilliance and display.

The effect, for instance, which a single chant by Christopher Gibbons had on him one weekday morning at matins was most marked: the beauty of this most simple of musical forms hit him, as they say, in the solar plexus causing tears, literally, of deepest pleasure and spiritual satisfaction. Undoubtedly the words (of Psalm 26) would also have played their part: 'I will wash my hands in innocency, O Lord, and so will I go to thine altar'. He had already set them in memorable style as an introit, and the aptness of the chant to which they were sung on that particular morning – a mere ten simple chords – produced an effect which, to him, was irresistible, and in such incomparable surroundings. It is perhaps worth pointing out that this chant, mostly diatonic, contains two chromatic notes, of which one provides a modulation to the key of the dominant – a common occurence; the other – a foreign one (G flat in the key of A flat) – produces a surprise, which is rare – or should be.

He would define romantic music as something strange and, at the same time, beautiful: that a Greek statue was beautiful but not strange: that a chemical reaction was strange but not beautiful: and (rather unchivalrously!) that the daily charlady was neither strange nor beautiful. The sudden placing of a triad of F major between two D major triads could provide a strange and beautiful effect, as at 'Hosanna in the highest' in the *Benedictus qui venit* of his D major communion service; and most tellingly, perhaps, in the final page of the anthem *Lord, thou hast been our refuge,* as well as elsewhere quite frequently in his compositions, following Stanford's lead in his song *The Fairy Lough.* This utterly simple device produced a powerfully evocative atmosphere as used by a composer some three centuries earlier, and it moved him deeply.

XI

The Perfectionist

IF A MAN IS A PERFECTIONIST, as Bairstow was, he becomes either ruthless or full of despair. There were times when Bairstow came near to despair, especially about tenors and contraltos; but he was mostly ruthless, and that meant what many people regarded as rudeness.

Perhaps the most memorable of his excursions into this troublous field occurred in 1928, when he visited Canada as a festival adjudicator at Winnipeg, and gave an organ recital in St. Andrew's Presbyterian Church, Fort William. Let us quote the Port Arthur News and Chronicle of 23 April 1928:

> The sensation was not in the music programme but in criticism, volunteered by Dr. Bairstow and directed toward the contributions of the two assisting artists, Mrs. H.W.Airth of Port Arthur, and Joe Ross of Fort William. These two outstanding vocalists had accepted invitations to contribute voice numbers in order to vary the program and were heard with the pleasure that always accompanies their appearance on any platform here.
>
> Mrs. Airth was programed for one number and sang *The Little Damozel* by Ivor Novello – a piece that has many times been sung by Galli Curci – responding to an encore with *Calm as the Night* by C. Bohm, another piece that is popular with artists of world fame. Mr. Ross was programed for one song and gave *The Bell in the Lighthouse Tower*, his encore being *Annie Laurie*. Both were accompanied upon the piano by Percival Kirby, organist of St. Andrew's.

It was noticeable to some in the audience that Dr. Bairstow appeared ill at ease while Mrs. Airth and Mr. Ross were singing. The vocalists occupied the pulpit platform and the visiting organist sat at the organ beyond. During the vocal numbers he seemed to be giving his attention to other things and actually, while Mrs. Airth was singing, turned his back towards her and looked towards the pipe organ, as if counting the pipes or giving it some other thought. He had been making it a practice to speak of his own numbers as he went from one to another on the program, explaining their nature or history, and it was while so speaking before his last number that he offered the unexpected criticism which so startled his hearers.

He said: 'You have listened with a great deal of patience to my portion of the program; more so than I have listened to yours'. Then he went on to say that his lack of patience was because of the character of the songs chosen by Mrs. Airth and Mr. Ross. He said they were very much unfitted to such a program and he referred to them as 'trashy stuff'. It was the first time, he said, that 'Annie Laurie' had ever been sung on one of his programs. He did not specifically name any of the other songs.

Dr. Bairstow's remarks were so unexpected and so startling that his hearers appeared almost stunned. Their full significance apparently was not immediately recognised, or at least the audience remained under self-restraint until after the organist's next and concluding number. Then, however, the incident became the one big topic of very animated discussion as the people left the church, everyone commenting in one way or another on the dramatic nature and the ethics of such a criticism offered by one musician to others on the same program.

Mrs. Airth and Mr. Ross were immediately surrounded by members of the committee who had, in arranging the program, invited them to sing, and by others expressing regret that they should have been made the centre of such an incident. Members of the committee, especially, offered such apologies as they could to the local artists. Mr. Ross and Mrs. Airth both sought out Dr. Bairstow and told him they resented his remarks, but little in the way of an apology was forthcoming from him.

'I pointed out to him' said Mr. Ross to the News Chronicle today, 'that *Annie Laurie* had been sung by artists who received all the way from $1,500 to $3,500 for one appearance, and told him it was too bad he had come all the way over here to be bored by our efforts to assist in his program. I asked him what he thought we were, over here, and I told him it was unfortunate that we had to send overseas for a man to come to criticise our music; that we had plenty of men of ability in Canada quite equal to his. I told him it was too bad he should permit jealousy to make him insulting. Mrs. Airth also paid her compliments to the Doctor and his program.' The Minister who had intended to speak at the conclusion of the program refrained from making a platform appearance."

B. Gunton Smalley, composer and conductor, said, 'On ninety-nine organ programs out of one hundred the contributions by Mrs. Airth and Mr. Ross would have been eminently fitting. Dr. Bairstow's was so unique in its character that it is true they were just a trifle out of place, but I was indeed surprised to hear the Doctor comment as he did. Dr. Bairstow's organ program was of a highly classical nature, including the works of several of the old masters, in the form of voluntaries and preludes by such composers as Gibbons, S. Wesley, Charles Wood, Bach, Louis Vierne, Karg-Elert and César Franck, together with one or two of his own compositions. He played with an excellent technique.'

'It was most discourteous, one of the rudest things I ever witnessed', said Percival Kirby, organist of St. Andrew's. 'It was distinctly out of place for Dr. Bairstow to say any such thing. The songs of which he spoke pleased the audience, even if they didn't please him. As for *Annie Laurie* it has taken its place among the classics, has been sung on the best programs for many years and will be so placed long after Dr. Bairstow is gone. Mrs. Airth's songs were of a very high class. If it was an occasion for criticism, there was opportunity for us to criticise Dr. Bairstow, but we didn't do it. I think he stepped far out of his sphere to speak as he did.'

'I must say that I did notice a certain incongruity as between the organ numbers and the vocal numbers', said A.F. Thornborough, choirmaster of Trinity United Church, Port Arthur. "There was a lack of harmony in the matter of choice. The proper procedure would have been for the principal to give his approval to the selections of the assisting artists before the program was adopted, but under the circumstances of Dr. Bairstow being enroute, traveling, this was largely impracticable. His remarks from the standpoint of critic or adjudicator, in which position he will be when he goes to Winnipeg to attend the musical festival there, were to a considerable extent justified, but since the purpose of his stop-over here was to entertain and not to criticise, he might very well have allowed the matter to rest without comment'.

When he returned from Canada in June, ECB gave the Yorkshire Post his views under the headline DR. BAIRSTOW SHOWN THE DOOR:

The chief object of my journey was to adjudicate at festivals in the four provinces of Manitoba, British Columbia, Saskatchewan and Alberta.

An amusing thing happened after I left New York. Several months before leaving England, I was asked to give an organ recital at Fort William, and when I arrived there I was most cordially received. The recital was in the church. On examining the programme I found there were to be two local singers – a man and a woman. They sang the most awful songs, finishing with 'Annie Laurie'. Before my last piece I congratulated the audience upon listening to my kind of music with more patience than I had listened to theirs. I tried to explain to them why the songs were "pot boilers" and said that as the singers had excellent voices I could not imagine why they had selected such songs.

In the vestry one of the singers (the lady) "went for me". She said she supposed I had come from the Old Country to show them how to do it, and I replied "That is what I was engaged for". After that we were all invited to the Minister's house for tea. I was introduced to the principal members of the congregation. At the table not a word of conversation took place. When I left to catch the train to Winnipeg, instead of being driven to the station I was taken to the front door, the host simply pointing to the road and saying "That is the way to the station", and I had to walk.

Subsequently I had a local paper sent to me containing a report of the recital, with these flaming headlines:

SENSATION AT ORGAN RECITAL
ONE ARTIST CRITICISES OTHERS
DR. E.C. BAIRSTOW OF YORK MINSTER, ENGLAND
SAYS MRS. AIRTH AND JOE ROSS SING TRASH

Canada can be put down as a music-loving place. The standard is high, the teaching very good indeed, and the choice of music of the very best. What impressed me was the number of business men who gave up their time to assist in organising the festivals, and the great desire they evinced to help in what Canada needs so much – cultural influence. There is a tendency to concentrate on material things, and to think of little but dollars. Many Canadians see that, and are doing their best to counteract it.

Looking back more than two generations it could appear that Bairstow's method of doing missionary work on behalf of his beloved music in a younger country might seem too bold. There are undoubtedly other ways of going about influencing people to modify their views, most of which would not leave an unpleasant legacy. But with his impulsive nature and his passion for truth, could it be that he foresaw that to cause a stir would bring home his message to a much wider audience? Who can tell what its ultimate effect could be? His courage in taking such a strong line is worthy of admiration: he seemed to feel that to spur people with a love of music was an uphill struggle at that time and that every means should be employed to bring it to effect no matter what the consequences might be.

So much for Canada. As for America, ECB was often liable to give vent to his feelings by somewhat violent castigations of that country and its products. It is not easy to determine why he should have felt thus, and it would seem a rather unreasonable stance to take. He would imitate the American pronunciation of the phrase 'as a matter of fact', deprived of most of its consonants and with the vowels running together to produce what sounded like one word. And we have already noted his opinion of going to live and work there as reported by Sir Ernest Bullock. He seems to have harboured this feeling for a long time. He told his audience in his presidential address at the Royal College of Organists in January 1929: "We live in an age of stunts. There is a craze for perversion

– for putting things to a use for which they were never intended. A certain nation that invented the word has infected us. It is a younger generation than ours. It is not their fault, perhaps, but their misfortune that they have no traditions. Like children they seize on any new thing and stunt with it. They use the wireless to advertise pork factories and the organ to reproduce the kitchen furniture of the orchestra. Their orchestral programmes are thickly sprinkled with stunting pieces, and their lighter music is constructed entirely of rhythmic stunts."

That word 'stunt' is defined by Cassell's dictionary as 'Chiefly American' and denotes 'a remarkable feat of strength, skill, etc., especially in public'. There are two further instances of ECB's use of it, the one more public than the other. To Sydney Nicholson, then organist of Westminster Abbey, who was compiling a collection of variations on hymns, he wrote on 20 December 1925:

> Dear Nicholson,
>
> I enclose five 'Hymn tunes with stunts'. As people complain that they cannot sing when the Minster Choir perform the simplest of descants, it seems to me that to write anything of this sort without "putting off" some of the congregation is an impossibility. The descants to "Praise to the holiest" and "Let saints on earth" have been sung many times in the Minster and elsewhere round here. The varied harmonies of "O come, O come Emmanuel" were written when I was at Norfolk Square in 1896, and these, too, have been used extensively. Send back what you don't want.
>
> Yours ever,
>
> E.C.Bairstow

The two remaining numbers were "Lord, thy word abideth" (Ravenshaw) and "Jesu, grant me this, I pray (Gibbons' Song 13, then called 'Canterbury' in A. & M.). Though provision was made for congregational participation, the latter arrangement was too elaborate for this purpose and too sensitive a conception for any other than good choirs. It has become widely accepted for use as a choir piece for solemn occasions. It was sung at Bairstow's funeral.

The other – the public – use of the word was at a Song School Speech Day in 1924 . "We have been engaged in a stunt with the choir. The aim is to achieve a better ensemble, such as would be expected in a concert room, and the choir and the organ are to begin together after a pause of indefinite length. This they do by instinct. Although not perfect, the results are remarkable, and it is a thing not hitherto done in a cathedral. The difficulties of ensemble at York are greater than in an 'ordinary' church because of the distance between organ and choir. Accompanying the choir in services held in the nave is now easier because of loud speakers in the organ loft". Before that, it must have been extremely difficult to achieve any unity, organist and choir being out of sight of each other and some ninety feet apart. We have noted, however, how he 'controlled' a large congregation from the screen console during the 1927 celebrations.

The console had been moved from the east to the south side of the organ during the 1903 rebuild, with the object of making possible accompaniment for both nave and choir services. Forty years before this, Dr. E.G. Monk had realised the necessity for an independent organ for the nave and had caused one to be erected in the north aisle. This was removed, however, by T.T. Noble who apparently did not consider the large distance between choir and organ a problem for coordination. The introduction of loudspeakers some years later only partially solved the problem. Fifty-seven years later the moveable nave console brought the matter a stage nearer solution, but as the source of sound was still in the same place, far away from the voices it was meant to support, the situation was still unresolved, and there is little doubt that Monk's arrangement of 1863, treating the nave and choir as separate buildings, was the most effective answer to the problem. The nave organ, a three-manual Hill of thirty-three stops, was sold to the church of St. Thomas, Radcliffe, Manchester where it still sounds splendidly, tonally hardly changed from its original state.

In the early part of 1929 the Minster organ went disastrously wrong. Bairstow explained in a Yorkshire Post article in April:

> About two months ago, partly through the unusually dry, hot atmosphere created by the new heating apparatus, the organ became quite unplayable, and although it has been temporarily repaired, fresh faults occur daily. Notes refuse to sound, or refuse to cease sounding; stops when drawn will not shut off again, or

will not draw at all; wind is escaping from cracks all over the organ.

The Dean and Chapter have done the only thing possible, for York Minster cannot be left without an organ. They have commissioned Messrs. Harrison and Harrison to make an entirely new mechanism at a cost of £2,892. As the organ will have to be dismantled and cleaned, a few additions, rearrangements of stops and other improvements can be effected now at a greatly reduced price. For instance, there is no bass to balance the great Tuba Mirabilis. A new pedal reed stop is asked for to supply this deficiency. There is no Viol d'Orchestre, or stop of that kind of tone in the organ. We hope to obtain this also. A few other alterations, difficult to explain to the lay mind, but very necessary, bring the total to £3,877.

There was, however, and still is, a Gamba on the Choir organ, of a fairly keen tone quality similar in tone to the Viol d'Orchestre, but unenclosed and without means of expression.

Finally, a characteristically straight injunction with a sting in its tail:

The congregations at the Minster number amongst them quite as many, if not more, visitors than York people. Surely there must be many of these visitors who have received pleasure and benefit from the Minster music, and will contribute something in return. The Dean and Chapter are hard put to it to find enough money for windows, roof and stonework, all badly in need of immediate attention. It is most unfortunate that the organ should have failed at this time. However, the Minster without an organ is unthinkable. Therefore let us emulate our fathers and show that we have not got incurably material.

In the same Yorkshire Post article of 16 April 1929 he describes the organ as it was when he arrived at York:

In 1903 Messrs. Walker and Sons reconstructed the organ and put much new work into it to a specification drawn up by Sir Walter Parratt and Mr. T. Tertius Noble, the organist. At that time there was a general outcry against over-large and blatant organs in churches, and in deference to this prevailing opinion the Minster organ was toned down considerably – in fact far too much. Nevertheless, there was a great deal to be said in favour of the 1903 organ.

Earlier G.S. Talbot had written:

The instrument was ... one of very great charm and extreme delicacy. Still there were several critics who considered that it had been robbed of much of its old grandeur and that it was deficient in top brilliancy and heavy pressure reeds. As the time had arrived for a thorough overhauling, it was very wisely decided to supply these deficiencies at the same time, and to entrust the work into the faithful hands of Messrs. Harrison & Harrison. The new tuba (which speaks like its predecessor in the Hill organ straight down the nave though not in fan shape projection) is on twenty-five inch wind pressure – two inches heavier than the tubas in St. Paul's Cathedral. In a building where the acoustic proper-ties are so excellent (largely owing to the lath and plaster roofs) the effect is certainly nothing short of stupendous. The Walker tuba is also retained with a pressure of eleven inches.

Obviously the rest of the instrument had to be strengthened up to keep the new giant in countenance. Consequently a large open diapason, No.1 (quite as remarkable in its way as the tuba), ditto, No.2, and octave, fifteenth, and nine ranks of mixture have been added. The two largest reeds on the Great have been 'put up' six notes, with new bottom pipes added, while the place on the old heavy-wind soundboard (vacated by the two reeds now on the twelve-inch pressure) is filled with one of the mixtures which is now of silvery brilliancy . . . It should also be mentioned that every stop in the organ has been revoiced by Mr. Arthur Harrison himself.

According to Mr. Scaife (Master of the Song School), E.C.B. said, characteristically: "This organ is a woman: I'm going to make it into a man." But in 1929, thirteen years after the gender of the organ was changed, and but twenty-six since the previous major rebuild by Walkers, here was a serious situation requiring much thought and consideration.

To a Leeds Mercury reporter, after "piloting" him through the interior of the organ, Bairstow confessed:

I don't think, if I had the chance of an entirely new organ, that I would have one. Every organist who has used it has praised it.

It was built by men who realised the importance of using the Minster as an auxiliary of the organ. Vaulted arches play their part as much as the (*organ*) builders' ingenuity.

When we added the new Tuba in 1917 (*really 1916*), we experimented with a trumpeter until we had ascertained the best direction in which to throw the sound. No, the organ itself, with its 90-odd stops is still pre-eminent, in a world where 150 stops are not reckoned too numerous. There are few, if any, of its size, which have the power, the dignity, ethereal quality, variety and beauty of tone, as this, although it has only 71 speaking stops. *The other 19 were couplers and tremulants.*

The organ was duly rebuilt, and was dedicated at Evensong on Saturday 28th March 1931. The first piece to be heard from it after a year's silence was the St. Anne Fugue by Bach. Then, on April 29th a series of recitals began, of which Doctor Bairstow's was the first and his Assistant, Owen le P. Franklin's, the last on August 5th. Between them came G.D. Cunningham, Doctors Alan Gray, W.G. Alcock, Stanley Marchant, Henry G. Ley and A.C. Tysoe, then organist of Leeds Parish Church. Each programme included a singer who had been trained by E.C.B. – a pupil, a songman or a chorister from the Minster choir.

His own programme began in rousing fashion with his Prelude in C, which was followed by the Adagio from Mozart's String Quintet in G minor and four chorale preludes, by Bach, Charles Wood, Bairstow and Karg-Elert (*Macht hoch die Tür*). Then came the first vocal item, *Et exultavit* from Bach's Magnificat, with Bach's Fantasia and Fugue in G minor, Bairstow's own Scherzo in A flat and the 'Trumpet Tune and Air' by Purcell arranged by Henry G. Ley. The Angel's Song from Gerontius was next, with Schumann's Sketch in D flat and, to end with, what must have been Stanford's Fantasia and Toccata, which is in D minor and a favourite piece of Bairstow's, though it appeared on the programme as Prelude and Toccata in D. There is no work of Stanford's with this title.

G.D. Cunningham was the only visiting recitalist in the series to include a piece by Bairstow – the Toccata-Prelude on 'Pange Lingua'. His final item was the Prelude and Fugue in C minor by Vaughan Williams, published the previous year, while Dr. Tysoe ended with the Dupré Prelude and Fugue in G minor, then only eleven years old. It is interesting to compare these with a programme given by "Mr. E.C. Bairstow, Mus.Bac., F.R.C.O." at All Saints, Norfolk Square on May 11th 1899 which was as follows:

Overture to Tannhaüser	Wagner
Reverie in $\frac{5}{4}$ time	Lemaire (sic)
Prelude to Act III and Banquet Dance from the incidental music to *The Tempest*	Sullivan
Finale from *Symphonie Pathétique*	Tchaikowsky
Evening Song	Ed. C. Bairstow
Overture *Ruy Blas*	Mendelssohn

Both Sullivan items were almost certainly his own arrangement: there is no manuscript or printed copy of the Banquet Dance, but the Prelude to Act III exists in his own hand. (It was published by Banks Music Publications in 1985.)

At the time of this recital at his London church, Bairstow was aged 24, and this programme contained but two pieces of genuine organ music. It was rarely that his choice of programme failed to include a transcription. Two recitals given on the same day for the opening of the large Harrison four-manual in Saint Mary Redcliffe, Bristol on 5 June 1912 were typical:

At 3.0 p.m.	Prelude and Fugue in G minor	Bach
	Elegy and Toccata-Prelude on *Pange Lingua*	Bairstow
	Four Sketches	Schumann
	Cantilène in A flat	Wolstenholme
	Introduction to Act III of *The Tempest*	Sullivan
	Choral Song and Fugue	Wesley
At 8.0 p.m.	Prelude in C	Bairstow
	New England Idyls, op. 62	MacDowell
	Chorale Preludes on *Vom Himmel hoch* as treated by Pachelbel and	Reger
	Berceuse	Arensky
	Scherzo in A flat	Bairstow
	Prelude to *Dream of Gerontius*	Elgar
	Finale to the New World Symphony	Dvorak

The opening of the three-manual Harrison of 31 stops in
Emmanuel Church, Southport on 19 March 1914 included the
same Macdowell piano pieces but some different Dvorak:

Toccata and Fugue in D minor	Bach
New England Idyls	MacDowell
Midwinter	
With Sweet Lavender	
In deep woods	
Elegy and Scherzo in A flat	Bairstow
Fantasy-Prelude	C. Macpherson
Four Sketches (for Pedal Piano)	Schumann
Pièce Héroique	Cèsar Franck
Overture *In der Natur*	Dvorak

The second of the five opening recitals on the 25-stop three-
manual Harrison in St. Margaret's, Durham on 5 February 1917
began with the same Bach G minor, followed by the same Pachelbel
chorale prelude and the second movement of Tchaikowsky's fourth
symphony. Next came his own three pieces published by Augener,

'*E.C.B., Bishop Frodsham and Arthur Harrison. Taken at the opening
recital and dedication of the organ at Halifax Parish Church, Oct. 1929*'

but in reverse order, beginning with *Pange Lingua,* and with *Vexilla Regis* coming third, after the Elegy. The rest was French: *Légende* and *Scherzetto* from Vierne's *24 Pièces en Style Libre* published five years earlier; and Franck's *Final.*

(His programme note quotes the fact that MacDowell is considered America's greatest composer. He continues: "Be that as it may...")

This Durham church is the one attended by the Harrison family, whose firm built the organ and donated part of it. E.C.B. was on friendly terms with Arthur Harrison and held him in great respect, regarding him as the finest organ builder in the country. He played many an opening recital on his organs, including that at Leigh in Lancashire, to which the following letter of 30th March 1921 refers:

My dear Harrison,

I am disengaged on the 27th, but if I came to Leigh it would mean putting off a day and a half's teaching, for I could not get back the same night. The Wednesday is my Leeds day and brings me in about £10. I would come for 15 guineas. I can't afford to be kind these days!

We are all fit and I hope you and yours are also. Look us up whenever you can.

He also opened the Willis organ in Sheffield City Hall on 12th January 1933, of which event there is a happy photograph of him seated at the console. He had acted as consultant, and a feature of the choice of stops, which would certainly have been his suggestion, was a horn in the swell organ. The York example, to which he was attached, was of a very smooth tone quality. The Sheffield one turned out to be more of a trumpet, but no comment from him on this has been recorded. In his programme for the opening recital he was supported by a soprano and a tenor from York, Mary Worth and Alfred Hepworth, and his choice of pieces was much as before – Pachelbel, Dvorak, the Mozart Adagio, Purcell/Ley, his own Scherzo and, for the beginning, his Prelude in C and the Franck *Final* for the end.

In 1925 the nearest thing to a transcription was the first item – a Handel Organ Concerto in B flat. This was the third of the

The official opening of the organ in the City Hall, Sheffield,
12 January 1933

opening recitals in Otley Parish Church after the renovation of the
organ, on Monday 23 February. This Abbot and Smith organ of
1902 had 33 speaking stops. At York, as we have seen, organ recitals
were held from time to time, to the great pleasure of many people
whose sources of music of any kind were few before the gramophone and wireless came along. An appreciative letter to the
Yorkshire Herald in October 1920 signed 'A Working Man'
expressed his gratitude to Dr. Bairstow:

> for his sympathetic and stimulating interpretations of the great
> masterpieces of musical composition which he gives at the close
> of Evensong at the Minster each Sunday. ... How can one
> forget...his really wonderful rendering yesterday afternoon of
> Mendelssohn's Sonata in D? It was worth more than words can
> express, and one at any rate who heard it felt that he could go
> back to the duties of life with a lighter heart, feeling the burden
> of existence to be a little less tangible and oppressive, and that
> there is, after all, some harmony and melody in this strange and
> baffling old world.

A recital of more than usual interest was given on 20 June 1933 by the violinist Jelly d'Aranyi in which she was accompanied on the organ by Sir Edward. The press critics were very appreciative. Reginald Rose of the Yorkshire Herald, though he would have preferred the piano for the Handel sonata, was nevertheless impressed by the soloist's position. 'Almost out of sight on the organ screen she held the large audience spellbound'. Herbert Thompson in the Yorkshire Post noted that Sir Edward 'made no attempt to imitate orchestral effects, and the diapasons of the instrument made a low-toned background through which the clear, penetrating tone of the violin came like a shaft of light into a darkened room.'

As for voluntaries after evensong, both on weekdays and Sundays, the Doctor was not always happy to be playing them in a noisy Minster. Soon after the modifications of 1916 he asked his audience if it was likely that the Dean and Chapter would spend £4,000 or £5,000 on an instrument to be used for covering up noises. Was it to be used for the same purpose as a restaurant orchestra? Was it courteous, if one could not appreciate music, to make such a noise that other people could not listen to it? If music did not have words, it did not make it any less sacred. Then, if music was a real offering of worship to God, it was only right that people should listen to it decently and in order. A hundred years or more ago, the nave was used as a public promenade. But they were getting better. The only way to do was for those who knew better to request people who talked and laughed not to do it, and all present could help in this way. (The speech day audience applauded here).

He returned to this subject now and again over the years, and finally, writing to me on 16 March 1945 "... I am not playing Voluntaries. People do not listen and make an infernal noise, so they can go without." This, though understandable, was a pity and no doubt a source of disappointment to organ lovers. He was undoubtedly a very fine player – authoritative, dramatic, sensitive and colourful. Moreover, whatever he played, whether in solo or accompaniment, had no suspicion of inaccuracy, in either notes or registration. With one exception – a notable one, to prove the rule, perhaps.

This happened one day at evensong when the canticles were being sung to Stanford in B flat. All went well until the beginning of the Nunc Dimittis when, to the complete surprise of everyone present, the first chord burst forth from the Tuba Mirabilis. The pipes of this stop – by far the loudest on the organ and one of the most powerful in the country – are placed horizontally along the parapet of the choir screen so that their tone is projected into the nave without any hindrance. As the service was in the nave the full force was directed straight at the worshippers, and the choristers were hard put to it to keep straight faces as the reverberation rang on for its full five seconds which seemed, on that wonderful day, to be even longer than usual. Nothing was said; and it is mere speculation to decide why such a salient *contretemps* could have occurred. The stop knob was certainly in a position where it was not always easy to see whether it was on or off, but as it was not used in the previous item, the Magnificat, it could not have been left on by accident. The organ usually functioned perfectly, as a Harrison and Harrison should, so the blame cannot be laid on the mechanism.

What was probably the only other incident of the same sort, however, was the organ's fault, when a cypher occurred on a pedal reed (the Fagotto with its wooden resonators, predecessor of the present stop of that name which was inserted in 1994) during the Balfour Gardiner anthem *Te Lucis* and stayed on throughout the long *diminuendo* to the hushed finish. The choir staunchly stuck to its guns against great odds. The cypher continued until the wind was turned off, when its dying throes seemed interminable. Not only did the Minster congregation undergo this rare experience, for it was broadcast. In the silence which followed, the priest's injunction 'Let us pray' was imbued with added significance.

The Times of 15 July 1929 reported that Dr. Bairstow had been appointed Professor of Music in the University of Durham. (See page 6) He was the third holder of the office, having been preceded by Joseph Cox Bridge, organist of Chester Cathedral and brother of Sir Frederick ('Westminster') Bridge. J.C. Bridge's term extended from 1907 until his death, on Good Friday, 1929. His predecessor was the first professor, Philip Armes, who held the office for ten years. He it was who instituted examinations for the

Gordon Slater, E.C.B. and William Ellis at Durham,
September 1936

'William Walton and E.C.B. after the Degree Ceremony, June, 1937
at Durham, when Walton received the degree of Mus. D., honoris causa.
The photograph was taken by Hilda Atkinson, the harpist, who
happened to be there'

musical degrees in 1890, before which year the only degrees awarded were honorary. The two doctorates were given to John Bacchus Dykes in 1862 and John Stainer in 1885. (There were, however, four musicians who were honoured with the degree of D.C.L.; George Grove 1875, Hubert Parry and Charles Villiers Stanford, both in 1894, and the same John Stainer in 1895). There were also four musicians, all of them well known composers, made honorary Doctors of Music during Bairstow's period as Professor; John Ireland 1932, Arnold Bax 1935, William Walton 1937, and Thomas F. Dunhill 1940. These were all presented to the Chancellor at the ceremony by the Professor of Music himself.

Late in August 1925, Dr. Bairstow made an appearance at a Promenade Concert in the Queen's Hall, London, during the thirty-first season, not as conductor (as on the previous Good Friday with the Royal Choral Society in Messiah) but as solo organist. Macpherson, Cunningham and Alcock were similarly employed in an experiment involving organ solos at these concerts. Bairstow's choice was Bach's Prelude and Fugue in B minor and, for an encore (which was not really allowed in the first half of the concert), the quiet chorale prelude on 'Come now, Saviour of the Gentiles'. The Yorkshire Post commented that 'the playing had an austere strength and beauty that concentrated attention on the essential splendour of the ideas and their treatment, and the effect of both was deeply impressive'.

XII

Dinners, Doctorates and Dubbing

'A DINNER GIVEN IN HONOUR of Dr. and Mrs. Edward C. Bairstow by Past and Present Pupils, Members of the Leeds Philharmonic Society and York Musical Society' took place in the Hotel Metropole, Leeds on Thursday July 26th 1928. There seems to have been no anniversary or jubilee to celebrate; just an act of devotion to a person held in high esteem by many people.

There were seven toasts including The King, and no fewer than 12 speeches. One wonders if a strict limit was placed on all the speakers and what was the effect on the chief guest at the end of it all.

Back at York, nineteen-thirty saw honour done to "the distinguished Chief Musician of the city" in the form of a concert of Bairstow's works organised by the York branch of the British Music Society. It is more than likely that the idea originated with Dennis Laughton, and that much of the organisation was carried out by him. He was a friend of Sir Edward's, a great supporter of York's music, and one of the prime movers in the founding (in 1922) of the British Music Society in the city, a body which still continues to flourish.

> Though he has never posed prominently as a creative musician (*wrote Herbert Thompson*) the pieces chosen showed the extent and variety of his compositions. There was nothing pretentious about this 'Evening with Dr. Bairstow's music', but it was a pleasant compliment to one who ranks high, not only in his native country, but among all the church musicians of his generation.

There were part-songs, for male and female voices respectively, and for both together, an anthem, introits sung by the Minster

177

Choir, instrumental pieces, Variations (for violin and piano) played by Sybil Eaton with the composer, and (for two pianos) by Cyril Jackson and Owen Franklin, as well as songs sung by Elsie Suddaby and Leslie Wright. The works ranged in date from 1896 to 1928.

> The programme was well carried out, but one is less inclined to dwell on the performances than on the spirit which animated the performers. No fewer than four different choirs took part, and their hearty co-operation may safely be interpreted as a desire to do honour to Dr. Bairstow, and another proof was to be seen in the large audience, which nearly filled the vast wilderness of a hall which has to serve as a makeshift concert-room till a hall worthy of the city is evolved.

Thus Herbert Thompson ended his review, these final comments referring to the skating rink attached to the Rialto cinema in Fishergate, since renamed Mecca.

Leslie Wright was a solicitor, and, during his choristership at the Minster, a notable soloist. The Reverend Cyril Jackson was then a Vicar Choral at the Minster: after the war he became Canon and Precentor of Salisbury Cathedral. The choirs taking part were the York Musical Society under Dr. Bairstow its regular conductor; the York Male Voice Choir conducted by Owen le P. Franklin, Assistant Organist at the Minster from 1929 to 1946; the York Old Priory Choir directed by Mr. J.H. Forster; and the Minster Choir. On their own, the choristers sang *The Blessed Virgin's Cradle Song* which was encored.

An editorial in the York Herald on the day of the concert, 6 February, maintained that:

> There are many people we know who seldom, if ever, enter York Minster, and who think of Dr. Bairstow, if they

TOAST LIST
▽

"THE KING"

"OUR GUEST"
Proposer: Dr. ERNEST BULLOCK
           (followed by a Presentation).
Reply: Dr. EDWARD C. BAIRSTOW

"MRS. BAIRSTOW"
Proposer: Mr. H. BACON SMITH
Reply: Mrs. BAIRSTOW

"MUSIC"
Proposer: THE VERY REV. THE DEAN OF YORK
Reply: Mr. H. PLUNKET GREENE

"THE LADIES"
Proposer: THE VICAR OF LEEDS
Reply: Miss ELSIE SUDDABY

"LEEDS PHILHARMONIC SOCIETY"
Proposer: Mr. GEORGE PARKER
Reply: Mr. ARTHUR HAINSWORTH

"YORK MUSICAL SOCIETY"
Proposer: Dr. GORDON SLATER
Reply: Miss L. VIOLET ARGLES

*Menu, Hotel Metropole,
26 June 1928*

ever think at all, as a remote and austere cathedral organist, high up in his organ loft far above us common creatures here below. It is given to a few, however, to know him well and to realise the striking and charming personality which lies behind the rather cold and stern figure of this notable musician. Dr. Bairstow is given to uttering statements which are inclined to lead the public to think that he is scarcely human and certainly as high as the highest of the highbrows. But nobody who hears his carol for boys' voices, *The Blessed Virgin's Cradle Song*, a glorious melody, which was written when the composer was only 21, can fail to appreciate the tenderness and human feeling of which Dr. Bairstow is capable.

In the birthday honours list of June 1932 appeared ECB's name. According to the Evening Standard he was the fifteenth musical knight (Elgar was included although he had become baronet a year earlier), and the only other cathedral organist was Ivor Atkins of Worcester. Sir Walford Davies, however, Master of the King's Music, organist of St. George's Chapel, Windsor Castle, popular broadcaster and one of the best known musicians of his day, is omitted from the list for some reason. The Belfast Newsletter, however, appeared to include him when, on 4 June, it noted that there were sixteen musicians who had received the honour of knighthood and that the oldest musical knight, created Knight Bachelor nearly forty years previously was Sir Alexander Mackenzie, then in his eighty-fourth year.

The Musical Times considered that the conferring of the knighthood would give pleasure "both on personal grounds and as a recognition of the important work done by holders of similar posts throughout the country", and that he is:

> a good deal more than a distinguished church musician. He is a skilful and inspiring teacher and conductor; an adjudicator whose candour is more than balanced by the practical and constructive nature of his criticism; a composer whose quality is best gauged by the general regret that his output is so severely restricted by his other activities; and (above all, perhaps) a personality who exerts a powerful influence over a wide area and in many directions. One may disagree with him on occasion, but there will be unanimous testimony as to the sincerity with which he pursues his ideals. Musical knighthoods go sometimes to distinguished

artists, sometimes (less often) to slogging hard workers: Sir Edward has richly earned his in both capacities.

The 'Listener' was of the opinion that the honour would please those who heard services and concerts of religious music which had been regularly relayed from York Minster, and remarked that Dr. Bairstow had recently become a member of the B.B.C. Advisory Committee.

"Those who are familiar with his capacity to discipline a large chorus" said the Yorkshire Post of 3 June 1932 "know how ruthlessly he can deal with mediocrity and, conversely, how generous and energising is his praise for good work." The conferment took place on Friday June 22, the Court Circular stating that *Mr.* Edward Bairstow, along with 34 other Gentlemen, had been 'introduced into His Majesty's presence by the Right Hon. Sir Philip Cunliffe-Lister, M.P. (Secretary of State for the Home Department)'. A day or two later we choristers were given a first-hand account of the proceedings in place of five minutes' work at the end of choir practice. We felt very privileged: the only blot on an otherwise memorable and enjoyable day was that the King had said 'Rise Sir Edward BARSTOW' – related to us with much scorn and nasal tone quality.

Two dinners in close succession were held in July 1932, that on the fourteenth in honour of Sir Edward and Lady Bairstow at the Hotel Great Central, N.W.1. It was, presumably, connected with the knighthood; the autographed menu shows a formidable list of the musical fraternity.

Autographs on Menu Card, Hotel Great Central, 14 July 1932

Four days later, and back on home territory, the York Musical Society honoured their conductor and his wife at a dinner for the

Autographs on Menu Card, Hotel De Vere, 8 October 1932

same purpose, to express the musical citizens' delight in their new knight and his lady.

The Royal College of Organists, its President and Council honoured Sir Edward – on his own – at the Kensington Hotel de Vere, close by the College. This was held on October eighth 1932. The menu contains the signatures of 21 of the top brass of the country's organ brotherhood – and no ladies ... .

One more press commentary on the knighthood, from the Yorkshire Post, is from a more personal angle:

> York people regard Dr. and Mrs. Bairstow as an ideal couple. They are of that enviable class of people who, after many years of married life, are still very much in love with one another, and don't mind who knows it. Each week after Dr. Bairstow has been to Leeds to conduct the practice of the Leeds Philharmonic Society, Mrs. Bairstow is on the platform at York to meet her husband. I once heard a ticket inspector say on York platform, after one of those occasions: 'They're real sweethearts, those two. I don't remember a time when she didn't come to meet him.'

In the same way, the Rover would drive up to the Song School gates on Monday morning at the end of choir practice, and Lady Bairstow (the driver) would appear in the practice room and convey her husband to the railway station for the ten o'clock train for a day's teaching in Leeds.

Exactly a week after the investiture – on St. Peter's Day, 29 June 1932 (the Minster's patronal festival) – the new Dean, Herbert Newell Bate, Dean of Bocking and Rector of Hadleigh, was installed in succession to Lionel Ford who had died on Easter Day.

On 24 June 1935, Harry Plunket Greene celebrated his seventieth birthday, and a dinner in his honour was given at the Savoy Hotel at which Sir Edward took the chair. It was a prestigious occasion, attended by practically every musician of note, as befitted one who, by his performances and his remarkable interpretations as well as by his writings, teaching and lecturing, had done so much in the cause of singing. Sir Hugh Allen announced Mr. Greene's election that day as a Fellow of the Royal College of Music (by the authority of the Prince of Wales), and an illuminated address was presented to him expressing 'affection, admiration and gratitude for a friend who never failed to help others in need and for an artist who made beautiful our own speech in song'.

ECB's friendship with HPG was of long standing, stemming from a love of song which was a potent influence in both their lives. Nearly ten years later (in January 1944) a tangible record of this appeared in book form under their joint authorship, entitled "Singing learned from Speech". Most of the text is by Sir Edward but it included most of what was left by Plunket Greene among his papers. Bairstow declares that HPG changed English singing from 'a bad imitation of the Italian style ... to a healthy native art', and that he did so primarily by his perfect diction. The approach made by the book is fundamentally a psychological and emotional one; its watchwords are 'The letter killeth but the spirit giveth life', and 'The nearer to laughter, the nearer to song'.

In 1936, Sir Edward was the recipient of the first of his two honorary degrees. That of D. Litt. was conferred by Leeds University. The second, at Oxford, came barely eleven months before his death and is related on page 224.

At Leeds the occasion was the opening of the Brotherton Library on 6 October. The presenter was Professor A. Hamilton Thompson, who spoke as follows:

My Lord Duke and Chancellor:

In Sir Edward Bairstow we recognize at one and the same time a musician whose reputation is known far and wide, and a native of Yorkshire whose life has been intimately connected with the musical activities of our own city. Born at Huddersfield, he became after a well-spent interval organist of Leeds Parish Church for eleven years, and during most of the period which has followed his translation to what is, in one sense at any rate, the more eminent position of organist and master of the music at York Minster, he has continued to watch over our fortunes as conductor of the Leeds Philharmonic Society. Nor has Yorkshire alone profited by his talents. He occupies the chair of music in the University of Durham, and in various towns of Lancashire choral societies, not inferior to our own in vocal dexterity and endurance, have enlarged their repertoires and flourished under his wise guidance. At York he has trained his choir to a degree of excellence worthy of the noble traditions of English Church music, with a deep understanding of the advantages afforded to the display of his art by the splendid sanctuary whose inspiration can be readily discovered in his own scholarly compositions. Not long since we welcomed the bestowal of a knighthood upon one to whom we owe a special debt. If we have no doctorate of Music to confer upon him, the degree which we offer has its appropriateness to a master of the virtues of harmony and rhythm and involves the fullest acknowledgement of our obligation which it is in our power to make.

My Lord Duke and Chancellor, I present to you Edward Cuthbert Bairstow for the degree of Doctor of Letters, *honoris causa*.

XIII

Relationships

I T MUST OFTEN HAVE struck people that, when Bairstow was faced with a choice between telling the truth and preserving a relationship, whether with a person or a body or institution, the lot fell upon the former. His concern for the welfare of choral societies led him to state that "Whilst the wireless has done a great deal to improve musical standards in the country, it has had the effect of putting out of existence no fewer than one thousand five hundred choral societies." The editor of the *Listener* of July 17 1932 wrote that "The supposedly disastrous effect of broadcasting upon the musical amateur is becoming one of the stock references of adjudicators at musical festivals", and that this was an example.

> Dr. Bairstow has his figures pat: where and how he obtained his figures it would be instructive to know. They have an exactitude which, in such obviously unchartable matters, is strange. Even if his figures were accurate, however, we should still remain unconvinced in his diagnosis of a cause. Authorities agree that the decline in members of amateur choral societies was noticeable even before the War, and from the obvious consequences of that catastrophe itself they have never recovered. So far is Dr. Bairstow wrong, indeed, that one might almost say the opposite is the truth: broadcasting has not only raised the musical intelligence, but has done everything that was possible to foster, rather than to destroy, the good amateur choral work being done up and down the country. In the North of England, where choral singing excels, repeatedly broadcasts have been given of the work of various societies ... whilst in the South, two recent instances alone should serve to show the helping hand that broadcasting gives to choral singing, viz., the successful relay from the

184

Petersfield Festival and the organisation of a new choral body, chosen from all over Kent, for the memorable festival at Canterbury. ... The truth would seem to be that Dr. Bairstow is flogging the wrong horse. It is fashionable today, when a defect is discovered in matters musical, to blame broadcasting – much as, a few years ago, it was blamed for the bad weather.

When he joined in a symposium on the future of the B.B.C. in the Morning Post a few days later, his opinions were scarcely less forceful. They were printed along with similar contributions from two of the most august and controversial personages of the decade, Bernard Shaw and Sir Thomas Beecham. The former was 'surprisingly kind' according to the Musical Times of September 1930. Sir Thomas started by remarking that, as an artist, he had very little to say about the B.B.C. "He then proceeded to say a great deal about it – presumably as a baronet."

"Dr. Bairstow's criticism was more constructive" the Musical Times continued:

'Taken at the resuscitation of the York, Durham and Ripon Cathedral Choirs Festival at Durham, 26 Sep. 1934. L. to R.: E.C.B., Dykes Bower, Moody, Ellis.'

He would like to see the Corporation doing something for choral music by relaying the concerts of the best provincial choirs. He regards the choice of singers as being not nearly stringent enough, and wishes the B.B.C. would vet the songs as well as the singers. 'There is no reason why such a mass of rubbish should be let loose as is now the case, to say nothing of the bad singing'. But I doubt the practicality of his suggestion that 'all the tripe and dance music should be broadcast from the same station, so that we can know what to avoid.' What of the owners of crystal sets that can pick up only one station satisfactorily? The plan would give some tripe enthusiasts none of their favourite fare, and some tripe-haters would get nothing else.

But Bairstow was certainly proved right not many years later when the Light Programme came into being.

During the nineteen-thirties, choral evensong was broadcast twice a week; from Westminster Abbey on Thursday and, on Tuesday, from York Minster. At the 1934 Speech Day, ECB said that these broadcasts were appreciated in an extraordinary way. Two years later, Dean Bate said " I still find, maybe on a diminished scale, that there is the keenest interest by a very large number of people, in what we do and what we sing at the Minster. Many people listen to our weekly broadcast and we have received letters of appreciation from the distant corners of the earth."

But at the end of 1933 a letter to the local newspaper from nearer home – from Bishopthorpe, two miles away – complained that the choir was noisy, "kicking the kneeling stools in standing and kneeling; the starts in responses, psalms and hymns (sic) were ragged; the microphone, admirably placed for the Vicar Choral and the lectern, was too far from the choir and organ so that the music and singing sounded remote and woolly. I understand Sir Edward was away; I cannot imagine that he would have allowed such distractions and faults to occur. ..." To which Sir Edward replied, on 1 January 1934:

I make it a general rule not to be drawn into newspaper correspondence, but the letter ... is so untrue and unjust to the Minster Choir that I must reply to it. The choir were not noisy. There are no 'kneeling stools' in the choir stalls, but one long kneeler, which is not moveable. *(True of the boys' stalls but not of the songmen's behind them.)* Evidently your correspondent's Christmas festivities had given him a bad indigestion, for I have two letters from people far from York, sending warm appreciation of that particular service, both of them musicians. My wife is a regular listener, and she asked me whether some improvement had been made in the position of the microphones ... as the service was so very well broadcast.

In 1936, however, there was considerable adverse criticism from both BBC programmes staff and from listeners, of the poor quality of the weekly broadcasts of evensong from York Minster. The following January, at the request of the North Regional senior staff, Director of Music (Sir Adrian Boult), members of music staff, and three members of the BBC's Central Music Advisory Panel listened to one of the broadcasts. Sir Adrian reported directly to Director of Religion (Dr. F.A. Iremonger) that they were unanimously horrified by the atrocious standard of performance, referring particularly to the mutilation of a Te Deum by Charles Wood – it "would have been a disgrace to a small village choir. I cannot think that Sir Edward Bairstow realizes how bad."

Sir Adrian and Dr. Iremonger realized that, in view of Bairstow's eminence, criticism must be well founded and its representation very tactfully handled. Sir Walford Davies, as the BBC's consultant on church music, was also asked to listen, and agreed in general terms with the criticisms. In February, Dr. Iremonger sent a full and frank letter to the Dean of York (the Very Reverend H.N.Bate) giving details of the reporting, noting that criticism came from listeners, North Regional staff, Director of Music's London staff and advisers of the calibre of Walford Davies, and asking the Dean to advise on a formal approach to Bairstow. As York was the parent church of the Northern Province, the BBC attached great importance to the weekly broadcast, and reasonably expected an exemplary standard in every aspect of the ceremony. (Simultaneously the North Regional Director, Mr. E.G.Liveing, wrote personally to Bairstow, presumably with London approval, expressing anxiety about the broadcasts in less detailed terms.)

In reply, the Dean said he was not surprised, as he had long been aware of some deterioration in the choral evensongs. As Dean, he had no effective *musical* control over Bairstow, who was very temperamental, resented criticism, and was irrationally hostile to the BBC although he was a member of the North Region Music Advisory Panel. He was, however, prepared to grasp the nettle, and sought yet another expert opinion from Dr. E.H.Fellowes who heard one evensong in the Minster, and later on, another transmission with Dr. Iremonger. Some improvement was noted in the latter. A later report by programme staff stated that there was a general improvement, and that their professional relationship with Bairstow also improved. There is no doubt that the Dean's tactful handling of a delicate issue had influenced him for good as regards co-operation and musical discipline.

Dean Bate, who was scholarly and witty, a good pianist, somewhat small in stature when compared with the monumental figure of his predecessor Lionel Ford, had decided views on church music. These did not accord with ECB's. For one thing, he considered Charles Wood a better composer of church music than Stanford. For another, the Dean had been known to cover his ears at some of the more ebullient moments, and this must have been hard for ECB to appreciate. He might even have gone so far as to regard it as a weakness, with which he would have had little or no patience.

On a certain day before the war, after I, a teenage student, had been left to play evensong, the Dean met me at the organ loft door. Unaccompanied items were conducted from a central position, which the Dean did not like. He wished it to be done less obtrusively and would like me to stand at the side and beat time with one finger. This put me in a difficult position, and I lost no time in reporting it to ECB. His reaction was immediate and somewhat strong. He told me to take no notice and that he would see the Dean about it. The manner in which he would do so may be imagined, with a certain deterioration in the relationship as a result. The Dean himself, of course, could have foreseen the result of his action in directly interfering in the Master of the Music's territory without any consultation.

At one stage, Dean Bate's dislike of ECB's conduct of the music at the Minster reached such a pitch that he determined to unseat him and to appoint his assistant in his place. According to Chancellor Harrison, who recounted the episode, a meeting of the

Chapter took place when this was to be carried out. Instead, Bairstow was upheld by the canons and the Dean's motion was defeated: whereupon the Dean arose and walked out, sadly shaking his head and saying "You've let me down, you've let me down". This was a bold move for a chapter to attempt, and shews that Dean Bate must have been unaware of the esteem in which Bairstow was held by the canons of York, not to mention the music world at large. Certainly a first class scandal must have ensued if the motion had been carried.

Arriving for a lesson one day, I found ECB in a state of some perturbation. Not long before I entered the music room he had received a telephone call from an official of a competitive festival somewhere in Wales enquiring if he could take the place of Julius Harrison who had for some reason withdrawn. His reaction was somewhat violent, though quite in character: "I told him I'm not playing second fiddle to Julius Harrison or anyone else". Harrison (1885-1963) was a well-known and respected conductor who had learnt the Wagner tradition from the same Hans Richter at Covent Garden and become conductor of the Hastings orchestra as well as a prolific composer. It occurred to me at the time that this was a rather unexpected statement for a student to hear from his tutor but felt flattered that he should take me into his confidence in such a way. It was no doubt intended as part of my tuition – an example of how to act in a similar situation.

We have noted ECB's methods in the training of choirs, particularly his straight talking. For most of his life choirs took what he had to say and either liked it or hated it. Those who weathered the storms emerged, no doubt, stronger and better.

An example of his direct way of expressing himself was witnessed by those attending the Annual General Meeting of the York Musical Society a day or two after his visit to Buckingham Palace to be knighted. He had some trenchant comments to make on fellow citizens and made an admission of his own uncompromising attitude in choir training. There was also a hint of an apology which was rare for him (perhaps because there was usually nothing to apologise for...) and he alluded to the difficulties encountered by societies which produced live music. In reply to appreciative remarks on his conducting he mentioned the many hundreds of letters of congratulation he had received which set much value on his work. However, when he first came to York concerts were much better patronized by the citizens, and there were two hundred singers in the chorus at his first concert. That number had gradually dwindled as had the subscribers. But York was not alone in that respect; there were many other towns and cities in which music was struggling for its existence.

On his methods of choir training – "It has been a case of kill or cure with me, and sometimes I have reproached myself for what I have said to you. The trouble is because there are so many people who do not regard music as I regard it myself. An old lady who congratulated my wife the other day remarked 'I think music has always been an 'obby to the Doctor'. Perhaps that was a nice way of putting it". Recalling his first experience of choral conducting at Petworth House – "they were so snobbish down there that even farmers' daughters were not allowed to join. No-one beneath the daughter of a doctor or a parson could get in. Yet I do not think I ever slated anyone as much as I slated those people, because they could not sing for nuts. But they took what I had to say like sportsmen and improved quite a lot. At York I have never minced my words and I often feel I have been too rough".

His next onslaught was on the many small choirs in York – too many of them. If the Musical Society went down through little choirs, singing little music in little halls in a little way, it would be a great pity, for although little part songs were beautiful they were not to be compared with the more ambitious works. "I am prepared to work my fingers to the bone for the society if only you will do the same, but I think there is a stupid sort of idea prevalent in this city. There are some people who feel that because they have sung a couple of songs at a concert they are altogether beyond a musical society. That is not so in the Leeds Philharmonic, in which there are a lot of people of the semi-professional class who are the mainstay of the chorus. It is necessary that we should have the best singers in the city".

Regarding the attendance of the public he said "… it is a fact that the better the music, the more difficult it is to get people to a concert. They will go to a circus or a tattoo where they just sit and look and allow others to think for them, but if they have to argue with themselves as to what the music they are hearing means to them and their souls, they will not go. What would the music of this country be like if we decided to give people exactly what they want? The music which is the expression of one age is not the expression of the next, and it is necessary with music, as with anything else that we should move with the times." As we have already seen, Bairstow was always ready to try out new works, as with Gerontius and the Hymn of Jesus.

In March 1938, past and present members of the Musical Society received a letter inviting them to subscribe towards a presentation to Sir Edward. The letter recalled that he had, in June 1913, accepted the conductorship of the YMS and that 'the history of the Society's musical achievements ... is an eloquent witness to the inspiration of his leadership. ... The whole history of this twenty-five years is one of unflagging idealism and unfailing devotion to the highest and best in the art of music'. And at the Annual General Meeting on 27 May 1938, the Archbishop, President of the Society, presented Sir Edward with 'a chiming grandfather clock to mark their appreciation on the completion of twenty-five years as honorary conductor. The occasion was used by individual members of the Society to express their appreciation.'

All too soon, however, the picture changed dramatically. During the following season the consequences of over-rough treatment of which he had spoken reached serious proportions. After so long a period of resounding success there arose dissatisfaction and disarray in the ranks. The minute book sets out the facts:

1. Discontent amongst chorus members due to treatment from Sir Edward.
2. Dropping off in attendance at rehearsals.
3. At the March concert chorus members sold scarcely any tickets.
4. Several pieces of music bought by members of the chorus and only used by the Little Choir.
5. Sir Edward on one occasion walked out on the Little Choir.

6. Mr. Franklin's letter to the Committee. In it he expressed the view that he would no longer tolerate in a voluntary capacity 'the strife, bewilderment and chaos' he had long endured.

7. Discouragement of the society's officers who were working for the financial benefit of the society.

The committee decided to send the following letter to Sir Edward:

> At a recent meeting of the committee extreme concern was expressed at the relationship during the past season between you and the chorus which, it was felt, would lead to the disintegration of the Society if no improvement could be effected. Full regard was heeded at this meeting to the slackness of the chorus at some rehearsals and the criticism which this had drawn from you was, in the Committee's opinion, justified in itself, but not in its degree. The musical diffidence and bad attendance which resulted, pointed to the ineffectiveness of certain methods of dealing with individuals.

The letter went on to say that the Committee appreciated the time and energy which Sir Edward had devoted to the Society, and they added that neither they nor the chorus had ever been backward in showing their regard for the work he had done, and their admiration for his high musical standards. It appeared to the Committee that:

> unless the conductor and chorus could work together in greater sympathy than during the past season, then the Society's expectation of life would be negligible. They felt strongly – and this was fully borne out by observation – that the response of the chorus to the stimulus of friendly direction would be wholehearted and effective in the same measure as the reaction to the unwise resentment and discouragement. It was in view of this, however, and having regard to the sense of frustration which the present relationship could but engender in those who had worked and were working for the betterment of the Society's financial position, its public relations, and as far as possible, as a musical force, that the Committee wrote to discover whether some understanding could be reached before the beginning of another season.

At the Annual General Meeting on 6 June 1939 the correspondence was read out at Sir Edward's request. His reply to the Committee's letter ran:

> There is only one thing that a self-respecting man can do when he receives such a letter as the one you have sent me and that is to resign. I should like to point out to the Committee that I have conducted choral societies in five large towns in the north of England for the past 40 years, and had nothing but pleasant relations with them.

On being asked to reconsider his decision to resign, Sir Edward declined to do so. Alan Gray's niece, Faith Gardner, thought the letter was insulting and 'too bold'. The Chairman, Alderman W.H.Birch, added that he knew Sir Edward appreciated straight talk and would much prefer that they should say exactly what they meant. Perhaps it was a surprise for the Committee to see the effect produced by their letter, and they may have thought their conductor's reaction in resigning was too drastic. But that, unfortunately, was the end of his connection with the YMS and he felt it keenly.

The relationship between a cathedral organist and the head master of the song school which provides choristers for the choir can have its difficulties, and requires tact and give-and-take between them. In 1940, at Speech Day, ECB said that his relations with Mr. Scaife, the Head Master, were better than ever, and paid tribute to Mr. Scaife's willingness always to help him. This brief reference to his colleague (which might, perhaps, have been expressed somewhat differently) could throw a little light on their association – allowing, of course, for the fact that this is not a complete report of the speech. Perhaps it had not always been a completely ideal one, notwithstanding Mr. Scaife's contention that he and ECB had 'never had a wrong word'. But it worked for thirty-three years, though only, perhaps, because Mr. Scaife realised that the only way to keep his colleague happy was to give way to his demands whatever they were; mostly for extra rehearsal time which must of necessity come out of school hours. It was not easy to resist or deny his wishes.

The boys' schooling had been in the hands of George Arthur Scaife who had run the school single-handed since its re-founding in 1903, with assistance only in later years. It was a remarkable achievement which came to an end with Mr. Scaife's retirement through ill-health in 1951. His colleague for the first ten years of his head mastership was Thomas Tertius Noble, with whom relations were completely cordial and smooth. It must have been disturbing, then, when a man of a quite different temperament came into his world. One of the changes Bairstow made soon after his arrival is clearly delineated in the Song School log book on 5 February 1914. Mr. Scaife's large, firm handwriting (which on this occasion seems larger and firmer than usual, perhaps indicating the strength of his feelings) tells how 'Dr. Bairstow, the new organist, wishes to have entire charge of all the music, and having obtained the Dean's consent thereto, the Theory of Music, which I have taught for the past eleven years and made a speciality of the school, and the entering of the boys for the examinations of Trinity College of Music, London, now cease, and the Theory of Music is no longer a part of the school curriculum.' It would appear that Dr. Bairstow brought this about without any consultation with Mr. Scaife. Not having had to work closely with a choir school up to this point, he was perhaps not fully aware of the delicacy of the situation. But afterwards the collaboration appeared to work well enough and was at any rate viable for the whole of the time they were together. The Head Master's attitude in encouraging the choristers always to give of their best to the music, whatever his feelings towards the choir, could not have been more helpful to the whole organisation.

As to the relationship of the Master of the Music with his choir, this was always on a formal basis. The choristers usually saw him only at rehearsal and service. He and Lady Bairstow sometimes gave a Christmas party for them at their house, which was well organised and consisted of games in different rooms, each presided over by a different member of the family and visited by each boy in turn. But his choristers did not know him intimately: there was neither time nor opportunity for this unless, of course, one was fortunate enough to be his pupil. So many things on his mind and irons in the fire kept him perpetually busy, not least the unending task of keeping up the Minster music to a high standard. He told the Old Choristers' reunion in 1940 that he was grateful for the 'spirit of friendliness that seems to have pervaded the Minster in recent years. Thinking as I do of the music as the first and most important thing, I realise that it has been a fault of mine to forget the other side, but I am now convinced how important it is.' What he meant by 'the other side' might have been a reference to the religious aspect, or perhaps to the pastoral side of a choir master's duties, with which he did not actively concern himself, but left to others. There were, in fact, few attempts of this kind by those responsible for the choristers' welfare. Long before the days of parents' associations, the choristers' parents were all but unknown to Mr. Scaife and probably never met Sir Edward during the whole of their sons' choristership.

This, however, did not deter him from telling them the truth as he saw it about the way they brought up their children. This he did usually during his address at the school speech day. On one of these occasions he expressed the opinion that:

> At present we have the most attractive and lovable set of boys that I ever remember. But for the last four years we have not had a first class solo boy. We have plenty of splendid voices: it is not a matter of voices. A solo boy must be absolutely without fear, and self-reliant, and in recent years they seem to have lost these qualities compared with former years. There is far more fear in boys than there used to be, and I attribute this partly to the fault of the parents, who are treating their boys with too much care and solicitude. Boys treated like this don't get very far in this world. I can assure parents that it is no kindness to treat their children so that they lose their self-reliance. I would like to see a little more courage from the boys when it comes to singing solos.
> (*Yorkshire Post 16 March 1940*)

Could it have been that it was his own attitude which was intimidating the boys? Perhaps a little less roughness and more gentle encouragement might have brought better results. Did it ever occur to him that the fault could partly have lain in him? But he may well have been right: who can tell?

Before this, in 1931, he had told the speech day audience:

> The boys are losing their self-consciousness and are becoming friendly and natural and noisy. I like them to be noisy: I don't

like quiet boys, but we still suffer to a certain extent by the spoilt child. It is not the poor little chap's fault, it is the fault of the parents in most cases, especially when the family is small. You put a burden on the boy's back, and he has to go through the world with it. It is very disappointing when you spend a lot of time on a boy and he does not repay you for it: it is not the sort of thing that is born in a boy. It is mostly due to the parents.

His last utterance in this vein was a report which, during his last illness, had to be read for him by his assistant, Owen le P. Franklin, and was printed in the Yorkshire Evening Press on the first of April 1946, exactly a month before he died. He urged parents not to spoil the boys who, as choristers, had to stand on their own feet. He was, by this time, in the Purey-Cust nursing home at the west end of the Minster where he could hear the bells ringing and chiming, and loud chords on the organ if the Minster doors happened to be open. We cannot but notice the familiar purport of his message on a subject which seems to have been constantly at the forefront of his mind. (See also page 222)

With the advent of a successor to Dean Bate, who had died in 1941, a relationship of a different kind sprang up for Sir Edward. Changes to the services had been made of which he disapproved. 'All goes well here' he wrote on 1 June, 'We put away most of the Dean's petty alterations in the ritual on the day after the funeral.'

The new dean was Eric Milner-White from King's College in Cambridge, a celibate and an enthusiast for everything beautiful, musical, artistic, architectural; a balletomane and a tireless worker for the Minster for the next twenty-two years. Six months later ECB wrote:

> The new Dean is a great success and gets on well with everybody. We are having the Festival of Nine Lessons on Christmas Eve which they have at King's. The choir boys, songmen and the Organist each have to read a lesson.

On 28 March 1942:

> The Minster goes splendidly. The new Dean has a kind heart and is extremely appreciative. We had a very nice speech day last Saturday.

And on 6 August 1942:

> The new Dean is a dear. He is very much interested in the music, knows all the boys by their Christian names, and makes us all feel happy. We have the most musical set of boys we have ever had just now. Several pianists and three excellent solo boys.

Much later, Dean Milner-White related how ECB was suspicious when the weekly music meeting on Monday evenings after dinner was instituted, for the purpose of choosing the service music for the ensuing week, and how Milner got his way and Bairstow was perfectly happy. Milner wanted rid of some of the feebler pieces from the repertoire as he had done at King's in Daddy Mann's time and as ECB and Talbot had already done at York nearly thirty years earlier. That he achieved this without a major confrontation speaks well for his powers of persuasion and his determination, both of which were considerable.

The relationship began well – on the rebound, one might say, after the preceding regime of frustration – and continued happily enough for all concerned. One cannot help feeling, though, that after the first flush it cooled a little, though not, perhaps, so much as a result of Bairstow's dislike of oppressive decanal orders as from his preference for plain and honest dealings. Milner's methods were honest enough but were at times tinged with a modicum of deviousness, delivered in elegant, flowery phraseology and were thus, one could assume, not always completely to Bairstow's taste. The Dean, however, whose regard for Sir Edward was of the highest, was most keen that his abilities as a composer should not be wasted, and did what he could to encourage him to write, choosing words for him to set to music.

His first Christmas present was E.H. Fellowes' book "English Cathedral Music" which, it seems, ECB did not already possess. It came with the following letter dated Christmas Eve 1941:

> My dear Sir Edward,
>
> You may well find in this more to criticise than to enjoy – if criticism be not in itself a pastime! But it is a serious work on what we both love; and if I may have the honour of putting it on your shelf may it be with the best wishes for Christmas, and profound thanks already for glories I shall continue to enjoy in the Minster.
>
> With best wishes also to Lady Bairstow – Ever yours sincerely
> Eric Milner-White

XIV

Second War Time

A T THE BEGINNING OF the war, Sir Edward gave a series of lectures at Hull University. It fell to my lot (recalls FJ) to drive him there in his Rover and to play the illustrations on the piano. He made sure there was no conversation by practically curling himself up in the passenger's seat and appearing to be asleep while I drove rather fast on roads which were almost devoid of traffic; but he seemed quite oblivious. True to his principles, he had given me

'R.V.W. and E.C.B. at a lecture by the former in York, Sep. 1939.'

a job to do and was trusting me completely and leaving me to get on with it.

He regarded these lectures, known as the Ferens Lectures (with their ninety-guinea fee) as providential, for he had suffered a substantial decrease in income through lost pupils on account of the war, but here was something to take its place. Pupils did, however, come to him later, as we shall see (letters 17 October 1943 and 4 February 1944 e.g.); a different and unexpected clientele. These lectures were afterwards published in book form by the Oxford University Press under the title *The Evolution of Musical Form* which, among several reviews, received a generous and well-reasoned one by Eric Blom. He considered that 'this companionable little book ... is just difficult enough to be stimulating, but never professionally or professorially overbearing.' While being suitable for those starting from scratch, it would also be enjoyed by professionals.

> They will find two kinds of pleasure in it: that of seeing certain points driven home more neatly than has been done elsewhere and that of occasionally disagreeing with an eminent author. Sometimes a thing that is obvious once it has been noticed seems nevertheless to have been said by Sir Edward for the first time, and even if it is not, he very neatly puts technicalities in their place for the reader whose notions about their nature and function are vague.

Ferruccio Bonavia in the Daily Telegraph of 27 March 1943 observed that:

> This close examination of the subject – his examples range from Guidetti to Vaughan Williams – should give the student much needed help in an age that prides itself on the disregard of every rule.

It was the opinion of the Times Educational Supplement that:

> Sir Edward's claim that he has made the subject of musical form human and friendly is abundantly justified. He also establishes its importance in musical education by stating, what is not generally realized, that the inability of English musicians of the nineteenth century to write extended movements, and so to lag behind Continental composers, was due to the neglect of form in their training.' The chapter on the evolution of sonata form, in which 'the limitations of the lecture are burst by the material'

have nevertheless 'served to focus it into a bird's-eye view at once fresh and authoritative.'

And the Musical Times reviewer thought that:

Sir Edward may surprise some people by an easier approach than might be expected of a university professor whose demands upon would-be graduates have always been very high. He has adapted himself to his auditory, without seeking the (shall we say?) Walfordian level.' *(This is a reference to the popular broadcasts by Sir Walford Davies on musical appreciation)*.

Bonavia continues:

Here is good, solid teaching, touching the imagination with quiet phrases of which one or two only can be quoted; on modern developments in composition – *Love is still the only thing which can cast out fear. When a new departure is due to the fearlessness of love it is good ... when it springs from the fear of being old-fashioned or plagiaristic, it is a failure'.* Of Bach – *'His technique was so subconscious that his mind could dwell undistracted on the main object of all music – the expression of human feeling (My underlining. FJ).*

The Cambridge Review was not so easily satisfied. HSM (Hubert Middleton? of Trinity) wrote:

If a curious reader expects to find in this book some account of the nature and growth of musical form he will be disappointed. Gustav Reese, in his *Music in the Middle Ages* requires 220 pages to examine the genesis of Form in Music. Within the limits of 110 pages there cannot be found room for a scientifically organised examination of the problem of genesis and development. We must be content to find in these lectures simple comments on some select specimens of music, and use the book as an index by means of which we may be encouraged to examine the problem for ourselves. To those people who had the good fortune to attend the Ferens Lectures in 1940 the book will appeal, for, in reading it, they will be enabled to recollect in the quiet of their homes some of the agreeable emotions they enjoyed on the occasions of the public delivery of the lectures.

The Musical Opinion's view was that 'here we have a book on a dull but very important subject that is as readable as a novel....'

Sir Edward provides insight into his life at this time in letters to FJ, then in the army in Hampshire. On 2 November 1940 he wrote:

> I enclose a little letter to R.V.W., whose address is:- The White Gates, Westcott Road, Dorking. I am sure he will be kind to you. Go and see him. All goes well here. We had a most interesting recital from Tertis in the Minster last Saturday, and the B.B.C. have just asked me to play for half an hour from 12 to 12.30 on December 6th. Perhaps you might hear that.' *(Lionel Tertis, born 1876, was the topmost violist of his day, and a propagandist for the viola as a solo instrument).*

Iris Lemare had recently arrived in York and was active on the music scene.

1 June 1941:

> (She) is full of beans, quite a good conductor, and tries to get more music going than she has time to organise for – but that is a good fault. The Leeds Philharmonic are doing Israel in Egypt on the 18 of this month, and the Minster Choir are joining with Leeds P.C. for a festal evensong on July 2. They are going to sing my *Prodigal Son.*

'Taken by Eve Fairfax, March 1941.'

14 December 1941:

> We had the Leeds Philharmonic Messiah yesterday. It was a great success, and we could have filled the Town Hall twice over. Hopkinsons *(ticket agency)* turned away over 500 people before the day itself!

8 February 1942:

> All goes well at the Minster though we are short of tenors. Yesterday and today we have had five altos – a record. *(Frederick Arthur)* Gutteridge turned up and *(Leonard)* Wreghitt *(both old Minster choristers)* has been discharged from the army and is now back

in the choir. You can imagine the noise they made! The new Dean is most sympathetic and keen on the music. The O.U.P. have at last published the book of Hymn Tunes *(Alternative harmonizations)*.

28 March 1942:

I wish I could let you have a copy of my service in G, but I am afraid it is too risky to try to send you one. ... We are both of us well, and have no undue excitements here. It is the Passion music tomorrow. The chorus is bigger than last year.

6 August 1942:

Publishing is a pretty hopeless job. The O.U.P. only sent the page-proofs of the book on the Evolution of Form – made from the six Hull lectures – the other day. They had managed to lose the foreword and the carefully compiled list of music referred to in the text. The whole of the last few days have been spent re-writing these two things. They also sent the proofs of my organ arrangement of the Purcell Trumpet Sonata. It is difficult, but effective on an organ such as ours. I fear it would not be much good on an organ without an enclosed reed of good quality and strength. I have also done a "Lamentation", the words from the Lamentations of Jeremiah, selected by the Dean. It is just a few chants of irregular pattern, and a refrain: but it is effective. This should be out soon.

We have had a few tip-and-run raiders over this week. On Sunday and Monday evensong had to be stopped. No damage was done to the Minster and not much elsewhere. The Blitz was alarming and many people were bombed out, amongst them Mr. Scaife. However, the recovery has been wonderful. I am going this afternoon to see Mr. Scaife's house now that it has had its roof and glass put in again and been redecorated. The most welcome addition to York music is not Iris Lemare but Richard Austin. You would like him tremendously. He has taken on the Northern Command orchestra and does wonders with it. They gave a concert one Sunday night in the theatre. He asked the choir to go. They sung my 'Lord thou hast been our refuge' with orchestral accompaniment. Although they were at the back of the stage and the orchestra in front, they came over splendidly. The accompaniment was beautifully played. Austin is the organiser for E.N.S.A.'s serious music for the North of England. .... I don't think the unmusical folk can ever understand what it means to a musician to be cut off from what is to him all that matters in the world. However, there is one bright spot. The composer who has never been through it and suffered, but has always had an easy life, never writes great music – not the real, soul-stirring stuff. That side of life is a closed book to him. I have always felt that our English music – even folk-song – has been too easy and smooth! Now keep your pecker up and do some more composition if you can.

27 September 1942:

The O.U.P. still hang fire with the little book on Form that I made out of the Hull lectures. However, the last proofs are now corrected, so that it should be out soon. When it is I will send you a copy. ... also the Purcell Sonata discovered in our library, for trumpet and strings, arr. for organ by me. It has a very short slow movement, which is one of the most moving bits of Purcell that I know.

26 October 1942:

We have been expecting a wire from Marlborough for the last day or two. It has just arrived to say that Nancy has got a girl baby. The boy is a grand little chap, so I am hoping the girl will be likewise. This is the fifth grandchild. ... There is not much musical news as far as I am concerned. We are having "Sleepers Wake" on the second Sunday in Advent and the Passion as usual. ... I am giving a recital at Leeds P.C. in November. I still feel rather stiff and uncomfortable, though I have done quite a lot of practice. Poor Tom Hallford has suffered an awful tragedy. His wife and child were safe at Alnwick, but they went on a visit to some friend at one of the East Coast towns and were killed in an air raid! *(His last appointment was as organist of Llandaff cathedral, where he died, having suffered another similar bereavement, in 1950 aged 38).* You and the other boys serving are constantly in my mind. I pray for you every night.

22 December 1942:

I'm sure that, after this bloody war is over, with all its ugliness of force and machinery, there will be an outcry for beauty in art. No wonder the German composers wrote music that breathed of threatenings and slaughter; they were so much inculcated with

those things that their music expressed them willy nilly. I hope
our English composers will turn out something that will show
that all sense of the beautiful is not lost. All goes well here. The
choir is at full strength again despite losses. Our new bass is a
blind man, *(William Gibson)* but he is a good musician and an
interesting solo singer. Poor old Elam is dead. *("Freddie" Elam,
alto, senior songman and choir librarian).* He would have had fifty
years in the choir if he had lived till July. He was a good soul.

11 February 1943:

At last the book on Form ... is published, and has received an
excellent notice by Eric Blom in the Birmingham Post; a whole
column in war-time! Owen *(Franklin)* turned up on Sunday clad
in the R.N. uniform of a Sub-Lieutenant. And, wonder of
wonders, a fortnight ago Laurie Slater *(Assistant organist before
Owen Franklin)* turned up, come from the States to join up. I
think he felt very 'good' about it, but has changed his tune now
that he has been sent for training with a mean lot, including, as
he says, a jail-bird.

11 May 1943:

Last Saturday we had a concert at Leeds which I was very
anxious about. The programme was Dyson's *In honour of the City*,
Brahms Violin Concerto (Sammons) Elgar's *Music Makers* and
Verdi's *Te Deum*. The chorus would not attend well and would
not get enthusiastic. I was afraid the band would not learn all
that in three hours. So I dug into the scores and learned them
really well. Everybody enjoyed it and it was played and sung much
better than I anticipated. ... you will have to start publishing with
things which are simple and attractive – not cheap. For publishers won't look at big and difficult stuff from an unknown pen.
This always seems hard lines in a way, for that is the most difficult thing to do – simple piano, violin, or organ pieces and unison
songs for schools, and yet not commonplace. The beginnings are
difficult, but if you have a message and are not easily depressed
by returned manuscripts, in the end you will get there.

All goes well here: the choir is in first class form, so is the
organ. I was asked to play last Saturday at the R.C.O. at a recep-
tion to Lord Lang. I couldn't go because of the Leeds concert,
so they asked Sir Walter Alcock. At 10.50 that night he broadcast a recital from St. Mark's, North Audley St. I heard him. It
was first rate. He is 81!

4 August 1943:

> Your orchestra reminds me of my first attempt at scoring. My
> first job was at a private school at Windsor. The band consisted
> of a flute, two violins, double bass and piano. I played the D.B.
> ... I had the Diocesan Festival (choir of 300 voices), and a *Messiah*
> performance at Doncaster, organised by C.E.M.A. from the
> Doncaster choirs and the surrounding villages. Some of them
> had been practising for a year, but the pity of it was that they
> were not used to singing to the beat. It was like "taking a jelly
> fish for a walk on an elastic lead". But they did enjoy it. An enor-
> mous cinema was packed to the eyes with 2,000 people. Canon
> Bell had his usual evening services in July also, for which I had
> to provide music. So you see July was a busy month. One Sunday
> I had the boys at 9.45, matins at 10.30, service for the land army
> at 2.30, evensong at 4.0, and Canon Bell's do at 8. This is a
> record' *(He omitted to include the 11.30 Eucharist, which always
> followed Matins on Sunday)*. I have just finished a singing primer,
> and am now thinking of starting a book of reminiscences.

From the Swan Hotel, Grasmere, he wrote on 17 August 1943
in reply to my description of a visit to Tunis cathedral three or four
days after the liberation. The feeling of gratitude to the allies was
such that those saying their private devotions rose to their feet each
time the English national anthem was played – at the suggestion of
a mischievous sacristan who enjoyed the spectacle several times.

> I got a letter from you dated June 6th just before I left York. Here
> goes to answer it. It was a most interesting letter, all about the
> Cavaillé-Coll organ in Tunis Cathedral. Arthur Harrison used
> to say that C.C. stocked organs of various sizes and sold them.
> I was much amused by your story of the National Anthem. It
> reminds me of a joint recital given at Westminster Abbey by all
> the organists who had either been pupils of S.S. Wesley or occu-
> pied posts where he had been organist. This was on the occasion
> of the centenary of his birth in 1910. Somebody played Wesley's
> variations on God Save the King – or Queen.When the theme
> was given out all the vast audience stood up. Afterwards, when-
> ever the theme was prominent, a few stood up, looked round
> rather sheepishly, and then sat down again. It also reminds me
> of Joan Elwes (no relation [*to Gervase Elwes, 1866-1921, famous
> tenor soloist*] but quite a well-known singer in her time). She told

me that for charity she had sung at a convent in Birmingham. Amongst other things she sang the Bach aria, "Jesus sleeps". At the word "Jesus" all the nuns knelt down. As this word comes in practically every phrase they had quite a lot of strenuous exercise, but spoilt the effect of the song. The French never seem to take much care of their organs. There was a large one in the west gallery of the beautiful cathedral at Trequier (*Tréguier*) in Brittany. The front pipes looked like the sketch (see page 211).

We have come here for a "parson's three weeks" till Aug 28. We had a hectic and very crowded journey. This year the population, having plenty of money, would not be put off with "Holidays at home". Crowds essayed the journey to Scarborough, Blackpool, or Morcambe and lots of other places. They even paid to sleep on the lawns of houses. I thought the Monday after Bank holiday monday would be easier, but was it! First of all our faithful taxi-man's car fell ill and he had to pass on his engagements to a friend. This gentleman never turned up. I got one from the station of all places at the last moment. On the station the loudspeaker was broadcasting the stimulating information that there had been an accident on the line, and that all Leeds trains were diverted via Selby. I foresaw missing the connection and the taxi ordered at Windermere to get us here. We had just a few minutes to change stations in Leeds, but there were no porters and we had to struggle through a seething mass of humanity carrying very heavy cases. It nearly did for poor Lady B. However, we caught our train and got 1 1/2 seats. Most of the way there were four people standing up down the middle of the carriage. This place is very lovely. It has such a wonderfully luxuriant growth of everything – rock plants, flowers, shrubs and trees. But the weather has been very unkind hitherto – we have been here just over a week and it has been either cold and windy, or hot gray and stuffy, with a few sunny intervals. We had Ken Andrews for a week – he went back this morning. Valerie Selby is coming on Friday. I am writing my reminiscences!! Such a number of people have encouraged me to do it, and I must say it is very amusing to do so. Ken seems depressed about his composition. I always thought he was spoilt by being pushed to write ultra modern music at the R.C.M. He never really liked it and is naturally more conservative than progressive. Since then he has never found himself, or acquired confidence or stimulus. He says he doesn't get any encouragement in Oxford, that they don't seem to like his church music at New College. I tried to cheer him up and encourage him.

Airgraph 17 October 1943:

I have been so busy that my 'war correspondence' has got all behind. However, the second of three lectures at the Mount School came off on Friday, and I have broken the back of indexing the Counterpoint book, which is having another edition printed; so that I can safely have a vigorous go at getting abreast with the letters today. All goes well at the Minster. The Dean has chosen a set of religious poems which he wants me to set en suite for solo and chorus. ... I have lots of boys stationed here who try to get in lessons when they can get leave for an hour or two, but it is very difficult to fit them in. Joan Wright, a pupil who has played a lot for C.E.M.A. and E.N.S.A. played a Concerto in the Minster with me, and we both did solos.

Here was the first intimation I had of what was to be his last major work. His letters of 4 February and 28 July 1944 give more details and report progress. Publication was not attained until 1954, ten years later, when five of the 'Six Songs of the Spirit' (the alliterative title being certainly thought up by the Dean, who seemed to enjoy sibilants) were seen through the press by Sir Ernest Bullock who orchestrated the last three numbers. 'The Veteran of Heaven' by Francis Thompson was omitted as it was considered not to fit well with the others from a literary point of view. The strongly rhythmic character of the music, however, is valuable from the musical angle as it provides needed contrast between the gentler fourth and sixth numbers.

Airgraph 16 December 1943 (typed in capitals):

I am sorry that there is such a big blank between my letters to you. The reason is that the counterpoint book has run through the first edition. Macmillans suddenly sprung this on me and asked for any corrections and for the index. This last proved to be a colossal job and took a lot of my precious spare moments. It was only sent off at the end of last week. I was quite prepared to hear from Macmillans that they had been unable to hold up the publication of the second edition any longer. However I heard this morning that they are including it. By then the correspon-

Choir practice for a war-time broadcast

dence work of four prospective Mus. D.'s had accumulated into
an enormous pile. I began to reduce it on Monday and sent off
the last package by 5 o'clock this evening. Now I am starting to
clear off a host of letters and airgraphs which had also accumulated. You are to be the first to be answered. The B.B.C. have
started a series of 'Church Music of our Time' and honoured
me by putting me on third the first two being Howells and Darke.
The Leeds Messiah was on Saturday, so I was away all day. The
broadcast was on Sunday at 1.55 p.m. The choir finished the
choral eucharist at 12.30, and rehearsed from 12.45 to 1.15. then
the Dean (who did the talking) gave the men lunch, and we
provided for the boys. We were back at 1.45, and the choir with
no fuss at all sang most beautifully. Dr. Harris wrote to say it was
"inspiring", and Dr. Bullock said it was "streets ahead of the
other two". I have had a very bad rheumatic pain down the left
leg since a week ago. You can imagine doing three hours
"Messiah" and a previous rehearsal under these circumstances.
But it is marvellous what you can do if you are put to it. I gave
them extracts from your letters at the Old Boys' Reunion. They

were very much amused and interested. Your last letter about the flautist *(Roger Cortet, then living in Algiers)* was very interesting too. It is a fine thing for you to be thrown up against so many good musicians of a foreign type. But I bet you keep a warm place in your heart for our English music nevertheless. I expect Christmas will have passed by the time you get this. I hope you will have a happy one. You will be remembered when we drink to absent friends on Christmas night. ...

Air Mail letter card, hand written, 4 February 1944:

I don't call your bandmaster to mind. I see a good many of them these days. There are four come for coaching for Durham. One is just writing his Bachelor's exercise, two are preparing for 2nd Mus. B., and one is actually working for the doctor's exam. He is the most musical of the lot – Norman Richardson. But they are all more or less 'army', which means that their music has more iron discipline in it, and more four-squareness than is necessary for freedom and initiative. However, they are good fellows and pleasant to work with.

You are a lucky dog to get such a lot of music – some of it excellent experience for you. A good many old pupils keep up a regular correspondence with me. Some, like David Hird, have been stationed near a piano or organ, or both for a while, and moved off into the desert. Others seem to have had none. Tom Hallford writes *(from where?)*: "Every place we go through is almost completely destroyed and there is never any electricity to blow the organ. But only last night I was playing on a magnificent concert grand piano at a competition held for H.M.F. All kinds of acts on the stage, the judging being done by the amount of applause from the audience." He goes on to say that he won the first prize with Liszt's second Hungarian Rhapsody.

All goes well here, except that I have had a dose of sciatica in my left leg. It seems to go and come back. It can be devilish, but luckily it is not often. Cold and pedalling it does not like, but get really warm and stick it up on the sofa and it will go to sleep for a bit. I have been doing a bit of composition lately. The Dean has fished out six religious poems .....I have done two and am just starting the third, but I don't get much time, alas.

Air Mail letter card, 8 May 1944, hand written:

When I was in Edinburgh for the Caird Trust, we went to the Royal British Hotel for dinner. The food was much better than the North British, but the snag was that they clear the middle of the dining room in the evenings, and push the tables and chairs to the sides, and then let loose a hideous jazz band. A few melancholy couples lounged through the slow and dismal dances. I thought of you, for there were two saxophones – I suppose a B and an E or F one. *(I had been teaching myself to play an alto in the desert)*. The gentleman who played the former sometimes swapped it for a Clarinet or a fiddle. The only other people were a pianist and a percussionist. The latter had to do the side drum with his hands, bass drum with his foot and cymbals with the other. He had some music and counted his bars, but as long as he had thumped out the first of the bar on one or other, he could easily have done without his part. I thought of the days when I was a boy and we used to romp through the Lancers, the men lifting the women clean off the floor when they waltzed them round. Often there was a first-rate band with no illegitimate instruments. They could thrill you to bits with Strauss's waltzes.

All goes well here. The choir keeps up, though we have patches of trouble when the men get ill. The Minster has been a grave or cellar through the cold weather. A propos of having queer combinations of instruments. In the days of German bands, Punch had a picture of a London Square with a member of a German band knocking at the front door of every house, collecting pennies. The only instrumentalists left to carry on the playing were a piccolo and a fellow with one of those enormous circular-helicon brass basses round his neck!

Air Mail letter card, hand written, 28 July 1944:

I fear I have neglected you lately. But, instead of work slacking off as the holdays draw near, it has increased. There has been a lot of teaching, much of it difficult to fit in, for people in the forces, or doing war work, do not seem to be able to come at regular hours. Then I have been working at "Six Songs of the Spirit" ... I have set them for Baritone Solo and chorus. One has women's chorus, one none at all, one is all chorus and two are mixed. I sweated at them to get them out in my 70th year, but alas! No publisher will take things on that scale now (chorus parts would have to be published). They all say they haven't even enough paper to republish things which have got out of print. Then I had a B.B.C. concert at Leeds with a massed choir of the Phil., Huddersfield Glee + Madrigal, the Sale choir + the

Scunthorpe male choir. I knew part-songs would be hopeless with a crowd like that under-rehearsed, and tried to get out of it, but the B.B.C. would not hear of it. It was a fearful sweat at rehearsal and a flop at performance. Wilfrid Pickles made things worse by announcing the wrong one. The choir could not hear what he said + I was helpless – I heard a good story from one of the B.B.C. men. A German airman in the Blitz period went to Goering + said, "Sir, I have bombed the B.B.C.". "Put him in a concentration camp" says Goering. "But, Sir, I hoped to be rewarded". "Nothing of the sort, you have set 10,000 men free to fight against us", says Goering. The Leeds concert must have cost them a pretty penny: they had to pay for rehearsal expenses, railway fares and a meal for the chorus, they brought over the North Regional orchestra, paid fees for me, Pickles + two singers and brought over an army of engineers, and hangers-on. Put on top of all this an organ recital on July 20 with Joan Wright (Schumann concerto, etc) and then next Thursday (home-holidays) and getting the September Durham papers off to the O.U.P. and you see I have been up to the eyes in it. ... I think the war will not last long.

XV

Seventieth Birthday Celebrations

SIR EDWARD'S SEVENTIETH BIRTHDAY provided a welcome cause
for celebration in the midst of so much wartime austerity. A
dinner and a concert of his works were arranged but, before these
took place on September 2, tributes appeared in the press. The first
of these, in the Musical Times at the beginning of August, was a
long, detailed and affectionate portrait by his pupil Ernest
Bradbury, music critic of the Yorkshire Post. Three weeks later, on
his birthday (August 22) the York paper, the Yorkshire Evening
Press, included the following appreciation by Dean Milner-White,
in his characteristic style:

> A seventieth birthday gives opportunity to a city to honour its
> great men. Sir Edward Bairstow is really great – as teacher and
> as executant, as conductor and as composer. He loves and lives
> for music; his profound scholarship centres not upon musical
> history, or musical criticism, but on *music itself;* he is a maker and
> evoker of *music,* and not the least of his gifts is the power to inspire
> others to love and to make music. We know how wide and strong
> his musical influence is in Yorkshire and the North of England:
> but to many it is an additional source of pleasure and pride that
> it proceeds from service to a Cathedral – from one of those ancient
> schools of music housed in the great churches of England as in
> no other country, and which themselves are renewed by servants
> so singlehearted and gifted. In wishing him many happy returns
> of the day, we gratefully salute one who has given York and the
> country deeper and better things even than happiness.

The same newspaper, the city of York's own, had, a day or two earlier, included an article by an erstwhile Minster chorister who was at that time a reporter on its staff. John Darby Tredger wrote of how he expected Sir Edward to spend his birthday – walking on the Yorkshire moors during his summer holidays. He writes of him as 'rather a frightening figure – austere, a fair but firm disciplinarian, keen to get the best out of a boy's voice, and endless in his efforts to create a perfect team'.

On his actual birthday the Yorkshire Post printed an Appreciation by his most famous and distinguished pupil Dr. Ernest Bullock, Principal of the Scottish National Academy of Music. As an extension of his more intimate preface to this book, we print some excerpts from this article – a public statement by one of his greatest friends of lifelong standing. He speaks of the love of song which has permeated Bairstow's life:

> It is the root and mainspring of his musical activity, and clearly traceable as a cause affecting his musical outlook, knowledge and experience. For example, was it merely fortuitous that his great friend Harry Plunket Greene, the man he loved as a brother, the one who influenced him probably more than any other man, with whom he discussed singing until they both finally reached a unity of view and purpose, was a singer of international repute?

> Was it by chance that most of Edward Bairstow's life was to be spent in training and conducting many choral societies in the North of England, and he was to be given charge of directing the music at two famous churches? How was it that he was to become interested in the teaching of singing, when he himself was never likely to become a professional singer, and be the magnet to attract pupils in a land blessed with a plentiful supply of singers?

> Apart from music and singing Sir Edward has inherited many Yorkshire traits and characteristics. He has the temperament of a musician combined with a shrewd common sense, for although he may be carried away by a fine performance, yet his judgment is never blinded, and he retains the power to give a just assessment and a reasoned criticism. He is direct in speech, commands attention and interest, even when his words are likely to cause embarrassment. He respects sincerity, but cannot bear pretentiousness and humbug. As host and hostess, he and Lady

Bairstow have always been warm hearted and generous. All who have enjoyed the pleasure of their hospitality at Minster Court will readily agree. He is loyal to his friends, and even makes excuses for those who are ungrateful, a fault which normally he cannot understand. He has a striking personality and a typical north-country determination, patience and sense of purpose. Above all he has a keen sense of humour and appreciates to the full a good story, especially a Yorkshire story.

Sir Ernest then makes the point that, had Sir Edward confined himself to song, he would not have become such an outstanding figure:

It is rather because of his marked ability as an all-round musician that he is honoured in his profession and is able to exert an influence to be reckoned with in music – especially in the North: as conductor, as trainer of the Minster choir, as accompanist, especially of the psalms, as extemporiser and as composer and writer as well as professor at Durham where he raised the standard of the examinations. But as a teacher his influence has been greatest – for a teacher lives again in his pupils. He has had a very large number of private pupils, to which can be added a still greater number who are, or have been, members of his church choirs, choral societies, or competitors at musical festivals.

It was Ernest Bullock who was charged with the presentation to E.C.B. of a cheque for £250 which had been subscribed by personal friends, professional colleagues, pupils past and present, former choristers and many others. This took place at the dinner which followed the afternoon concert of his works, reporting on which Alice Knight wrote in the newspaper:

The hall of St. William's College was full to overflowing and among those present were Herbert Howells, Gordon Slater and H.K. Andrews. The programme was excellently chosen to show the wide variety of Sir Edward's gifts as a composer, instrumental music, songs and choral items all displaying the same technical command of the medium, used in the service of profound musical thought and feeling.

The variations for two pianos were played by Joan Wright and Cyril Jackson, and two of the Six Songs of the Spirit were sung for the first time in public by George Parker. The Minster Choir, out of sight in the gallery, sang the three introits, conducted by the composer, and the concluding item (which is one of his most eloquent and deeply felt inspirations) the Six Variations on an Original Theme for violin and piano, was played by Sybil Eaton to whom they were dedicated nearly thirty years earlier. In this and in the songs, the piano was played by Norman Franklin. Songs were also contributed by Elsie Suddaby.

The Yorkshire Post correspondent reported that the Dean 'expressed the affection of the gathering for one who has done so much, given so much, and taught us so much in the realm of sacred and other forms of music. Sir Edward responded by thanking the artists who had given up their time to rehearsals and had travelled to York to give the concert. With characteristic humour he remarked that the music, whatever it was worth, was extremely difficult to play.'

The Times thought that:

> In listening to this one-composer programme it was at once noticeable how little the music of Edward Bairstow is imprinted with any mannerisms of style that would stamp it as the work of one man. The approach to each work is fresh and the works are individual, so that there is constant variety. It was perhaps a pity that both the purely instrumental works performed had the same musical form, the "theme and variation", but there was nothing of the academic in their treatment, and the themes themselves were of that lyrical quality in which the composer excels.

The October issue of English Church Music, the organ of the Royal School of Church Music, ended its concise and penetrating tribute with a sentiment that was always in the mind of Dean Milner-White:

> Sir Edward's activities stretch well beyond the confines of the Ridings for there can be few churches who do not use his music to enrich their services. His writing never panders to laziness, spiritual or musical, and is taut with sinew and bone: his texts are always Christian, never merely theistic, and he adorns them with a beauty which makes one never again able to think of the words without recalling the music. If with our necessarily belated birthday greetings we may mingle a complaint, it is that he does not write more.

In one of his three articles in the Yorkshire Post in 1944, H.P. Dixon reminded Sir Edward about the Dean's wish for him to compose more than he did. He replied 'I was compelled to neglect composition when I had a growing family, but now – we have five grandchildren, you know – I have more time ... what I would also like to do is write a string quartet. I have made eight or nine starts on such a work and torn them up, just as I tore up six or seven attempts at an organ sonata, before I produced my one in E flat'. It was his belief that, in composition, all progress is made from the position of things left by those who have gone before. There must be a foundation for music or it will not stand. 'Some of the moderns have no roots'. His feelings regarding atonal music were that it was retrogressive to overthrow wilfully the tonal system which was well tried and proved and had taken so long to evolve. To do so was to deprive music of one of its most valuable means of contrast and variety. Time seems to have proved that his attitude was prophetic.

An unexpected by-product of the birthday celebrations was the beginning of the series of evening canticle settings produced by Herbert Howells which began with that entitled *Collegium Regale* in 1945 and with the Gloucester service close on its heels. "For something to say" in his speech (as he told FJ) the Dean advanced the idea that a *Magnificat* might portray the mood of the Annunciation and Mary's bewilderment; likewise the Song of Simeon on first beholding the Saviour – *Nunc Dimittis*. This was typical of Milner-White's original and unusual ideas (which were plentiful), the end result of which in this instance he could not have foreseen. The notion was not entirely original, as he acknowledged, bearing in mind Stanford's delectable inspiration in G major of forty years previously where Mary sings Magnificat seated, like Gretchen, at the spinning-wheel.

His own account of the celebrations comes in two letters to FJ. 18.viii.44:

> Here we are at the Mallyan Spout Hotel Goathland in wizard weather, having an excellent time. Many thanks for your congratulations. Elsie is singing some of my songs on the wireless on the 22nd. The big celebration is to be in York on Sep 2nd. A concert of my humble efforts followed by a dinner. The two

sets of variations, the songs and some church music by the Minster Choir, Sybil Eaton, Elsie Suddaby, George Parker, Joan Wright and Cyril Jackson. I don't know why they should do all this, but it just shows what amazing affection and loyalty they have. I really have a wonderful set of old pupils. When you get to my age you will appreciate what all this means to me. It is most heartening.

September 10.1944:

The birthday celebrations were amazing and took my breath away. ... On the morning of August 22nd about 20 telegrams arrived. The hotel manager informed me that there would be 1/6 to pay extra on each of them! Later in the day a young lady in the York Telegraph office was quick enough to appreciate that 1/6 multiplied by 100 is rather a large sum, so she rung me up at the hotel and asked me what to do with the rest. I told her to put them in an envelope and post them. I answered by hand about 20 important letters and cards. Then they began to come in shoals, so Olive Atkin got a type-script letter duplicated and Valerie *(Selby)* and I sent off about 120 of these. They still keep coming in. The concert at York was most moving. You will probably get a programme. They all played and sang most beautifully, especially Sybil Eaton who has never played the violin variations so well in my hearing. The dinner was marvellous. Herbert Hey was in charge. We had sherry and gin and bitters before, and hock and burgundy with the food – unheard of in wartime. The Station Hotel excelled themselves over the food. The speeches from the Dean, Sybil, Slater, and Ernest Bullock made me feel like a wet rag. I could hardly stumble out my reply at the end. I wish you could have been there.

Autographs on Menu Card,
Station Hotel,
2 September 1944

The organ piece *(FJ's birthday present)* sounds as if you were more cheerful and in better form. At any rate we can all see that the end is coming. I don't think it will be long now. God's mercies to us have been wonderful = this house and the Minster never touched, the choir at full strength, and no casualties amongst the family and close friends.

L'Envoy

Airgraph, York 25.xii.44:

THIS BEING CHRISTMAS DAY, 2.45 p.m. I feel especially sympathetic for all you dear boys out at the front, for I am
literally wallowing in good things and good fortune. First, we
have got Peter home! He suddenly appeared a fortnight ago from
Holland. He is posted to Malton where he will be training troops
for the next two months. He is going to see your Mother. He is

November 1944

actually in York for today. He brought back all sorts of nice things from Antwerp, where apparently you can buy anything except food. So tonight we shall be able to drink to 'absent friends' – you included – in real fizz! *(Marcel)* Kruger, the late head boy, who has been having organ lessons, turned up with a marvellous cake which his father (head confectioner at Rowntrees) had made. It had a Father Christmas, a little house, three carol singers with a lantern and some snow heaps all done in sugar. Another choir boy whose people had a farm at Tockwith, turned up with a pre-war pork pie and some brawn and sausages. They had killed a pig the day before. Lots of other kindnesses have warmed our hearts. And so I turn to answering your letters and Air-graph Christmas greetings – one from Melville Cook in India. The poor Parish Church have got an old stop-gap from Harrogate named Yeomans who has let things down badly. Melville will have some up-hill work when he comes back.

The music at the Minster keeps up to a respectable standard despite difficulties with new men who don't read very well, and don't all like being told off.

Lady B. keeps going splendidly and does a lot of work for the Soldiers, Sailors + Airmen's Families Association. ...

Air letter, hand written, Jan. 8.45:

This is the first day of the choir holiday. Of course I woke promptly at seven, but I soon realised that breakfast wasn't till 8.30. It is snowing hard which makes me more thankful still that I can hug the fire and write to you instead of rehearsing a peculiarly stupid set of boys and then enduring the freezing Minster till 10.45! Of course it is nobody's fault except Hitler's, but the Minster has been purgatory this winter. The stained glass with its outward protection of plain glass made double protection against the cold. Fuel economy has reduced us to two furnaces instead of four. How the choir stick it on a Sunday morning from 10.30 to 12.30 I don't know, but they do, and are singing beautifully despite casualties. You know I always said that Providence has watched over us to get men for the choir. Well, we have had a Cambridge Mus. B. singing tenor for about six months. He was in the meteorological branch of the R.A.F. but had an operation and was discharged. He got a job as second music master at Uppingham and cleared off on Dec. 31st. On Saturday a boy of

24 appeared from Leeds. He was grade 4 and is a grocer's manager in a branch shop. He has a lovely free tenor voice, is very artistic, was brought up as a choir boy at St. Aidan's and is dying to join the choir!!

Airgraph, hand written, 30.1.45:

> I envy you your stay in Rome. Somebody gave me a magnificent History of Architecture with splendid illustrations for my birthday. I have just got to the section on Renaissance period, and have been reading up S.Peters and other Roman buildings just lately. ... Your description of the organ reminds me of the one in Lausanne cathedral, upon which I once gave a recital. There the ostensible draw-knobs would not move, but above and below them were black knobs which you had to pull out and push down into a slot. They went in on a spring. The one above the white ones brought on the stop, those below put it out of action on the pistons and pedals of which there were six, which acted on the whole organ. You could not get the full Swell without the full pedal organ and Tuba. There was a crescendo pedal and a duplicating set of drawer (sic) knobs which acted as on the organ you describe. The fourth manual was an echo organ up the central tower (the organ was in a West gallery and was pneumatic). You could play an octave of a rapid scale on this before you heard a sound, so slow was the action! We are having terrible cold and snow, but are well.

It is probable that the recital was given during the international conference at Lausanne in 1930. The intervening fifteen years had done nothing to dim his memory of the organ's peculiarities.

As a member of the committee of the Church Music Society, Sir Edward was a co-signatory (along with the president, Archbishop Lang, Dr. E.H. Fellowes, Dean Duncan Jones of Chichester, Stanley Roper and Dr. W.H. Harris) of a letter to the Times emphasising the importance of 'preserving the true cathedral service since it is one of the most important contributions which the Church of England can make to the religious and aesthetic life of the country'. The Dean and Chapter of Ripon had decided to abandon cathedral music at matins, and to substitute music suited to a parochial service, greatly to the disquiet of the organist Dr. C.H.Moody who instituted legal proceedings against his employers. A leading article in the same issue (9 September

1943) remembered that in the Great War the singing of matins had
been discontinued in many cathedrals and never restored:

> The fear of those who care for the centuries-old cathedral
> service and its rich heritage of our own native music is that
> modifications made here and there to meet passing needs, though
> possibly small in themselves, constitute a threat to a priceless
> tradition, for which its present administrators are trustees to
> future generations. ... If the traditional music of our cathedrals
> falls into neglect we lose something unique – unique in English
> history, unique in European music....

Air Letter, March 11th 1945:

> Thanks for your air-letter. I also heard from Alan Wood. I sup-
> pose you heard from him that he hopes to become a parson. He
> seems to have a little spirit which most of them lack. I have just
> answered an S.O.S. from *(Frederick)* Hudson at Alnwick, where
> the new vicar is making his life miserable by trying to strip the
> service of its traditional beauty. The Ripon case came up in the
> Chancery Court last month, but the Judge took away piles of
> documents and reserved his judgment. They had never had a
> similar case in that Court, and did not seem to know whether
> they had any power to enforce a verdict. I have heard nothing
> since except a rumour that the judge is consulting 'someone who
> would be acceptable to both sides'. This might be Lord Lang.
> There is another rumour that the case will come on in an
> 'Ecclesiastical Court'.
>
> I was much amused by your description of the local Cathedral
> congregation wading through an endless litany. ... Our two new
> tenors are shaping well: they are both keen and good musicians,
> the boys are a disappointing and stupid lot at present. Yesterday
> at the Speech Day I had a good whack at the parents: they are
> to blame for a lot of the easily daunted and timid inefficiency.
>
> It can't be long before you come home now, surely ... Leeds
> concert on Saturday with Handel's Acis + Bach's Magnificat.
> Then Durham and then the Passion.

Air letter, May 8 York:

> ... I want to go to the Transvaal for three months to see Stephen
> but cannot leave the Minster with only Miss Milvain. I wonder
> when you will be available. We are celebrating V.E. day here today
> and tomorrow so I am free from teaching. ...

In the Choir Practice Room, 1945

The following month Sir Edward was in Oxford to receive the honorary degree of Doctor of Music. This prestigious honour was a great pleasure to him, according him, as it did, recognition of his work not only as an academician (notably for his book *Counterpoint and Harmony*) but also as a national figure, active in the musical establishment, spending a whole lifetime in the Church, and for being, himself, a living example of the all-round musician he wished his pupils to become. In the Sheldonian Theatre on 8 June 1945 the public orator proclaimed as much to the world in his Latin oration:

Degree of D. Mus

SIR EDWARD BAIRSTOW, F.R.C.O.

UTINAM ne sola oratoris vox hospitem musicis gratissimum salutaret, sed multiplex potius ille sonus quem fundere organis Sancta Caecilia fertur docuisse: cuius ad modulationem utinam lectissimi chori symphonia carmine prorsus triumphali totum Theatrum personaret! adest enim qui artem illam caelesti munere traditam in maius usque provexit; qui Eboraci in ecclesia cathedrali fistulis adsidens vocalibus ea sollertia simul claves digitis percurrit, simul variat continui spiritus moras, ut nusquam suavius sollemnia murmura diffundantur. Cantorum ibidem Magister factus, duplici munere annos iam functus bis sedecim id feliciter egit, ut concentus amabiles antiqua Aedis tecta circumsonent, mundi totius Dominum Deum numeroso mulcentes alloquio. signifer idem musicae artis novem paullo plus lustra assidue militavit, nunc in frequentes Lancastriae urbes vocatus, qui choros omnigenos virga nutuque moderetur, nunc in natalem reversus comitatum, ubi tanto fructu organicorum et canentium rexit sodalitates ut censeant nonnulli musices palmam Eboracensibus esse deferendem. missa tamen quaestione tam invidiosa, id solum dicam quod ab universis conceditur, huius unius consilio inniti, tanquam robori studiorum ac firmamento, collegas eius omnes operisque consortes; hunc etiam praeter ceteros effecisse ut populares eius, quid sublime sit edocti, severioribus carminum exemplis admodum delectentur. quid quod ipse 'melopoeus' numerandus est insignis? quod tam in scientiam musices, ut compluria eius scripta testantur, quam in artem ipsam incubuit? quod Professor discipulos profectu vel maximo ad omnem excellentiam informavit? sed quid moramur!

praesento vobis Angliae septentrionalis Musageten, Edwardum
Bairstow, Equitem auratum, apud Ledesiensis in litteris
Doctorem, apud Dunelmenses artis musicae Professorem, ut
admittatur honoris causa ad gradum Doctoris in musica.

Which, being interpreted, runs as follows:

Would that a guest so welcome to musicians could have been
saluted here not by the voice of an orator alone but by the richly
textured organ tone which was Saint Caecilia's gift to us, so we
are told: and would that, then, to the organ's measure the finest
choir that we could choose could have been making the whole
Sheldonian ring with truly triumphal song!

For we have among us one who has ever carried further that
Art which came to us from heaven: who, seated at the organ in
York Minster, with such skill fingers the keys and simultaneously
varies the stops of the unceasing wind that solemn murmurings
pour from it, unrivalled in the world for sweetness. Made Master
of the Choir in that same place, for thirty-two years he has
performed the twofold function with felicity, to make the
Minster's roofs resound with delectable song and charm the Lord
God of the whole earth with harmonious address.

So, too, for something over forty-five years in this service of
her, he has assiduously carried music's banner – called sometimes to the populous towns of Lancashire to conduct with baton
and nod every kind of chorus, and returning then to his native
county, where he ruled the fellowship of organists and singers to
such effect that many would say that music's palm should be
awarded to the people of Yorkshire.

Let so invidious a question pass. I will confine myself to what
all alike would concede: that on this one man's wisdom, as the
strength and stay of their profession, all his colleagues and his
fellow-workers lean. And it is his preeminent achievement, they
would say, that the members of his school, taught by him the
meaning of 'sublime', take pleasure now, in high degree, in the
more demanding modes of song.

What of the fact that he himself is to be numbered as a distinguished 'maker of song'? or that, as his many writings witness,
he has devoted himself as much to the science of music as to the
art of it itself? or that as Professor he has with the greatest
success shaped his pupils to every excellence?

But why delay? I present to you the Chief Musician of Northern England, Edward Bairstow, Knight, Doctor of Letters in Leeds, Professor of Music in Durham, to be admitted *Honoris Causa* to the degree of Doctor of Music.

On 3 January 1946 Sir Edward wrote to his pupil David Hird in the Middle East:

> ... Your letter finds me in bed where I was sent by the doctor on Christmas Eve with a temperature. I managed to get through the Carol Service. Thank goodness my temperature has gone back to normal, and I am to be allowed up for tea tomorrow, but I am still coughing up a lot from the bronchial tubes.'

To me on 19 February:

> An abcess on the lung often requires two operations. They try to do with one, which occasionally suffices, but nearly always there has to be a second which means an incision and a tube to drain the thing off.'

The next hand-written letter from the Purey-Cust Nursing Home was dated 23 March 1946:

> ... I am really very well if only this stupid lung would stop discharging. It does it much less than it used to, but it must cease before I can be up and about again.

Finally, on 1 April:

> ... I have had a very long stretch of illness which is not over now. Last Thursday they made a further incision and took another bit of rib away to drain the bottom of the lung. It was the most severe of the lot and has made me feeble. But both local doctor and specialist seem satisfied, and say I shall soon be out of this Nursing Home.

Alas, this was not to be. He gradually became weaker and died on the first day of May (1946), a day of perfect spring weather, warm and bright with a slight mist, full of hope and promise. Lady Bairstow telephoned me at Malton (as it was the choir's day off and I was spending it at my Mother's) telling me of the funeral arrangements.

Many obituaries appeared, paying him high tribute. Thus *The Times*:

York Minster loses an organist and master of the choir who stands high in distinction in a long line, Durham University its Professor of Music, and Yorkshire a great choral conductor. Bairstow, who refused all temptations to come to the south, thus contributed over many years to the vigour of musical life in the north. ... The Dean and Precentor of York, writing to *The Times* in 1938 to initiate a testimonial to Bairstow to commemorate his 25 years' tenure of the organistship, said: *Those who have worshipped in our Cathedral, or listened to the broadcasts of our services, are well aware of the pre-eminent service which during a quarter of a century he has rendered to the cause of English church music.* Bairstow's church compositions, anthems, and services place him in the line of Wesley, Stanford, and Charles Wood. He was a great church musician partly because he was not only a church musician . ... Bairstow was an exigent conductor, a firm disciplinarian, and a musician whose sure judgment and tact justified the exigence of his demands . ... In his concert programmes he took pains to enlarge the repertory of his choral societies beyond the acknowledged masterpieces with works of fine quality by modern composers.'

The Musical Times:

He had no use for the lukewarm or the humbug – he was him-self direct and outspoken, and unpleasant truth lost nothing of its unpleasantness when delivered in his, at times, grating voice. But his sincerity, his fine musicianship and judgment made it an enviable privilege to work under him and he inspired in his pupils a deep affection and loyalty. As an adjudicator he never minced his words in giving unfavourable criticism, but warm praise, or indeed praise of any sort, from him was worth having.'

Doctor F.H. Wood (in 'Music and Education' July-August 1946) wrote of the 'last glimpse of all', sent to him by a mutual friend of his own and ECB's, Mr. Eric Furrell of Hampstead, who was the husband of Maud, sister of William Wolstenholme and, according to *The Musical Times* of 1931, an enthusiastic London chorister. 'I went to York for the funeral' he wrote. 'The Minster was full except for the side aisles. Dr. Bullock played, and Jackson conducted the choir. The boys especially were magnificent, par-ticularly in *Save us, O Lord*. The streets outside the Minster were crowded.' As the coffin was carried down the nave and out through

the Great West Door Doctor Bullock played one of the two Bach
pieces which Sir Edward most admired (along with the Great G
minor), the Prelude and Fugue in B minor. Dr. Wood continued:

> Bairstow excelled in all he undertook. Had he concentrated upon
> composition, he might have written a Gerontius or some other
> enduring masterpiece. Posterity ... will decide whether (he)
> lessened his chances of ultimate fame as a composer by scatter-
> ing his energies. Personally I think he did right to scatter them.
> It was the way for him to go. His temperament was like a high-
> powered electric grid which drives energy and light over many
> counties at once. ... During the eighteen years of his professor-
> ship at Durham the standard was steadily raised until the Durham
> degrees became the most difficult in the world. For that he had
> many critics and made a few enemies, but he was ever quick to
> appreciate merit and to help deserving students. Even rejected
> exercises carried back encouragement to their composers, and
> often these comments embodied a valuable lesson on construc-
> tion and form. As a man there lay under that hard exterior a kind
> heart and a sympathetic nature.'

The Yorkshire Gazette reported from a reader who knew Sir
Edward well that:

> The service ... which marked the passing of one of the greatest
> figures of his time in British music, was beautifully austere.
> Nothing could have been more moving than the first anthem
> written by Sir Edward, *Save us, O Lord*, which is sung up and
> down the land in English parish churches, and the devotional
> rendering ... of the Gibbons-Bairstow hymn, *Jesu, grant me this*.
> ... Sir Edward's grave at Huntington is under the spreading
> branches of a beech tree. He lies at rest to the west of the church.
> Many people, no doubt, have wondered why Huntington was
> chosen. In his last public speech Sir Edward mentioned
> Huntington Parish Church for its beautiful choir singing on the
> occasion some years ago when he attended a service there. It is
> scarcely possible to visit Huntington churchyard without being
> charmed by the steeple among the trees.

On Sunday the fifth of May, the day after the funeral, Canon
Frederick Harrison, Chancellor of the Minster, and a long-stand-
ing admirer of ECB, gave a characteristic and moving address:

Those who were present yesterday afternoon at the funeral service of Sir Edward Bairstow, for 33 years organist and master of the music of this cathedral and metropolitical church of St. Peter in York, must have been conscious of a surge of love and thankfulness welling up from a thousand hearts for one who had given almost one-half, and those the best years, of his life to the service of God in this great church. It is fitting that, at the earliest opportunity, there should be paid from this pulpit a tribute to the work of a great musician, an inspired artist, a stimulating companion, a loyal friend and, most of all, a man of deep piety. Of the 30 years during which I knew him, I worked in close touch with him for 20; and probably unknown to him, I followed the music chord by chord and almost note by note, and in so doing I became his devoted disciple.

I think that very many who come here, and doubtless to other cathedral churches, even for fleeting visits, gain inspiration from the music which they hear. It would be untrue to claim that the music anywhere is always at its best. Choirs have their ups and downs, and the thing which is commonly called temperament can, and often does, move in mysterious ways. But Sir Edward always taught his pupils that, whatever medium they used, their efforts would be of no avail unless they had a message and tried to deliver it. To this end, certain qualities were essential – sincerity, unselfconsciousness, unselfishness, and honesty. The frank and open honesty and sincerity that is supposed to be one of the characteristics of north-country people had been born in him from the West-Riding stock to which he belonged. Those who resented this honesty and this sincerity in him may not have realised that, anyhow, he told them the worst about themselves, and that he kept nothing from them. It is this quality that made it possible for him to interpret music as the composer intended, and I do not doubt that composers would often have been surprised to realise how much their music meant when sung by his choir. Thus, as we here all know, (and thank God for it), our eyes were always being opened to new beauties in music. Did anybody else ever reveal the meaning of a Bach chorale as he did? Shall we ever forget the singing of the chorales in the St. Matthew Passion on Palm Sunday year by year? Can the memory ever fade of the rendering of the phrase,'Truly this was the Son of ' – and then a pause of two or three seconds, followed by the almost

whisperedly-reverent singing of the most sacred of all words –
'God'? We shall never forget these things. Nor the ineffable beauty
of the singing by our choir of his arrangement of the lovely tune
of Orlando Gibbons to the hymn, 'Jesu, grant me this, I pray'.
First the trebles, then the tenors, then the second trebles have
the melody. Then, in the last verse, by a daring venture, the basses
sing the melody. 'Death will come to me one day; Jesu, cast me
not away; Dying, let me still abide, Hidden in thy wounded side.'
All this in a tense *pianissimo* – and then the gradual fall of the
cadence of the *Amen* until we can almost see with our very eyes
the sinking of a departing soul to its rest.

With all this went a reverence that was as sincere as it was
deep. I remember being present at a rehearsal of the Minster
choir, probably 20 years ago, when the hymn was being practised: Bread of the world, in mercy broken, Wine of the soul, in
mercy shed.

Suddenly he stopped the choir. "No! No!" he said, somewhat sadly, "You are singing of food for the body. This bread and
wine are food for the soul. This is the mystery of the Holy
Communion."

For Sir Edward Bairstow was all the things that he was –
organist, choir-trainer, contrapuntalist, (who could play two
melodies against each other as he could!), composer, teacher,
husband, father, and friend, – (he was all these things) – because
he was a devout, simple, and humble man of God. He was a
regular communicant here, and those of us who, during his long
illness, administered to him the Sacrament of Holy Communion,
will never lose the memory of his simple and honest piety. It was
because his religion was the foundation of his life that he was the
man he was. Why have the musicians of the Church seldom been
canonised?

I want to say something now to the members, past and
present, of the Minster choir. During Sir Edward's 33 years here,
not far short of 200 boys have passed through his choir, and probably about 50 Songmen. Not a single one of these would ever
have described Sir Edward as anything but strict and exacting.
But our present choristers and songmen ought to know that never
at any time did he allow criticism of his choir to pass without a
spirited defence. In every boy and man who did his best, worked

hard, and was honest and sincere, Sir Edward found a friend and ally, to be championed through thick and thin. It is therefore no cause for wonder that he held them in the greatest and deepest affection. For six days of every week his choir had his freshest morning energy. Any case of hardship or suffering amongst them he at once brought to the notice of the dean and chapter.

And he loved this place. He was part and parcel of it. It was the background of his life. Somehow, he fitted into it, for, even though not a man of commanding stature, he was built on a magnificent scale. There was nothing mean about him. He super-intended the re-building of the great organ here, and made it just the right instrument for the building. He knew how every stop and every one of the more usual combinations of stops sounded in the building. The organ was his friend, an external part of himself, as it were. From here he turned out interpreters and creators of sacred music, and many of his pupils have occupied the position of organist at great churches, including Westminster Abbey and many cathedrals. To his pupils he was the great Maestro, but always their friend.

Let me end by relating an incident that happened 8 years ago, when he had been organist here for 25 years. With his characteristic generosity, he entertained at dinner the songmen and the resident clergy of the Minster. The date was the 14th day of the month. On that day 25 years earlier, he had played his first service at Evensong in the Minster. He told us that, as he played the psalms for that evening, verses 22 and 23 impressed themselves on his mind. As he quoted these two verses he was so far overcome with emotion that his words were almost inaudible. Few people knew, I may add in parenthesis, that it was no uncommon thing for him to be moved to tears as he was playing the accompaniment to the psalms. Perhaps this was why he accompanied them as nobody else did, or could, or perhaps ever will. Well, these two verses remained his inspiration. They reveal the secret of his life and of his influence over his fellow-men, through the divine gift of music.

> 22. Nevertheless, thou art always by me:
> For thou hast holden me by my right hand.
> 23. Thou shalt guide me with thy counsel:
> And after that receive me with glory.

As we recall the sad, but glorious and triumphal scene in the nave yesterday, and as we contemplate the loss which is ours, we can take comfort that our friend has been received with that glory, a foretaste of which it was his life's mission to give to us.

THANKS BE TO GOD

The next day a memorial service took place in Leeds Parish Church at which the sermon was preached by the Reverend Morris O. Hodson, former Precentor and close associate of ECB's who was a member of the selection committee choosing him as organist exactly forty years previously.

The following year a meeting was held in St. William's College (at the east end of the Minster) to launch an appeal for £5,000 whose purpose was to provide musical instruction for deserving choristers of Wigan, Leeds and York. It was attended by many notable figures of the musical world, but unfortunately the target was not reached. Due perhaps to the depressed state of the post-war economy, less than one thousand pounds was subscribed. It was shared between Leeds and Wigan, where the Bairstow Memorial Fund happily exists in pursuance of its original aims.

A tablet in Sir Edward's memory was placed in Wigan Parish Church and can be seen on one of the south pillars of the chancel.

His Leeds memorial reads:

Remembering with gratitude
the life and inspiration of
EDWARD CUTHBERT BAIRSTOW
1874-1946
Organist and Choirmaster of this Church
from 1906 to 1913
This tablet was placed here in the
year of the fiftieth anniversary of his death
by the Organists, Boy Choristers and
Gentlemen of the Choir
". . . . as they shout exultingly the hymn:
Alleluia, Alleluia, Alleluia!"
(from "Let all mortal flesh keep silence" 1906)

At York, the Minster holds two memorials. A tablet containing the names of Minster organists from the year 1475 is on the wall of the north choir aisle. It was given by the Friends of the Minster in the centenary of his birth and was unveiled by his daughter, Mrs. George Brown, in the presence of several members of his family on the patronal festival of Saint Peter, June twenty-ninth 1974.

The chamber organ standing in the Lady Chapel, with its four stops, the work of Henry Lincoln, bears the following inscription, composed by Dean Milner-White:

This Organ, 1801, commemorates
SIR EDWARD CUTHBERT BAIRSTOW
Doctor and Professor of Music at the University of Durham
Hon. D. Mus. Oxon: Litt. D. Leeds: F.R.C.O.
Eminent alike as teacher and composer:
As a man, beloved.

On a visit to her daughter and son-in-law in London,
Lady Bairstow died on February twenty-first 1950.
Her funeral took place in the Minster at York
and she was buried with her husband
in the churchyard at Huntington.

Epilogue

by Nancy Brown

M Y FATHER WAS SMALL and thin, with twinkling brown eyes, and a most expressive face dominated by a large nose. He was a perfectionist and expected his pupils to reach his high standards. If they didn't work hard enough, or were obviously having lessons for their own enjoyment with no intention of giving pleasure to other people, they were soon told to go, as they were wasting his time and their money.

My elder brother was born when my father was organist of Wigan Parish Church, and I was born three years later after my father had been appointed organist of Leeds Parish Church.

My earliest recollections of my father were coupled with Ernest Bullock, my father's assistant who lived with us at that time. Both seemed full of energy and brimming over with fun. We adored them! I remember the elaborate firework displays on Guy Fawkes Day, which gave much more pleasure to them than to us. We usually retreated indoors cold and scared! They got so much pleasure out of playing with our toys that we began to wonder if they had bought them for their enjoyment! We had an enormous box of German bricks made of some composition – like stone – I can remember the smell of them to this day! The box was far too heavy for any child to lift; it had four trays of bricks – the smallest on the top, and the largest, with arches and pillars, on the bottom row. My father and Ernest built the most intricate bridges and baroque churches from the plans given with the bricks, and often they went one better and began making their own designs. I remember a real gem of a Norman church they were very proud of, but all my brother and I were allowed to do was to put the bricks away. Each layer had a plan, and woe betide us if we deviated one brick from the plan! Then there was the electric train covering half the music room floor, where they played some absorbing game seeing who could make up a goods train with the fewest number of shunts. Occasionally we were allowed to move the points, but we soon got bored. Even the Meccano sets were used to make a grandfather clock which went for twelve hours. He entered this for a competition and won a prize; he received a number of letters of congratulation from grown-ups who thought he was a small boy.

My father always had the whole of August on holiday – the only time in the whole year he was really free, Saturdays and Sundays included. In the early days, before we owned a car, this was a time of great preparation when the whole family was upset and tempers were frayed. We rented a furnished cottage at Sandsend just north of Whitby. The cook, the housemaid and the nurse came with us – not to mention trunks of linen, trunks of clothes, bassinets, deck chairs, cots, hat boxes, bundles of rugs wound round umbrellas and tennis racquets. Though it was only a short journey, it involved a change at Malton and a change of station in Whitby. My father marshalled us on and off trains, then off to the luggage van with a list of various items of luggage in one hand and a child's chair with a hole in it over the other arm!

Once we reached our destination, it took the best part of a week for him to unwind and begin to enjoy himself. Not for him the lazy hours spent in a deck chair on the beach most parents enjoyed; he was either playing tennis or climbing the Rig – a flat-topped hill where we went blackberrying or practising golf – or walking up to Lythe church to practise the organ for the yearly organ recital he was asked to give. My brother and I had to climb this long hill, 1 in 4 in parts, and to pump the organ for him for which we were given sixpence! The village organ blower took over the task for the recital. I shall never forget the memorable occasion when, working up to the final crescendo, the wind gave out and a dreadful wail started high up the scale and ended with a cough in the bass. The organ blower had fallen asleep!

FAMOUS ORGANIST WHO MAKES MODELS.

DR. BAIRSTOW'S HOBBY.

SKILL IN BUILDING TINY MOTOR VAN.

It is seldom one comes across a musician, the composer of many beautiful songs and much church music, who confesses to an ardent love of things mechanical

Such a one is Dr E. C. Bairstow, the well-known musician and organist of York Minster. Although a busy man, Dr. Bairstow finds time to construct elaborate working models for his six-year-old son.

This week (writes a "Yorkshire Evening Post" representative) he showed me ingenious proof of his mechanical aptitude. He is at present engaged on a model motor delivery van, complete with left-hand drive, accurate steering, two forward gears, and a reverse. The body is the only part which is not "Meccano," being constructed of three-ply wood.

Dr. Bairstow explained with enthusiasm the principles of his model. On the polished floor of his capacious music room he demonstrated, on hands and knees, how the motor would not on top gear climb a rug, but when he put it into low gear, it made light of the task.

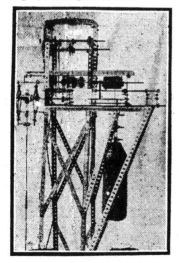

A MODEL GRANDFATHER CLOCK MADE BY DR. BAIRSTOW.

A Successful Competitor

We have pleasure in publishing a photograph of Dr. E. C. Bairstow, who will be well known to many readers of the "M.M." as the organist of York Minster. Dr. Bairstow was successful in sharing the first prize in Section "C" (cash £20) with another competitor in our recent Competition. We feel sure that Meccano boys will be interested in reading the following remarks from this well-known musician, and join us in congratulating him on his recent success.

"YORK.

"It has always been my custom to have on hand something that, whilst appealing to the imagination and general interest is in complete contrast to my usual work. The building of original models in Meccano has been the pleasantest of my hobbies during the last twelve years. The most interesting experience of all has been the building of the clock which won me the prize. There were many problems to solve and the solution of each one had to be attempted by several different methods before success was finally attained."

Meccano Magazine,
November 1922

Yorkshire Post:
date not known

The Meccano Clock

Whatever my father bought it had to be the very best and certainly his bicycle was a real gem. It was a Lea Francis and besides having the most modern gears and excellent brakes, it had all sorts of gadgets – one handle grip unscrewed to reveal an oil can, the other a repair outfit. We trundled slowly round the flat dusty lanes, our pace being set by the youngest member of the family who had the little fixed wheel bicycle on which we all had first learnt to ride.

He taught us all to row and I remember long hot summer afternoons when we rowed up to Nun Monkton or down to Bishopthorpe where we had an excellent tea in a cottage garden. Then there were the Sunday walks – rather solemn affairs which took place between Evensong and supper. At first we used to take a stroll along the river bank, but later when we owned a car we went further afield. My father used to try out his lectures on us and we were brought up to believe that fear was evil and to be avoided. If a singer had fear, the muscles tightened, the throat became rigid, the breath failed and disaster followed. Love was the most important thing in our lives: we must love our work, love giving pleasure to other people and then all would be well. The other favourite theme was *rhythm:* everything in nature had its own rhythm and woe betide the unrhythmical person, who embodied both faults – having no rhythm and being full of fear. Very often this fear was engendered by him, himself!

Rather surprisingly one of his timid pupils was given the task of teaching us the piano. We soon sensed this fear and as soon as the first interest had subsided we did as little work as possible. My brother escaped further tuition by going to boarding school but my father decided he would give me lessons. I am afraid I was a great disappointment to him. I didn't reach anywhere near the standard of most of his pupils. The lessons were stormy, and quite often ended in my retiring in tears!

The youngest member of the family – Peter – was born in February 1917. My father was conducting a performance of Mendelssohn's *Elijah* at the time of the birth. Wondering what name would be given him, a witty friend (*H. Bacon Smith*) suggested he should "Call him louder" – Elijah's repeated suggestion to the priests of Baal. Everyone enjoyed having a baby in the house and

I am afraid Peter got rather spoilt; Stephen and I squashed him firmly if he started showing off in front of us!

My father had a dynamic personality and life was never dull. There were days when the family relaxed: my father had had a successful concert or a pupil had made a name for himself, or the choristers were a particularly intelligent group. But of course there were periods of depression; my brothers and I had to tread warily otherwise we might bring the full blast of his anger on our heads! My mother was the stabilizing factor in our family; she managed to keep calm and soothe the victim and distract my father by suggesting a game of Patience.

Though he had been brought up in a strict Methodist family where playing-cards were thought of as "The Devil's Pasteboards", he found card games a delightful relaxation. The cards were arranged in the same order and my mother and father would see who could get the patience out, or in the event of its not being finished, the winner was the person with the most cards on the aces. Whenever possible they played a game after lunch, then my father had five minutes' sleep after which he could carry on with his tremendous round of activities.

One of the most extraordinary things about my father was, that except for playing the organ and conducting, he had very little exercise. Yet I never once heard him complain of feeling stiff after the strenuous exercise he took on holiday, playing endless sets of tennis in the morning, and perhaps climbing a fell in the afternoon! I have never known anyone work harder than my father, and as the years went by he seemed to take on more and more work. There was always a group of pupils being coached for their Mus. Bac. listening to the daily choir practices, having organ lessons, and occasionally being allowed to play an organ voluntary after Evening Service. At one time there were six cathedral organists – all his former pupils.

My father was full of fun and he had a fund of very good stories, but there were occasions when my mother quite unconsciously produced an unforgettable family joke. To say the least of it my mother was rather large. One Good Friday she went to the Three Hours Service and stayed until the end. Coming home with a rapt expression on her face she announced, "You know, darlings, very few men can hold me for three hours!" On holiday in Ireland it was our custom to bathe in the beautiful clear deep pools after undressing in some secluded nook among the rocks. One morning my mother had been sitting knitting some way off and, seeing us go down to the pool to bathe, scrambled over the rocks towards us. When she had nearly reached us she called out, "Darlings, I've come all this way to see you". Unfortunately there were two naked men at her feet!

Each year my father tried to make my mother an April Fool but quite unsuccessfully, as she could tell by the expression on his face what was coming. One year, however, my father hit on a wonderful idea. We had an extension of the telephone from the hall to the music room. On April's Fool Day he rang the music room from the hall and the conversation went something like this:

Father (in broad Yorkshire): Is that Bairstows?
Mother (haughtily) : This is Dr. Bairstow's.
Father : Uz wants to know doos 'e give lessons in t'banjo?
Mother (angrily ringing off): Certainly not.

It wasn't until he came upstairs with a broad grin on his face that she realised at last she had been caught!

At Christmas my mother and I would go over to Leeds to the Philharmonic Society's annual performance of Handel's Messiah. We arrived in time to hear most of the rehearsal in the afternoon, then with some of the soloists we went to an Italian restaurant patronised by my father. He always had a glass of champagne before a concert. The Town Hall was always packed and the whole atmosphere was one of excitement and happiness. The Yorkshire audience just loved every minute of the performance and so did I! We went to the artists' room during the interval and I was fascinated by the elaborate dresses worn by the ladies: they all seemed large and pink and white rather like a doll's. I remember being fascinated by a contralto whose diamanté shoulder straps just disappeared into fat!

Every Palm Sunday there was a performance of Bach's St. Matthew Passion in the Minster. I think if I describe this event it will give you an idea of my father's vitality. Our guests would arrive on the Saturday. They usually included Sybil Eaton who led the orchestra and played the solo violin part in the beautiful aria following Peter's betrayal, and Steuart Wilson who sang the part of the Evangelist. The moment the latter arrived the tempo began to quicken! As soon as he was safely ensconced in the drawing room my brothers and I would rush downstairs to see the year's flamboyant garment – a sombrero or an overcoat with enormous checks. One year, to our huge delight, it was a black cloak! From the moment he arrived we were kept in fits of laughter over his fund of amusing stories or his description of his latest tour abroad. The sounds began to increase: a bass practising in one room, my father with the solo choristers practising in the music room, and Sybil playing the fiddle in the drawing room! After dinner my father and Sybil played violin sonatas the entire evening.

The day itself started with a choir practice followed by Matins and Choral Eucharist; then home for a quick lunch and back to the Minster for a rehearsal which only finished as the people began to arrive for the performance. This finished after five and was followed by a grand tea party for the soloists; about six tenors from the Leeds Philharmonic, who came each year to help out, and about the same number of members of the Hallé orchestra who also came each year. I met one of them not many years ago and he told me he first played for my father when he (my father) conducted the Blackburn Choral Society – which must have been before 1913. We had a wonderful natter about old times. After supper, my father playing the piano and all the rest of us singing, it was the tradition to sing the oratorio called *Ruth* written by some earnest musician and dedicated to Queen Victoria. It had every possible fault and was very amusing. I think there were at least twelve pages saying – "His name was Boaz". Ruth gleaning was also given the full treatment – at least four pages – "She went out empty, she came back full".

It usually ended with us all collapsing with laughter. This was followed by the gossip about fellow musicians and the telling of the latest stories – always one about Sir Thomas Beecham! I think the best one was when he was very much in debt. He was taking a rehearsal and it was interrupted by a visit from the Official Receiver. "I am sorry, gentlemen, I have to see the Official Receiver, and for what he is about to receive may the Lord make him truly thankful!"

We rather dreaded entertaining foreign musicians because my father had the idea that if you spoke very slowly in broken English they were bound to understand. You can imagine how hard it was for the family to hide their amusement when my father started the meal with "Vill you 'ave a leetle meat Monsieur?".

When father was knighted in 1932, people were so very kind and seemed so genuinely pleased at this honour. I don't remember my father having a day's illness, except for a nervous breakdown in 1911. Even when he went into the nursing home in his last illness he was busy trying desperately to finish his autobiography. He turned to my mother for comfort; both seemed so peacefully happy after their stormy and exciting life together.

XVIII

The Compositions

ORGAN

Andante for Organ	MS	?
Evening Song	Lengnick	1900
Nocturne	Lengnick	1903
Scherzo in A flat	Novello	1906
Prelude in C	(Collard Moutrie) Cramer	1907
Meditation	Collard Moutrie	1907
Legend in A flat	Stainer & Bell	1907
Prelude on *Vexilla Regis*	(Augener) Stainer & Bell	1911
Elegy	(Augener) Stainer & Bell	1911
Toccata-Prelude on *Pange Lingua*	(Augener) Stainer & Bell	1911
Sonata in E flat	Oxford University Press	1937
Three Short Preludes op. post.	Oxford University Press	1947
i D minor-F major		
ii A major		
iii Veni Emmanuel		
Prelude to Act 3 of 'The Tempest'(Sullivan)	Banks	1985
Banquet Dance (from the same)	MS (lost)	19??
Trumpet Sonata (Purcell)	OUP	1942

ANTHEMS

Thou hidden love of God	ATTB (T solo) Organ	MS	?
The Blessed Virgin's Cradle Song	SS Organ	Novello	1900
Blessed be thou, Lord God of Israel	SATB Organ	Novello	1901

242

Come ye Gentles	SATB Organ	Novello	1902
Save us, O Lord	SATB Organ	Novello	1902
The promise which was made	SATB & div. Organ	Novello	1903
The earth has grown old	SAT(T)B Organ	Vincent	1904
Know ye not	SATB Organ	Novello	1906
God who at sundry times	SATB Organ	Novello	1909
If the Lord had not helped me	SATB Organ	Novello	1910
Sing ye to the Lord	SATB Organ	Novello	1911
I will greatly rejoice	SATB Organ	Novello	1913
Of the Father's love begotten	SATB Organ	Novello	1913
Blessed City, Heavenly Salem	SATB Organ	Banks	1914
Lord, I call upon thee	SATB Organ	Novello	1916
Lord, thou hast been our refuge	SATB Orch (Organ)	Novello	1917
Let all mortal flesh keep silence 1906	SATB	S & B	1925
Three Introits:	SATB	OUP	1925
I sat down under his shadow			
I will wash my hands in innocency			
Jesu, the very thought of thee			
Jesu, grant me this (Gibbons) 1925	SATB (Org. optional)	Banks	1929
The day draws on with golden light	SATB Organ	OUP	1930
As Moses lifted up the serpent	SATB	OUP	1931
The King of love (St. Columba)	SATB Organ	OUP	1931
Our Father in the Heavens	SSAATTBB	OUP	1932
Though I speak with the tongues of men	SA(T)B Organ	OUP	1934
Let my prayer come up into thy presence	SATB & div. Orchestra (Organ)	OUP	1937
While shepherds watched their flocks	SATB Organ	OUP	1947
Jesus died for us	SATB	MS	?

SERVICES

Te Deum and Benedictus in D	SATB & div Organ	S & B	1925
The same – original version?	SATB SATB Organ optional	MS	?
Communion Service in D	SATB & div.	Novello	1913
Magnificat and Nunc Dimittis in D	SATB Org.(Orch.)	Novello	1906
Benedicite in E flat	SATB Organ	Novello	1900
Te Deum and Benedictus in E flat	Unison Organ	OUP	1923
Communion Service in E flat	Unison Organ	OUP	1923
Evening Service in E flat	Unison Organ	OUP	1923
Evening Service in G	SATB Organ	OUP	1940
The Lamentation	SATB Organ optional	OUP	1942
Threefold Kyrie in A flat	SATB	MS	1942
Kyrie Eleison in F	SATB Organ	MS	1942
Benedictus and Agnus Dei (mixolydian)	SATB & divisions	MS	1942
Merbecke: harmonization of Responses, Sursum Corda and Lord's Prayer	SATB Privately printed		?

PSALMS AND CHANTS

Double chant in A flat (Psalms 97 & 145)		
All Saints Norfolk Square book (p. 311)	MS	1896
Quadruple chant (Psalm 78) *ibid*	MS	1898

The English Psalter; a speech-rhythm pointing of the psalms in co-operation with Percy Buck and Charles Macpherson, Novello 1925.

Fifteen chants (7 single, 8 double) in the York Minster Chant Book, privately printed by Novello.

Others in the Westminster Chant Book, Novello's chant books etc.
    Psalm 114   Church Music Society 1996

HYMN TUNES and DESCANTS

O perfect love (two treble parts only)	MS 189?
Hymn for the springtime (O little birds that all day long...)	189?

Seven tunes in "Twenty Hymns for National use
  in time of War"   Banks and S&B 1914
'Bedford'   (O help us, Lord) Fa-burden –
           melody in bass   Songs of Praise 1931
'Clamavi'   (Thou hidden love of God)   A & M 1904
'Dundee'*   (Let saints on earth) descant for
           Archbishop Temple's enthronement,
           1928, with brass and timpani (see p. 320)   MS 1925
'Eboracum'   (Through the night of doubt and sorrow)
           Diocesan Musical Festival 1941
Untitled   (Hail thee, festival day)   MS   ?
'Huntington'   (Let us sing out our praises to the Lord)   1910
'London New' (God moves in a mysterious way) descant
           Diocesan Musical Festival 1930
'Memento Mori'
           (Lord! how fast the minutes fly)
           Westminster Abbey Hymn Book 1897
'Minster Court'
           (Know ye the Lord hath borne away)
           A & M 2nd Supplement 1916
'Moscow'   (Thou whose almighty word) descant
           Diocesan Musical Festival 1934
'O God of Love'
           (O for a thousand tongues) descant
           Diocesan Musical Festival 1928
'Praise my soul'
           (Praise my soul the king of heaven) descant
           Diocesan Musical Festival 1932
'Ravenshaw*   (Lord, thy word abideth)   MS 1925
'Richmond'*   (City of God) descant† and Faux Bourdon
           Diocesan Musical Festival 1928
'St. Oran'   (O frail spirit, vital spark)
           Westminster Abbey Hymn Book 1897
†*This descant was used in the opening service of the 1927 festival, and is included in the following:*

ORGAN ACCOMPANIMENTS TO THE UNISON VERSES OF TWENTY-FOUR HYMN-TUNES FROM THE ENGLISH HYMNAL, OUP 1941.

* See letter, page 164

Hyfrydol, Miles Lane, Old Hundredth, Stuttgart, Richmond, St. George, Old 104th, Folkingham, Llanfair, Dent Dale, Rhuddlan, Picardy, Monkland, Helmsley, Adeste Fideles, St. Anne, Hanover, Hast du denn Jesu, In Babilone, Aurelia, Aeterna Christi Munera, Leoni, Capetown, Ebenezer (Ton-y-botel).

HYMN ACCOMPANIMENTS

'Forty days and forty nights (Hymn 92 A & M) with original accompaniments by Ed. C. Bairstow'	MS 189?
'O come, O come Emmanuel set for organ with original harmonies by E. C. Bairstow' (see p. 164)	MS 1896
Old Hundredth for brass and organ, for the enthronement of Archbishop Temple	MS 1928

EDITIONS and ARRANGEMENTS (Sacred)

S.S. Wesley	To my request and earnest cry	Novello	1906
S.S. Wesley	Let us lift up our heart	Bayley and Ferguson	1914
S.S. Wesley	Praise the Lord O my soul	Banks	1931
Schubert	Lord thy glory fills the skies (arr. for SATB)	S & B	
Handel	Holy, holy, holy (Art thou troubled)	OUP	1930
Nares	The souls of the righteous	Banks	1933

CHORAL

'O how amiable'	Chorus and orchestra (strings)	B.Mus.	1894
'By the waters of Babylon'	Tenor solo, chorus, orchestra	D.Mus.	1900

Three short works for Durham:

Ode: Salve, salve	T Bar B	MS	(date ?)
Anxia quisquis	TTBB & orchestra	Printed by Banks	1931
Ode in praise of Durham	TTBB	MS	(date?)

'The Prodigal Son' – Choral Ballad	OUP	1939
SATB & small orchestra		

Alternative accompaniments for: Strings and Piano
Organ and Piano

'Five Poems of the Spirit'
    op. post.   Novello   1954
    i. Come, lovely Name (Crashaw)   Baritone solo, Chorus SSC
    ii. O Lord, in me there lieth naught (Mary Sidney)   Bar, solo
    iii. Praise (George Herbert)   Chorus SATB
    iv. Purse and Scrip (Walter Raleigh)   Bar, Chorus SATB
    v. L'Envoy (George Herbert) *(King of glory, king of peace)*
                                      Bar Chorus SATB
      The Veteran of Heaven (Francis Thompson)   MS
                                      Bar Chorus TTBB
      This was originally placed between iv and v. (See p. 299)

ORCHESTRAL

CORONATION MARCH for the 1902 coronation and submitted under the pseudonym 'Dum spiro spero'. Full orchestra. Also an arrangement for piano.

The Pevensey Pageant: incidental music, with J.R.Dear and others 1908

INSTRUMENTAL

Variations on an original theme for two pianos	OUP	1932
Six variations on an original theme for violin and piano	OUP	1931
Two impromptus on Irish airs for violin and piano	MS	19??
'The dear Irish girl'		
'The snowy-breasted pearl'		

SONGS

Daffodils in the grass	MS	19??
Lord I am small	MS	19??
Sweet day, so cool	MS	19??
Pack clouds away	Joseph Williams	1903
The sea hath its pearls	do.	
The pine tree	do.	
I arise from dreams of thee	do.	
A prayer for light	do.	
Daphnis and Chloe	do.	
The Hostel (arrangement of air by Alexander Ewing)	S & B	1918

When I heard the learned astronomer		Enoch	1919
Orpheus with his lute		S & B	1919
Come lovers, follow me		S & B	1922
So sweet is she (arrangement)		do.	
At night		S & B	1924
To morning		do.	
The lonesome girl		S & B	1926
The oak tree bough		Cramer	1926
The buryin'		S & B	1927

PART SONGS

Sweet day, so cool	SATB	Novello	1897
The dawn of song	SATB	Novello	1901
Her eyes the glow-worm lend thee	TTBB	S & B	1908
I dare not ask a kiss	TTBB	S & B	1908
Where shall the lover rest	SSAATTBB	Novello	1914
The oak tree bough	Unison	Cramer	1924
The oak and the ash (arrangement)	SATB	OUP	1928
Music when soft voices die	TTBB		1929
On a poet's lips I slept	SSC	Winthrop Rogers	1929
The poacher	?	OUP	1929
El dorado	T Bar B	OUP	1937
Listening	do.	OUP	1937
Gifts	do.	OUP	1937
The frog and the mouse (arrangement)	Unison	OUP	1937

ARRANGEMENTS (Secular)

Nineteen Schubert songs arranged for various choral combinations, with English words by Paul England.		S & B	1927-8
In the pine-wood *Im Haine* opus 56/3			Unison
Lullaby *Wiegenlied* 98/2			Unison
The miller's song *Das Wandern* 25/1			Unison
Trust in the springtime *Frühlingsglaube* 20/2			Unison

Spring's return		
An den Frühling	172/5	Two-part, equal voices
What the birds think		– do –
Laughter and tears		
Lachen und Weinen	59/4	SSA
The mother's song		
Wiegenlied	105/2	SSA
Waterlily		SSAA
A song for marching		
Die Wetterfahne	56 /3	SATB
Evening glow *Abendröte* (1820)		SATB
First love *Erster Verlust*	5/4	SATB
The fishermaiden		SATB
The wayside inn		
Das Wirtshaus	89	SATB
To music *An die Musik*	88/4	SATB
My love hath left me lonely		
Die Liebe hat gelogen	23/1	TTBB
On lonely heights		
Über Wildemann	108/1	TTBB
A wiseman's song		
Greisegesang	60/1	TTBB
Victory		TTBB

No German titles – and few opus numbers – appear on the copies, making it impossible to identify every one of the arrangements, many of which are no longer available.

LITERARY WORKS

'Handel's Oratorio *The Messiah*'	OUP 1928
'Counterpoint and Harmony'	Macmillan 1937/1945
'The evolution of musical form'	OUP 1943
'Singing learned from speech'(with H.Plunket Greene)	
	Macmillan/Stainer & Bell 1945

XIX

Commentaries

a. THE ORGAN WORKS

Bairstow's compositions for the organ are comparatively few. They come from two periods, the earlier part of his life and, after quite a gap, towards the end. All were published in his lifetime except the Three Short Preludes (which appeared posthumously: see Addenda p. 327) and an Andante in F, an early attempt which remains in manuscript and is strongly in the mould of the many pieces by Victorian composers which failed to stand the test of time. It contains no pre-echoes of his more mature compositions, and the handwriting is the most juvenile to be found in any of his extant manuscripts. Though unremarkable, it has a certain touching simplicity as a teenage effort, and is no worse than some pieces of the period which found their way into print.

The promise offered by the first six pieces, dated between 1900 and 1907, was not fulfilled – numerically, that is – as might have been hoped. Four years passed before the next set of three appeared in 1911, and after this an astonishingly long interval was to elapse before the arrival of his last and finest organ work, the Sonata in E flat of 1937. There may be a variety of reasons for his silence; the war; his move to York in 1913, with his increasing involvement in many different activities. But it may also have been an underlying feeling that to write for the organ is difficult, and opportunities for giving recitals were so rare that it was hardly worth the trouble.

Before the second world war recitals in churches were not so frequent as they later became, a fact due to the rise in popularity of the organ as it embraced classical principles of design and voicing. There is little room for doubt that the heavy-pressure, leathered-diapason type of organ with its opaque, ponderous tones

– the instrument which, with the new century, was becoming more and more common – was to become a vehicle to provide rather less music than sheer sound. And so it came about that the organist had to develop, as an essential part of his technique, the ability to change stops constantly in order to maintain interest and to provide relief. This was the type of organ which Bairstow and most other organists of the period liked and which he caused to be installed in Leeds Parish Church by Arthur Harrison in 1913 as he was on the point of moving to York. And having arrived there he proceeded to have the Minster organ modified in the same way.

Before this, he had been associated with the fine Hill at Westminster Abbey. At Wigan, where he went in 1900, the organ was rebuilt by Norman and Beard in 1907. All three – Wigan, Leeds and York – must have been milder and more transparent in texture before he had them modified to more Wagnerian tonal proportions, characteristics he would not have found on the Abbey organ.

So we notice that, up to 1911, his compositions were produced before he came to possess his ideal romantic organ (with the exception of a brief period at Wigan). Whether this would have made much difference is hard to say, but he may have been hankering after the full-blooded sounds he heard elsewhere and which expressed his own deep feelings and aspirations. It is nevertheless an interesting fact that, having attained the organ of his desire – after the publication of the three pieces of 1911 – it was more than a quarter of a century before he was able to compose again for the instrument.

Here it should be remarked that the three posthumous preludes published in 1947 cannot be dated. They were seen through the press by Ernest Bullock. The third of them, on *Veni Emmanuel*, was in existence in 1930 and probably well before then; indeed it could be contemporaneous with the free accompaniments for the hymn which he wrote in 1896. No doubt he was fascinated, as others have been, by the wonderful melody which would come round each Advent and stir his imagination with its potential for composition.

There was also another piece which was not published, a *Basso Ostinato* in duple time with a short repeated motif in the pedals, with a rather unpromising beginning and, not surprisingly, a lack of fulfilment. The whereabouts of the manuscript are unknown.

This leaves us with the published works, eleven in number (counting the three preludes as one); nearly as many as César Franck's and considerably more than those of Duruflé. *Evening Song* was his first published organ piece and was soon to become his most popular organ work, being widely used. T.T. Noble often played it both before and after his move to America. This acceptance must have gratified its composer, but in later life he had slight regrets at having to acknowledge the authorship. After the privations of the Great War and the havoc it wrought to the former settled way of life, it was attributes such as sincerity and reliability which were counted as of most value. Music had to reflect this, as had the musicians themselves, and anything of a sentimental nature, like *Evening Song*, was somewhat frowned upon. However, it was Lady Bairstow's privilege on her birthday to have her request for a performance granted each year, at the end of evensong.

Its life began as a cello solo with piano accompaniment and was written for a *soirée* at a private house during the composer's time as organist of All Saints, Norfolk Square, a church demolished in 1961. In his own words, he 'did it out' for organ and, though in the outer sections it is not difficult to guess at what the cello played and how the piano accompanied, the more energetic middle section does not readily provide clues. In the organ version the organist needs to play expressively and, in the central section, rhythmically. He or she will find that three manuals would be more convenient than two, though with a neat change of registration it is perfectly feasible on the latter. It was published in 1900 but was in existence at least as early as the previous May. (See page 169)

Nocturne, of 1903, is laid out for three manuals but can, with slight adaptations, be played on two. The title denotes its lineal descent from Chopin, as does the music. It is dedicated 'To my friend William Wolstenholme Esq.' who had succeeded Bairstow at Norfolk Square. Like *Evening Song* it is a long reed melody with accompaniment, but in compound time, on a broader scale and with a wider sweep. A contrasting middle section in the tonic minor of C sharp has a regretful, sighing feel with continuously moving quavers in the pedals against crotchet chords across the beat (3/4 against 6/8). The final section is a verbatim restatement of the first, ending with a two-bar echo of the pedal quavers for coda. It is a very beautiful piece, deeply felt and unjustly neglected. Though lasting some eight or nine minutes it is the ideal foil to follow a tempestuous or discordant piece in a recital, to say nothing of its undoubted use as a prelude to a service, to set a mood of repose and contemplation.

When writing in this vein – and in others too – Bairstow's music is the very reverse of note-spinning. Never would he write for the sake of writing. Every note had to be imbued with the fullest meaning, such as are found in the anthems 'If the Lord had not helped me' and 'Lord, I call upon thee' as well as the violin variations.

Next came the *Scherzo in A flat*, his only piece to be published by Novello, in 1906. In a programme note he declared it to be 'a light and humorous piece, using the word humorous in its broadest and best sense.' Later, in an unguarded moment he said 'It's flick music' and, again, not quite the kind of product he would like to look back on during the more austere post-war years. But later, when the value of a lighter style came to be appreciated, its waltzing lilt and fine craftsmanship are such as many composers would have been happy enough to acknowledge. The middle section, in the same tempo, is a contrast both thematically and tonally, with its firm *forte legato* diapason combination, the outer sections being played on flutes and a solo oboe. The coda, taking up the whole of the last page, is playful and contains some delightful surprises. It was recorded on a player roll by William Wolstenholme.

Three pieces appeared in 1907. *Prelude in C* is a forthright statement in the manner of a *toccata* with a strong diatonic tune in the pedals, the *toccata* figuration being derived from it. A central section based on the same theme, but well contrasted, alternates imposing chorale-like phrases on the diapasons with passages of the *toccata* semiquavers on the full swell. It ends with a burst of tuba in the neapolitan key of D flat, a rapid upward *arpeggio* over almost the complete manual compass, and a decisive double tonic chord to finish. (See page 146)

Meditation, of the same year, is headed by the first verse of Wesley's hymn 'Thou hidden love of God'. Bairstow had already set this hymn as a male voice anthem and had also provided a tune for it in the 1904 A&M hymn book. The words would seem to have had a deep effect on him. The solemn repeated tonic chord of A major which starts the piece suggests the wonder of the love 'whose height, Whose depth, unfathomed, no man knows', and Bairstow's favourite device of juxtaposing triads (here of A G B A-minor and F) heightens the effect. Suddenly, though, a *più moto* descending succession of diminished sevenths, beginning *sforzando*, allude surely to 'My heart is pained', and an unquiet oboe solo seems to point to the remaining words 'Nor can it be At rest, till it find rest in thee'. It ends as it began, solemnly and peacefully. There is much beauty in this piece and, as with the *Nocturne*, it can engender a suitable pre-service mood.

The remaining piece from 1907 is *Legend*: here again it is tune and accompaniment. The latter consists of arpeggiated chords in a one-bar syncopated figure which persists throughout the first and third sections. The second and fourth are tempestuous and employ the same method of repetition, this time with a two-bar figure. Rachmaninoff and Tschaikowsky are not far distant in this rather symphonic piece; indeed the style of writing could well suggest an orchestral transcription.

Prelude, Elegy and *Toccata-Prelude* followed in 1911. With the lapse of a mere four years, Bairstow's style has matured. The two preludes, on plainsong tunes *Vexilla Regis* and *Pange Lingua,* are fine examples of his vivid, forthright manner in which every note is in its right place. The latter is one of the best organ pieces of its period and, with its scintillating staccato figuration in five-four time, must have had an electrifying effect when it first burst upon the world. Even today it retains this same power. Before this date very few chorale preludes had been written in this country, and Parry's first set, as well as the two books by Charles Wood, came out the year after these of Bairstow's.

Like the *Prelude in C, Pange Lingua* begins as a *toccata* with the theme strongly in the bass. The first section ends with a *diminuendo* and a pause, to be followed by a complete contrast in the shape of soft *legato* chords which then become more chromatic. Gradually life begins to return with the *toccata* motif and with a *crescendo* which terminates in a dazzling flourish down the keyboard and up again – 'the bit they all got right' at the RCO exam, as he once said in a slightly mischievous mood – and this ushers in the recapitulation. This is a very characteristic work, brimming with vitality, with sharp contrasts. Registration can present problems which nowadays can, of course, be abolished by general pistons. As to interpretation, a temptation can present itself to slacken the tempo in the central section which begins on the third page. No mention is made in the copy, of any alteration of tempo, and none should be attempted. The composer was always insistent that the printed text should be faithfully adhered to. Had he wanted a different speed he would assuredly have indicated as much.

Vexilla Regis is quite different. Starting softly it gradually generates energy and finishes on full organ with ascending tuba octaves in the left hand. It follows the form used by Pachelbel in which each line of the tune is used for a *fughetta* which culminates in a statement of that line as a *cantus firmus*. It is romantic writing, requiring additions and subtractions of stops for the frequent dynamic changes, and thumbing is employed for the purpose of highlighting the chorale at one point, for which the music is written on four staves. Though it is apparently intended to be played by the left hand, it would seem wise to distribute the notes between both thumbs. (The four-stave layout makes the part-writing clear and could, incidentally, be a help to one's score-reading prowess.) As the music increases in excitement, from crotchets to quavers and then to triplet quavers, the harmony becomes more chromatic and shows Bairstow's facility in using chromaticism for virility, almost asperity, rather than for near-sentimentality as sometimes in the quiet pieces.

Between the two preludes stands the *Elegy* as a sharp contrast. It begins and ends in B flat minor with sad melodic strains on string tone and Cor Anglais. The central section consists of two elements – a flowing phrase already heard in the pedals, and a chorale on the Echo Gamba marked *ppp* as if to suggest the singing of a distant choir. Again the writing is orchestral but the choral element is an additional feature which does not occur elsewhere in Bairstow's *oeuvre*. The most notable orchestral effect is a muffled drum imitation. Instructions are given in a footnote: 'Heavy 16ft. Diapasons and Bourdon; put all in except Bourdon, at the *pianissimo*' which is positioned just after the first beat of the bar. This, from the start, sets the tone of what is a heavy-laden elegiac piece which very much lives up to its title. Though it was, at one time, thought little of by its composer, it is a fine piece, extremely appropriate on memorial occasions.

It had long been Bairstow's ambition to write an organ sonata – to write several, in fact, so that at least one of them would survive. At last he got round to composing the first – and only – one, composing a good deal of it while on holiday in the Isle of Arran in August 1937, the month of his sixty-third birthday. The *Sonata in E flat* was published in the following spring by Oxford University Press and received its first performance by Doctor Willis Grant in Manchester Town Hall on 2 March 1938. In the following month, during Easter week, it was played for the second time (by FJ) for the Cathedral Organists' Conference, in session at York.

By coincidence it was published at the same time as the *Sonata in A minor* by William H. Harris, and both were reviewed in *The Organ* of January 1939: 'Both', it thought, 'are characterised by those feelings of restraint, of serenity and good taste that are widely described as *English*, – a term perhaps difficult to define, but none the less apparent in its implications. ... The grave serene charm of much of the first movement and the elegiac ending of the final fugue strike us as the most beautiful parts of this attractive work.' Harvey Grace in *Musical Times* was analytical and highly enthusiastic, rating the third movement highest.

Unfortunately it did not become widely used and had only occasional performances in recital programmes. Thus it was allowed to go out of print for some years except, happily, the middle movement which, standing alone, acquired the title *Scherzo*, this on the grounds that its composer used to refer to it by that name. However, more happily still, the complete work was issued again, in an attractive cover similar to the well-known pre-war Oxford design. This undoubtedly enabled it to become better known, and a change in the prevailing climate encouraged more organists to take it into their repertoire. It may have been the war that had discouraged its dissemination, as well as the preoccupation with modern music of a very different nature – neo-classical – twelve-tone – against which romantic works were dismissed as out-of-date. After more than half a century it becomes possible to regard a work historically, and, in the same way as in 1937 we could look at the later works of Brahms and Liszt, the Franck Chorals or the Elgar sonata, so the Bairstow sonata is seen, after a similar lapse of time, as thoroughly characteristic of its late romantic period, the work of a composer brought up during the last years of Victoria's reign who had imbibed its influences and those of Edwardian England as well as of Brahms and Debussy, and had himself pursued a continuous quest for, above all things, beauty in music. Not only do these echoes appear in the sonata (the whole-tone scale in three places) but prowess in invention – augmentation, diminution, inversion and suchlike – is given full scope in the fugue, sonata form being clearly presented in the first movement. Such formulae, though, are used only for expressive purpose, as a framework on which to hang his poetical ideas and not for the sake of mere academicism.

The outer movements are slow and quiet at their beginnings and endings, rising to a climax in between. The central movement, *allegro giocoso,* does the opposite, starting vigorously and extremely rhythmically in the mediant key of G major and settling down to a more sober mood in the middle, to rise from thence once more to the initial busyness by way of a short and rather spectacular pedal solo, and ending with a triumphant prance. Bairstow had wanted his *Scherzo* to be – as he put it – 'a real devil' and he surely succeeded so far as its energetic and mischievous side is concerned and because it is none too easy to play. The sonata is romantic organ music at its best, making use, as it does, of the changing colours of the palette without posing undue problems of stop control, and producing music which sounds like organ music rather than a transcription from an orchestral score.

b. CHURCH MUSIC
1. Anthems

We know the date of publication but not always when a work was composed. Most of them, one assumes, were sent off to publishers immediately on completion, but a notable exception was one of his finest anthems, *Let all mortal flesh keep silence,* which bears the date 1925. It was, in fact, composed in 1906, a remarkable circumstance since it was in the midst of his youthful flamboyance, and contemporary with the evening service in D with which it has very little, if anything, in common. He was then thirty-two. This anthem is prophetic of his later period, when his music became simpler and less showy. It is quite innocent, too, of the Victorian-Edwardian chromaticisms which he used in the early years of the new century and which, later, became anathema to him. Its outstanding quality is without doubt due to the effect on him of the mystical nature of the words, a very different matter from some of his other *libretti*. It is the only one of the pre-war period, moreover, which has no organ accompaniment. Was this, perhaps, one reason for its being unacceptable for publication in the opulent days of comfortable Edwardian living when unaccompanied singing could have been too spartan, and before the sixteenth century composers had been revived without any organ to support the voices? It was only after the Great War that he wrote any more unaccompanied pieces, and this was due, perhaps, to the effect of the Tudor and Stuart compositions which were, around that time, emerging from their long oblivion. There is an interesting alteration made by the composer on his manuscript copy which resides at Leeds Parish Church. It is in the second chord of the second *Alleluia* where the tenors sing an E: this was originally an E sharp. Its original key, too, was F minor. Perhaps it was too low for the basses, and, in the higher key the altos could reach the high C sharp (which he did, however, make optional for those who found it difficult).

The effect of words can be seen elsewhere – in the 1910 anthem *If the Lord had not helped me*, the genesis of which he describes on page 80. It is intensely serious, in its E flat minor key, for the words 'it had not failed but my soul had been put to silence'. But after an energetic middle section working up to a galvanising climax and a dramatic silence, a recapitulation in C minor is ushered in by a bass solo, and tension finally releases for 'thy mercy, O Lord, held me up'. This is all very deeply felt and is one of the best of his anthems. A practical point of interest concerns the *accelerando* on page 7 leading to the *Allegro con spirito* section. In his performances at York the composer used to double the speed immediately the 4/2 tempo was reached, obviating any need for a gradual speeding-up and effectively starting the *minim=120* two bars earlier than indicated in the score.

The words of *Come ye gentles* are of a different calibre. 'Come ye gentles, hear the story How the blessed mother maid Bare on earth the king of glory Lowly in a manger laid'. They are the work of the Reverend Edgar Rogers M.A. whose words he used elsewhere. Here, what is described as a Carol-anthem portrays the rocking of the cradle in 9/8 time, provides a suggestion of harps at the mention of angels, and, after a *pianissimo* mention of swaddling clothes, bursts *fortissimo* into 'saving us from death and hell'. This work was not in the repertoire at York, along with the anthems of 1901, 1903, 1904, 1906, 1909, 1911 and *I will greatly rejoice* from 1913.

The attractive and ingenuous carol for treble voices with solo, entitled *The Blessed Virgin's Cradle Song*, was written in his late teenage period and was one for which he always retained an affection. It has great appeal, and the words are by the same Mr. Rogers, his clerical colleague of the Wigan days. Every Christmas saw it as the prime favourite in the Festival of Nine Lessons and Carols at York. After rehearsing it one day, ECB was very pleased when Darby Tredger (one of the choristers) said to him "You must have been feeling very happy when you wrote that, Sir". "He's just about got it right", was the composer's delighted comment.

The male voice anthem *Thou hidden love of God* has all the indications of being written at the turn of the century – the calligraphy (similar to that of his D. Mus. exercise), some Victorian harmonies, a throbbing syncopated accompanimental figuration, and a rather flamboyant, operatic tenor solo such as was in favour at that period. The reason for its existence is less easy to determine. It has some of the composer's distinctive hallmarks, notably the careful attention to the meaning of words, the sense of puzzlement in the second line – 'Whose depth unfathomed no man knows', and the confident tone of the last verse 'Then shall my heart from earth be free, When it hath found repose in Thee', the music of which is a reprise of the beginning but with a passionate climax. We note his attachment to these words of Wesley in connexion with the organ piece *Meditation* and the hymn tune *Clamavi*.

The words of the early anthems *God who at sundry times* and *Blessed be thou, Lord God of Israel* were selected from holy writ and end with a poem or hymn. Three verses of 'Angels from the realms of glory', the well-known words of James Montgomery, conclude the former; and the latter, composed for the reopening of the Wigan organ in 1902, calls again upon the work of Rogers for its final section. At the age of twenty-eight the composer's characteristic style is clearly apparent, and such early compositions, though not equal to his greatest achievements, are by no means negligible in quality and deserve serious consideration: the perfectionist was discernible at this tender age. These pieces have a well-written organ part which, as always, is not easy, inclining towards complexity, needing careful practice and preparation: also good vocal writing, singable but containing an occasional infelicitous underlay with slightly awkward accentuation. As he gained in experience, however, such minor blemishes disappear and his word-setting becomes faultless. He is always at pains to express fully the meaning of the text: 'Let all mortal flesh' is earthbound and austere, sung by deep basses in octaves with the tenors, but is followed by the upper voices, now in harmony, lifting us above all earthly thought. In *God who at sundry times,* a Christmas anthem of 1909, the words (from the epistle for the day) 'who, being the brightness of his glory' are given poetic treatment by three-part alto-soprano chords which go up the *arpeggio* and down again. In *Save us, O Lord* 'Save us waking' is sung by the high voices, and 'guard us sleeping' softly an octave lower by the tenors and basses. Twenty-eight years later, and aged fifty-six, he similarly treats the word 'fear' in the Easter anthem *The day draws on with golden light,* one of his favourite sudden chromatic chords making the point. *Save us, O Lord* was written for the Wigan and District Church Choral Association in 1902 and has retained its popularity ever since, despite – or because of – its period flavour and on account of its reasonable standard of difficulty with which most church choirs of moderate attainment can cope.

A less successful attempt was published two years later by the Vincent Music Company, a Christmas carol with words by Bishop Phillips Brookes, author of *O little town of Bethlehem.* It begins:

> The earth has grown old with its burden of care,
> But at Christmas it always is young:
> The heart of the jewel burns lustrous and fair,
> And its soul full of music breaks forth on the air,
> When the song of the angels is sung.

Though there are welcome modulations, the overall style is somewhat commonplace, and the unremitting rhythm of crotchet and two quavers brings about some infelicitous word accentuations.

Another early anthem – of 1903 – *The promise which was made,* takes its words from Acts 13, the gospel for Easter Tuesday. After a substantial introduction declaimed in a broad unison, with joyful high chords for 'He raised up Jesus again', a treble solo sings the well-known passage from the Song of Solomon, 'For lo, the winter is past ...' the accompaniment providing a suitable background suggestive of springtime. After a reprise of the first part a short *fugato* brings an affirmative ending.

Then followed, three years later, another Easter anthem with words from Romans and Colossians – 'Know ye not'. It begins with a recitative section and then moves into a substantial soprano solo (*andante religioso)* joined by trebles and altos in a trio. This ends conclusively in E flat and a bright *allegro con spirito* in G major follows, an independent movement owing nothing to what has gone before.

By 1911, and with cheerful Easter words, he begins *Sing ye to the Lord* with an arresting trumpet fanfare in his bold, confident fashion. Soon come the makings of a tune, presented tentatively, but eventually burgeoning into fullest unison magnificence. The ending is a triumphant reprise of the beginning.

I will greatly rejoice was published around the time Bairstow moved from Leeds to York. A harvest anthem, it has noble tunes with warm, colourful harmonies in the Edwardian manner. The greater part is occupied with the words used by Parry in *Hear my words –* 'For as the earth bringeth forth her bud...' with the appropriate upward leap at 'to spring forth'.

On his transferring to York in 1913, his first anthem written there was one that has become universally known and loved – *Blessed city* – founded on the Mode II melody and an object-lesson in the use of a somewhat lengthy text avoiding any danger of discursiveness. On the contrary, the composition hangs together in a wonderful way. It is really a set of variations which are contrasted and characterised to suit each situation as it comes along, beginning

with the explosive beginning announcing the theme, and continuing with a treble section whose first note is not of the tune but a
far more arresting one a third higher; a brilliant men's verse, again
starting on the higher note, and with strong organ chords to accompany; leading to 'pain and tribulation' with a most descriptive
discord; then a tense passage which gives place to a vigorous chorus
depicting the building of the heavenly kingdom, succeeded by an
organ interlude carrying on the climax to its utmost height, then
gradually diminishing and leading into the calm of the final verse
in which the melody is conveyed by the lower voices in slow block
chords which support a solo treble's arabesque: one of Bairstow's
finest thoughts. This was written for churches in Heaton, Bradford,
in 1914 and has a version of accompaniment for string orchestra
(with a part for piano at the climax) which was probably done for
some special situation. The powerful music, though, seems to call
out for greater resources – a full orchestra at least or, failing that,
the addition of a potent organ to the string version.

In the same way *Lord, I call upon thee* shows him at his most
poetic, with rising clouds of incense portrayed in the accompaniment as well as some delectable Debussyan harmonies (see p. 152).
This was 1916. The following year *Lord, thou hast been our refuge*
was commissioned for the Festival of the Sons of the Clergy at St.
Paul's Cathedral. It has accompaniment for full orchestra and is
one of his biggest anthems, full of melody, colourful harmony and
dramatic treatment of the words, especially at 'man is like a thing
of nought, his time passeth away like a shadow', the last word
uttered in a breathy whisper. Some may say it is over-sentimental,
or too pompous; others, that it is nothing more or less than a very
imaginative account of these words from Psalm 90. It is the high
point, the apotheosis and summation of an Edwardian composer,
writing in the darkest days of war-torn Britain.

After this, as we have noted, Bairstow's style becomes less
elaborate and, perhaps as a result, more meaningful and expressive. The three unaccompanied introits of 1925 capture in a
nutshell the kernel of the music's message. The first, *I sat down
under his shadow* begins with alternating triads of E major and G
major, the tenor tune being accompanied by the other voices in
their lowest register. The altos next take the melody and the full

choir then sings in delectable harmonies of the sweet taste of the fruit. A passionate climax is soon reached and a return to the opening music for a hushed ending.

Jesu, the very thought of thee is the longest although it uses only the first verse of Saint Bernard's hymn. In his characteristic way – each word being given the utmost consideration – 'thought' appears in a sudden *pianissimo*, the trebles' high note to which it is set appearing as a mere whisper – twice – the second time a step higher. 'Sweetness' receives exactly the right amount of harmonic colour, and 'sweeter far' leads on to the climax at 'thy face to see'. The peaceful final bars are utterly expressive of repose, including four whole beats of silence – a daring gesture but amply justified.

I will wash my hands in innocency begins with a quasi recitative in which the major triads of B (the tonic) and D are juxtaposed – to express innocence. A brief ecstatic climax soon comes for 'tell of all thy wondrous works', then a contemplative contrapuntal four bars speak of love of the habitation 'and the place where thine honour dwelleth'. Four words of firm unison recitative – 'my foot standeth right' – give place to a brilliant ending in harmony with all voices in their high register.

Slight in length, so designed for the start of the eucharist, each one of the introits is a masterpiece of the highest quality, containing more inspiration than is sometimes found in many a work of far greater length.

Though I speak with the tongues of men has been widely sung: it depicts all the aspects of Saint Paul's words – sounding brass and tinkling cymbal, the *kindness* of charity. This last word, 'charity', has its own *leitmotif*, a falling phrase which is always heard with it. ECB was aware that this work might be compared to Brahms' setting of the same words – probably unfavourably – but took the risk. It is, of course, quite different and in another medium: it has been welcomed and, so far as is known, without criticism.

For Holy Week he wrote *As Moses lifted up the serpent* in 1931. As the basses sing the opening words to a rising phrase suggestive of a serpent – and including the augmented fourth (the *diabolus in musica*) – the trebles and altos accompany by leapfrogging each other and resolving the resulting intervals of a second. Then there is a central section in nine-eight time for the words 'For God so loved the world' which he chose in the hope that it would provide an alternative to Stainer's setting which he did not like. This, however, has not come about. It is, however, a fine, unusual and original piece with a strong atmosphere completely in accord with the penitential season and is not easy, intonation being the main problem.

Another anthem, again unaccompanied, from the following year (1932) was probably thought too difficult, even for the average cathedral choir of the time. *Our Father in the heavens* is in F sharp major (G flat at the recapitulation..) and has divisions in all voices with some awkward (not unpleasant) harmonic quirks. It certainly needs a confident choir and is very effective when well sung. The words are a metrical paraphrase of the Lord's Prayer by J.Leask and are probably different enough to allow of their being sung as an anthem in a service where the normal version already appears. As a concert item it is first class.

The introit he composed for the 1937 coronation, *Let my prayer come up into thy presence,* though a miniature, is one of his most perfect conceptions. Here, for the second time, he suggests the rising clouds of incense by upward-curling rosalias in the accompaniment (which is originally for orchestra) and employs some choice harmonies. The idea occurred to him while he was in the bath, from which he called for music paper to write it down before he could forget it.

As well as *Blessed City* and *The day draws on with golden light* three other anthems are founded on hymns. The earliest of them, *Of the Father's love begotten,* dates from 1913 and is, like its successor, a series of variations, this time on the 1582 melody from *Piae Cantiones* known as *Divinum Mysterium.* The men sing the first verse and are followed by a beautiful counter melody for trebles in *siciliano* rhythm with the tune in the bass as a *cantus firmus* in long notes, hardly discernible except to the initiated. The words 'O that birth for ever blessed' are sung in hushed tones with the utmost reverence and the ending is a rousing and exciting chorus with a climactic buildup to the final *Amen.*

Jesu, grant me this, I pray came into being as descants and *faux-bourdons* were being considered with Sydney Nicholson, then at Westminster Abbey. This turned out to be beyond the scope of a congregation, but it became a greatly valued choir piece. The first verse is sung straight; the second is a *faux-bourdon*; verse three has the tune in the tenor part and some quite elaborate embroidery in the other voices. The last verse – 'Death will come to me one day' – has the tune in the bass, with moving effect. (See page 164)

The day draws on is a sensitive and poetical impression of a calm ending to an eastertide day when contentment and thankfulness are uppermost in the mind. It is conceived as for a choir weak in tenors and is in three voice parts except for one phrase. The lovely Angers melody lends itself admirably to the composer's subtle treatment in his characteristic style, contrasting 'glad songs ... echoing through the height' (high voices) with the moanings of the deep (bass and tenor) in suitable chromatic organ chords, the whole suffused with a golden glow of peace and tranquillity as the day draws to its close.

The King of Love is well known. Founded on the tune *Saint Columba* it begins with a solo line on the organ suggesting a shepherd's pipe – and ends with the same and a high six-four chord to make the finish indeterminate so that it continues in the listener's mind. Verse two is a canon; the men's voices are heard bravely confronting the situation in death's dark vale; the spreading of the table with unction is full of comfort; and the trebles, next, have a counterpoint against the tune played high on the organ, each phrase closely following the mood suggested by the words – 'gently on his shoulder laid' is almost a caress, and the dotted figure, illustrative of happiness and rejoicing. This piece was written on holiday when no text was available, which accounts for the wrong order of the verses (see page 311). From experience it can be declared that half a century of association with the piece, and constant performances, failed to reveal the fact to at any rate one choirmaster!

Described as a Christmas Hymn, *While shepherds watched* was published posthumously. One is inclined to ask why the old favourite tunes had to be supplanted in favour of an entirely new one – in a pastoral six-eight time. It is a quite different approach, not without success, and bears the composer's imprint in the alternative harmonizations of the six verses – 'mighty dread' and 'troubled mind' for example. The first verse is given to the upper voices, the next three to the men in unison. The fifth verse, 'Thus spake the seraph' begins with a commanding descant, soon to be joined by the hymn tune in an ingenious canon between the upper and lower voices. Only the last verse is in four-part harmony. This is certainly not a negligible product and would be very welcome in many churches.

2. Services

Bairstow's service settings are of interest as illustrating each a different facet of his output, that in D major the first period, the E flat post-war, and the Evening in G six years before his death. This last has very gradually gained ground and become better known since it was first published in 1940. As with the Organ Sonata, the war was probably one reason for its failure to be taken up more widely. It may be considered by some to be more acceptable than the *Magnificat* and *Nunc Dimittis* in D, composed thirty-four years earlier, as being less showy and extrovert, quieter and more devotional. It took this form in reaction against a setting shewn him by H.K. Andrews which he thought alien to the spirit of the canticle. Although stated to be in the key of G, there is a flat in the key signature rather than a sharp as might reasonably be expected, making it look like F major or D minor. It is, in fact, in a transposed Dorian mode. The *Nunc Dimittis* is appropriately solemn, yet positive in feeling, the trebles being given an optional high E on the word *peace* at the end of the first phrase, which aptly sets the mood. A dotted-note motif in a six-four bar is a valuable germ which repeats several times as a one-bar *ostinato*, and there is a build-up to an imposing ending. The *Gloria*, common to both canticles, is a canon between choir and organ and, in its quicker tempo, comes joyfully after what has gone before.

The date of composition of the Morning Service in D is not known, but was probably during his early York years. It was originally for double choir, in which form he always performed it at York, from single-part manuscript copies (made by Freddie Elam). It was published by Stainer and Bell in 1925 in a four-part version with divisions. This adaptation does not adversely affect the music, which is some of his finest (but see p. 326). It is grand, descriptive and dramatic, but in a more controlled way than in the Evening Service. It is an interesting fusion of measured notes and speech rhythm, founded on what is really an anglican chant, starting on the tonic, moving by two steps up to the mediant, then back to the tonic. It is then given to different voices and moved to various degrees of the scale, displacing the semitones – a method he used more than once and which proved fruitful, especially in the *Te Deum*. The treatment of 'in glory everlasting' is characteristic, pointing the mystical nature of the words; and the piece ends, not on the tonic, but on a chord of the dominant. The *Benedictus* is similarly treated, using material from the *Te Deum* for part of the *Gloria*. Both these canticles can be sung without accompaniment: the *Te Deum* was used regularly in this manner at York at the end of evensong on Easter Day.

The Communion Service in D is one of ECB's biggest, boldest efforts deserving to be better known and more frequently used. It could be dubbed 'Wagnerian' not only in the nature of its harmonies, but also in its scale, and its ebullience. As such, to more ascetic tastes it is anathema: Dean Milner-White found it hard to take and needed some persuasion to allow performances at York. On page 86 the composer speaks of the motivation for writing the work – the opening of the Leeds organ in 1913 – and mentions his use of the *leitmotif*, quoting not Wagner, however, but Elgar as the main influence. The first of the themes is introduced in the Responses to the Commandments, 'Lord, have mercy upon us'. This rises a fourth by steps and then falls by a fourth and a minor third. It reappears at the same words in the *Gloria in Excelsis* complete with its evocative harmony.

The second – and main – theme is in the organ introduction to the Creed. Later it is altered, beginning on the third note, to become the *ostinato* which underpins the *Sanctus*. Here it is in the relative minor key, and in six-four time, with a noticeable triplet and dotted-note figure. This gives it a slightly jaunty aspect which, since the appearance of, say, Poulenc's religious music some half-century later, may not now offend as once it might have done. Against this the choir, in unison at first, intones a solemn low tune which gradually increases in pitch and volume, to a blaze of major key at 'Heaven and earth are full of thy glory', the *ostinato* persisting until the very end. This is followed by the *Benedictus* (see page 158) in complete contrast, its gentle introduction suggestive of distant bells, the upper voices entering in three parts in contemplative mood. This is suddenly dispelled, however, as the tenors and basses enter, confidently, in unison: but the magical ending is achieved with the never-failing juxtaposition of triads (here F and D).

The *Gloria* has its slightly operatic moments in somewhat emotional solos by the same three voices as in the *Agnus Dei* (bass, tenor, treble) for the same words 'Thou that takest away the sins of the world', and the *kyrie* theme appears for 'Have mercy upon us': the *Sanctus ostinato* is used, appropriately, for 'For thou only art holy'. Altogether, this is an inspired *magnum opus* by an Edwardian composer at the height of his powers, exulting in the joy of creating music for a fine new modern organ and a magnificent choir which possessed the necessary stamina to do it full justice, especially at climactic points such as that in the Creed where the choir divides into two for 'And the third day he rose again'. Indeed, perhaps for its fullest effect, a sizeable choral society (which is more or less what the Leeds Parish Church Choir at that period seems to have resembled) or a joining of three or more cathedral choirs, would be a realistic notion, supported by a powerful, colourful organ, or, perhaps better still, by an orchestra – with organ – if such an arrangement could be achieved.

The D major evening service was, as we have noted, written in the same year as *Let all mortal flesh keep silence*, unlike which piece it is ebullient and Wagnerian. He was fond of relating how, at an early performance, the priest, who was hearing it for the first time, was so overcome with the excitement of the *Gloria* of the *Nunc Dimittis* that he was for a while unable to start the Creed. The composer's own performances of this used to include an alteration in the fourth bar from the end where he doubled the note values, producing an extra bar. Thus are the orchestral parts written – those that survive, namely the string parts and an organ part containing a few bars at climaxes and a few soft thirty-two-foot notes elsewhere. But it is obvious that a fuller orchestra was intended, as is shewn in the introduction to the *Magnificat* where the topmost voice of the accompaniment does not appear in the string parts. This would presumably be played by the woodwind. Any score that would have existed has been lost. Some of the surviving band parts are in the handwriting of Freddie Elam (see letter 22 December 1942, page 204) which could indicate that the orchestration was made after Bairstow's move to York in 1913 – seven or more years after its publication – and it could have been done especially for the patronal festival at Saint Paul's Cathedral on 25 January 1922. An orchestra was usually used for this occasion together with a selection from Mendelssohn's *Oratorio*. This fact also provides a clue to the size of orchestra which might have been employed for the canticles.

The following year the service in D appeared again in the annual Festival of the Sons of the Clergy on 29 May along with *A Song of Praise* by Benjamin Dale. No doubt it was due to Bairstow's friendship with Charles Macpherson that his music was chosen for these occasions. Macpherson was appointed to Saint Paul's in 1916, and the following year Bairstow's commissioned anthem *Lord, thou hast been our refuge* was sung in the same festival service.

Orchestra was also used over in the west country, at the opening service of the Three Choirs' Festival. Bairstow in D, though, was not used there. He seems to have had very little, if any, connexion with this organisation, unlike his York predecessor, T.T. Noble, who in 1934 came to Gloucester and conducted his B minor evening service clad in his full dress Oxford (Lambeth) robes. When I told ECB that I had been present and had witnessed this, he did not seem to be aware that Noble in B minor had been orchestrated. 'It's not worth it' was his immediate and characteristic reaction.

The first of the E-flat canticles dates from 1900. This is a *Benedicite* and it followed the usual pattern of the period, including every word. The tune, or chant, is given *faux-bourdon* treatment, appearing in turn in all voices, and there is descriptive writing where appropriate. For present-day use some cuts are needed, to avoid tiresome repetition. This is possible now that it is not considered impolite to truncate holy writings, and accordingly such a version has been prepared which retains all the essential features and preserves a colourful period setting for this somewhat awkward canticle; but it is not published.

The rest of the E flat service appeared in 1923. This, though it may at first seem a modest achievement, is seen, on closer acquaintance, to contain the full fruition of Bairstow's genius and experience. The music is assured, poised, and always appropriate to the words, with no over-emphasis on descriptiveness. The *Te Deum*, like that in D, is a mixture of recitative and measured notes, the latter appearing for the first time at the words 'Holy, holy, holy, Lord God of Sabaoth' on a falling octave against strong diatonic discords. This is the same music as that of the *Sanctus* of the Communion Service. 'We therefore pray thee help thy servants' is set to an affecting tune which slowly rises and then falls in an expressive manner. Further use is made of it, and the falling octave is heard again at 'Vouchsafe, O Lord' before a crescendo leads to a confident affirmation of the last sentence. The method of using elements of psalm-singing in what is a very long canticle and tricky to set to music, was deployed with complete success in these two instances and in no way diminished the grandeur of the concept.

The *Benedictus* begins with an engagingly fresh, rising theme, which is extended and repeated, rondo-wise until, at the words 'And thou, child, shalt be called the prophet of the highest' an ingenious canon by inversion is played on the organ pedals against the voices. The first theme is recapitulated at the words 'Through the tender mercy of our God', though by the organ, the singers pursuing another course more suitable to the verbal accents. The *Gloria*, which is used again for both evening canticles, is terse and rhythmical, making significant use of the flattened seventh of the scale.

The Communion Service contains the usual five movements as well as the responses to the Commandments. These last contain several different harmonisations of the same melody to supply variety in a repetitive exercise. They have provided material, along with part of the *Sanctus,* for a nine-fold *Kyrie Eleison* (the work of other hands) which is now included in the printed copy. The Creed is built on the opening intonation, following Stanford's procedure in his service in B flat. Here again the music is direct and positive but is at pains to point the mystery of the incarnation with characteristic romantic chromaticisms.

The nobility of the *Sanctus* is followed by a contrasting *Benedictus qui venit* of a gently light-hearted nature in seven-four time, an original idea at that period which is in complete accord with the spirit and metre of the words. The *Agnus Dei* is extremely simple vocally, with expressive interludes between each strain. The *Gloria in excelsis* begins in brisk six-four time, and for the central section the voices change to two minims in the bar while the organ continues the threes of the original tempo. That so much artifice and inspiration should have gone into the making of what was no doubt intended by the publishers to be an easy setting for incomplete choirs is an illustration of Bairstow's determination to make as perfect as possible whatever he undertook. The music throughout is some of his best, and it is a pity that four-part choirs could be discouraged from making full and regular use of it. Another factor against its use, this time by village choirs, is the undue difficulty of the organ part – a usual situation as we have already seen in his works. Perhaps there is a case for some judicious rearrangement of parts of this unison service so that its fine music may reach wider acceptance by competent four-part choirs and their organists, for, though it may at first seem beneath the dignity of a highly trained choir to waste its talent on something so apparently simple, closer acquaintance will surely commend to the perceptive musician what is undoubtedly a splendid work which ought to be universally known and appreciated. The evening canticles are of the same high standard as the rest of the service. Doctor George Gray related how, as a student, he saw at his weekly lesson, a little more of the music as it was produced, and quoted him as saying 'My music is wrung out of me bar by bar'. But Bairstow in E flat is splendid music and bears no hint of any such difficulty.

It may be thought unfortunate that he did not write more services. However, here are three, each with its own distinct character and of a high degree of excellence. This makes the invidious task of selection unnecessary, for all of them are worthy of a permanent place in the repertoire, providing music of various moods as needed.

The two *Kyries* were written to supply a need caused by the substitution of the Summary of the Law in place of the

Commandments, a move made by the new Dean, Eric Milner-White. They are a contrasting pair, the one unaccompanied, with diatonic discords, the other in a flowing triple time with leisurely organ interludes. Both have a devotional feeling appropriate to the text. Neither was published. Also remaining in manuscript are the unaccompanied *Benedictus qui venit* and *Agnus Dei* which are mostly in block chords with divided voices. His harmonisations of the Merbecke *Lord's Prayer* and *Sursum Corda*, today considered unnecessary, are nevertheless beautifully done and are an object-lesson in discretion and economy. They were privately printed sometime during the nineteen-thirties, long before the days of easy desk-top publishing.

3. Hymn Tunes (by Donald Webster)

Despite his subsequent high regard for English Hymnal, Bairstow's earliest tunes to be published in a major hymnal were *Clamavi* (8.8.8.8.8.8) set in the 1904 edition of Hymns Ancient and Modern to 'Thou hidden love of God' – one of John Wesley's greatest hymns; and *Minster Court* (8.8.7.7.7.7.4) set in the 1916 edition to H. Twells' hymn 'Know ye the Lord hath borne away'.

The former flirts initially with the Mixolydian mode, a mannerism one finds in other of ECB's compositions, and the dactylic rhythm at the beginning of each of the last four lines avoids monotony. Unfortunately there are some instances of unhappy marriage between these words and the music. Even so, the near-sequential treatment of lines three and four gives shape to the tune, and it could be a useful companion to a more metrically flexible text. Apart from alternation of unison and harmony lines there is little of merit in *Minster Court* as it meanders for long stretches around a few notes. His tune *Eboracum* makes interesting points in its 8.7.8.7 metre, but the overall effect is too contrived and lacking in spontaneity for it to be a rival to *Marching* – or even to *St. Oswald* or *Rustington*.

A collection of Twenty Hymns for National use in Time of War, published jointly by Stainer and Bell and Banks of York in 1914 contains seven tunes by Bairstow. Unfortunately, none is given a name or has found its way into other collections.

No. 1. A spacious L.M. tune exploits tonic and dominant thematic relationships between lines one and two, and three and four.

No. 2. A seven-line tune – 6.6.6.4.8.8.4 – Lines five and six are treated sequentially, but in truth the melodic idea is insufficiently strong to bear such treatment.

No. 5. Of six lines – 6.6.8.4.8.8 – Melodically rather poverty-stricken, and containing two patches of weak, static harmony.

No. 15. A Litany – 7.7.7.6 – Lines one and two are treated sequentially, but once again, in his fear of the obvious, Bairstow has had to resort to calculation.

No. 16. An unpretentious S.M. tune which could well be revived.

No. 18. A 10.10.10.10 tune that has shape of a rather unappealing kind. It was, no doubt, written with these rather mawkish words in mind – or so they appear to our generation.

No. 20. A Requiem about which much the same might be said.

But Bairstow was not the only distinguished composer who experienced difficulty in writing hymn tunes. Stanford with *Engelberg* and Howells with *Michael* achieved greatness only once, so far as the hymn-singing public was concerned, and each had to wait a long time to attain it. Posthumous glory, though, surely awaits *Huntington* despite its fortuitous career. In its original form it was part of a Coronation Hymn Collection of 1911 and was set to words whose imperial pretensions betray their date all too clearly. Mr. Nelson Walmsley showed the tune to Mr. Simon Lindley. He and Dr. Jackson decided that with minor alteration, chiefly in metre, Bairstow's opus could be a solid joy and a lasting treasure to the Church's hymnody. The unusual metre – 10.7.10.7.10.8.10.8 – would obviously pose problems for a versifier, but the Reverend Caryl Micklem's beautiful paraphrase of Psalm 95 fits the music with ease and distinction. Its first performance took place at the 1994 Yorkshire Three Choirs Festival, where it was received with the utmost enthusiasm.

For one who admires Bairstow as both musician and composer, an examination of his original hymn tunes (apart from this one exception), is rather a depressing experience. Since he showed in his treatment of pre-existing material immense affection for hymnody, notably in his anthems 'Blessed City' and 'The King of Love' as well as in several descants and free harmonisations, this is all the more surprising. *Richmond* seems to have been a great favourite, and perhaps the sequential third line offers some clue, for he wrote a *faux bourdon*, a descant, and a free organ harmonisation for it, all of first class quality. He was, of course, not a pioneer in the writing of descants, but he must have been among the first to write imitative or rhythmically free settings. These demonstrate that search for spontaneous freedom that he was clearly looking for in his original hymn tunes and so seldom found.

For the York Diocesan Festival of 1932, the descant he wrote for Goss's 'Praise my soul the king of heaven' uses the composer's harmonies for the last verse. It might be deemed a pity that, for the last phrase, the descant disappears and joins the tune descending to the low final note. A little invention could evolve something more spectacular, but Bairstow probably did what he did for a good reason. He may have thought that dignity was preferable to brilliance and was better achieved by a firm and solid unison. A musicianly fa-burden for *Bedford* appeared in the 1931 *Songs of Praise*. All his descants, except *Dundee,* begin after the tune, *Richmond* on the second beat, the others on the second bar, two of them (*Moscow* and *O God of Love*) imitating the melody. *Dundee* in its version for brass accompaniment does, however, begin its trumpet descant on the third note. For singing, however, two additional notes – dominant and tonic – were placed to begin simultaneously with the tune.

The Organ Accompaniments to the Unison Verses of 24 Hymns from the English Hymnal, published in 1941 by the Oxford University Press, represent his greatest success in this branch of church music, and remain a testament to the way hymns were considered at their best fifty years ago. Their elaborate treatment presupposes the resources of a large organ and a resonant acoustic, and shows the sedate *tempi* at which hymns were sung in those days. Rhythmic alertness is wholly consonant with a steady tempo, and what are progressions in their own right, even on half beats, should be allowed time to make their point, rather than be rushed over as though they were mere passing notes.

Of the matters that arouse particular interest is Bairstow's ability to combine the first and final lines of *Adeste Fideles; Aeterna Christi Munera* treated as a mini-anthem over a span of five verses; two treatments of *Old 104th* remind us that it was clearly not the arranger's intention that these could be played at sight following a cursory glance during the sermon; *Picardy* could form an effective Communion anthem; *Old 100th* ante-dates Vaughan Williams by twelve years and has been unduly overshadowed by the latter's Coronation setting; and *Rhuddlan. Hanover, Folkingham, St. Anne* and *Leoni* all have multi-verse treatment. It is interesting to compare this collection with Eric Thiman's less elaborate essays of 1937. These are hardly outclassed in craftsmanship, but Bairstow's more ornate settings call forth skilled care and attention, attention that in our world of changed values will still bring its reward.

There are some striking progressions in *Lasst uns erfreuen*, and one imagines that the arrangement of *Dundee* for brass could still send shivers down the spine. Only those who heard Bairstow's own hymn accompaniments frequently would know how often they were improvised, but the ones that have been preserved show a skilled hand where the texture and harmonic resource are concerned, even if some end products would achieve an uncertain effect in contemporary cathedral worship.

His free harmonisations of the five verses of *Veni Emmanuel* date from 1896 – pre-Wigan, when he was still a Mister! Even so, the twenty-two-year-old arranger shows an original mind that impinged on our national music to telling and more significant effect in later years. The textural elaboration makes it unsuitable for use today, not merely because of the necessary slow tempo but because the romantic harmonies, when used to accompany singing, would strike a jarring note. Even so, they could be worked into an effective organ piece, and as such would offer a fascinating comparison with the (one suspects, since there is no date) later third organ prelude which is based on this tune.   D.W.

F.J. The similar treatment he accords the tune *Heinlein* is perhaps more practical. The tune is slow and dignified, leaving more room for the elaborations given to the organ. The tune also lends itself more readily to a colourful chromatic background than does a plainsong melody or the like. Of the six verses the third is to be sung unaccompanied: in the other five the melody is given as a kind of *cantus firmus*, but by whom to be sung is not stated. Being too involved for congregational use, this setting would make a perfectly acceptable anthem just as the composer left it.

Also from this period comes *A hymn for the spring-time*, by 'Ed. C. Bairstow, Mus. Bac.' A copy is to be found in the Wolstenholme archive at Blackburn. The hymn – more of a carol – is directed 'To be sung during the month of May'. It appears to be printed as a leaflet, for permission is given, for any who might wish, to take it away; but the tune is not to be printed in any other collection: 'It is copyright'. The words, whose authorship is not divulged, are clearly for small children: "O little birds that all day long Carol in every tree, What is the secret of your song, The meaning of your glee? You are so very, very glad, How loving God must be". The music is of a similar stamp and, once again, typical of its period.

In the same collection also is a single page containing a setting, for two trebles and obviously incomplete, of *O perfect love*. It is in E major and in three-two time but with neither accompaniment nor other voice parts. Once more, it seems to belong to Bairstow's sojourn at Norfolk Square.

In the Westminster Abbey Hymn Book of 1897 are two of ECB's early excursions into hymn tune writing. *St. Oran*, to some emotional, doom-laden words by A.P. Stanley – 'O frail spirit, vital spark' – stretching over twelve stanzas of eight lines each, exists in two versions, major and minor, and is very much in the style of the period. Permission, incidentally, is given for the omission of three verses 'if the hymn is thought too long'. The other, *Memento Mori*, is for Palgrave's hymn 'Lord! how fast the minutes fly' with its nine six-line stanzas, and is in a similar portentous mood. The tune is of no great distinction.

There is, however, a later and more adventurous effort, un-named, which is typical of his more mature style. In manuscript, it is for the processional hymn 'Hail thee, festival day', and is clearly designed for unaccompanied singing in the vast spaces of York

Minster. The refrain is in G major, in six-four time and laid out for five voices, the trebles being divided. The intervening verses are in four voice parts, the even ones for tenors and basses, the odd verses for trebles and altos. The former are in B flat, the latter in E flat. This has a momentary plunge into G flat, with a return via A flat to a cunning cadence which leads back to the refrain in G. The date of composition is not known. If it was ever used, it had, by 1929 at any rate, given place to Vaughan Williams' popular *Salve Festa Dies*.

4. Psalter and Chant

The Lamentation is almost in a category of its own, being a fusion of chants 'of irregular pattern' (see page 202) and measured notes. It is undoubtedly a piece *sui generis* and is likely to remain thus, for, like God Save the Queen or Zadok the Priest, it is difficult to imagine the words set in any other way. This remarkable composition, composed when Bairstow was approaching his sixty ninth year, is a distillation of the style formed throughout his lifetime and somewhat of a contrast to his efforts of half a century earlier. We find his treatment of the leavy-laden words perfectly matched by music which, with extreme economy, contains just sufficient chromaticism for the purpose and which is skilfully balanced by diatonic chords.

Bairstow's guiding principle in composition was that every word should find appropriate expression in the music, and he achieved it with astonishing effect in what the Musical Times called 'a fine, impressive little work. The writing throughout', it said, ' is deeply expressive and, though not difficult (!), calls for sensitive singing'. The main hazard is intonation by reason of the chromatic intervals, particularly in the tenor part.

The Lamentation takes its text from Jeremiah and was chosen by Dean Milner-White, its purpose being to provide an alternative to the Benedicite in Lent. Its effectiveness is heightened, however, by being used somewhat sparingly. At York it was kept for lenten Fridays, Passion Sunday, and Holy Week matins. Once, on a certain Friday morning, the Archbishop, Doctor Cyril Garbett, made an unexpected and unwanted appearance for the purpose of giving his approval for the Lamentation to be included in the revised orders of service which were occupying the Dean and the Liturgical Commission at the time.

Its construction is of the simplest – variations on a single chant which, at first, begins on the dominant of C minor, and ends on the tonic: the first variation begins on the sub-dominant and ends on the dominant. The refrain 'Jerusalem, Jerusalem, return unto the Lord, thy God' is presented loudly in bold C-major chords – and not eschewing the opposing triad of A major, his favourite device once more. The first chant then returns and there are unison verses as appropriate. After a repeat of the refrain, the chant becomes a double one in the refreshing new major key of A flat, and the chanting continues, ending in the confident affirmation 'Thou hast redeemed my life'. Then follows the master stroke which brings the work to a close – the refrain is heard again, but now *pianissimo*, its sudden return to the home key contributing to the magical ending. The work can be sung either with organ or unaccompanied. Though described in the review as a 'little' work, its stature, like that of the three introits, is far greater than could be expected, bearing in mind the modest means employed, such is the concentrated power contained in the music. It has become universally used and cherished and takes its place alongside others of the composer's imperishable masterpieces.

The movement towards speech rhythm in psalm-singing to anglican chants threw up several versions of pointing, each in its own style. In the nineteen-twenties, Robert Bridges the Poet Laureate joined forces with Sir Walford Davies, Steuart Wilson and others to produce *The Psalter Newly Pointed*. Bairstow, Percy Buck and Charles Macpherson were anxious that their *English Psalter* should be first in the field, so a race was joined which the latter narrowly won. Its title could indicate that it was intended to be a companion to the English Hymnal, then and ever since very much in favour.

It was introduced at York forthwith and at Exeter during Dr. Bullock's time there, as well as at other places. At York it was in use until around 1950. Its main aim was to distribute the words more evenly through the chant, rather than putting all but the last

3 (or 5) syllables on to the reciting note. It was an interesting idea
and was, no doubt, expected to provide the ultimate and complete
cure for the thumping of the ending of each half verse as in the old
system. This it certainly achieved but, over-stepping the mark as it
did, had the opposite effect of encouraging gabble as in verses like
the fourth of Psalm 1:

> *and look, whatso | ever .he | doeth . it shall | prosper*

the first of the *Venite:*

> *let us heartily re | joice . in the | strength of . our sal | vation*

or verse 8 of Psalm 7:

> *and ac | cording . to the | innocency . that is | in me*

in all of which the first barline is placed a whole bar earlier than
had hitherto been the practice. It all became too easy, and choirs
could only with difficulty be restrained from adopting too rapid a
pace. Looking back at the 'old' pointing – *The Cathedral Psalter* –
it could be seen that there was basically little wrong with it, and
that the successful new versions were merely more or less modifications of it. Another feature of the English Psalter which proved
to be unacceptable was the frequent joining togther of two verses
which, by themselves, were considered too short to allow of the
early-barline, multi-syllable treatment which was a basic characteristic of the new style (e.g. see Psalm CXIV on page 316).

Bairstow also, over the years, wrote several fine chants of which
fifteen are to be found in the York Minster Chant Book – eight of
them double and seven single. The best known ones are both in E
flat, that to Psalm 5 whose melody begins on the dominant and
proceeds to the flattened seventh, and the one for Psalm 85 which
proceeds upwards by step from the mediant and has a colourful
chord of the minor ninth at the start of its final quarter. Psalm 107
changes between a double chant and a single chant in D major with
two harmonisations of its D minor version. But undoubtedly the
most imaginative and spectacular is the single chant for Psalm 114
'When Israel came out of Egypt' which first appeared in the 1929
revision of the Minster chant book. It consists of four variants,
specially moulded to the words of each of the eight verses, of which
the third (What aileth thee, O thou sea, that thou fleddest?) is sung
softly a fifth lower in the subdominant minor key, to be succeeded
by a sudden *fortissimo* (and the lowest note of the thirty-two-foot

pedal reed) at the words 'Tremble thou earth at the presence of the Lord'. There is also a marvellous upward leap for the 'springing well' (or 'welling spring' as in an antipodean service book and the R.E.B.) This setting is one of Bairstow's happiest inspirations, and is prophetic of the Lamentation of thirteen years later.

Worthy of mention, also, is the *faux bourdon* for the refrain in psalms 42 and 43 (Why art thou so heavy, O my soul?) in which divided trebles and altos ask the question, in a poignant mood, with a diminished seventh on 'soul' (Wesley's melody being in the second treble part), and are answered by the full choir with the tune in the bass part and a brilliant descant by the trebles. The chant in C minor, which must have been especially written with the solemn words of psalm 139 in mind, has a strong atmosphere which is entirely appropriate and most effective for its purpose (see p. 316). It bursts the bounds of the anglican chant, however, both in its excessive crotchet movement and – what must surely be unique – a dotted minim and a crotchet in the fifth bar, for all four voices, rather than the time-honoured couple of minim chords. (W. Bayley in his E flat chant does the same but a bar earlier, that is to say, on the reciting note). It is almost a 'work' in itself, albeit of very miniscule proportions, probably inviting some kind of attention from composers of variations or the like. Bairstow's chant in G major which is set to the last section of psalm 78 (and was probably composed especially for it) is used for the E flat Te Deum, with one altered note.

What is probably his earliest chant of all is in the All Saints Norfolk Square manuscript collection. It is double, in A flat, and is dated *1896* (p. 313). The book in question is to be found in the Wolstenholme archive in Blackburn Central Library. It was brought to my attention by Douglas Carrington its archivist. Also in the same book is a quadruple chant in G major for the fifteenth evening, straightforward, carefully organised, passing through the relative and mediant minors and the dominant and subdominant majors, the second half being a variant of the first (*ibid*).   F.J.

c. SONGS (by Gordon Pullin)

The Oxford Companion to Music, 'reprinted with corrections in 1956', does not admit that Bairstow wrote songs. Few other musical dictionaries do that, not even the 1940 Grove, published when he was one of the most distinguished musicians in the country. There are perhaps two reasons for this: first, his church music tended to overwhelm the rest of his output; and secondly, he was born at a time when 'English Song' emerged from Victorian bathos and sentimentality into a genuine art form. Also born in the 1870s were Vaughan Williams, Holst, Coleridge-Taylor, Quilter, Bridge, Cyril Scott and John Ireland. Already alive were Parry, Stanford, Elgar and Delius, let alone Somervell and Bantock. And before the nineteenth century ended can be added the names of Bax, Butterworth, Gurney, Bliss, Howells and Warlock. And that list is by no means exhaustive.

Around the turn of the century both composers and performers found the writing and performing of songs quite a rewarding financial exercise (even the singers could receive royalties by promoting the songs), and as a result many songs were written for immediate consumption, and are therefore decried today, even though no little skill was required to compose them. Bairstow suffers as heavily as anyone from this judgment, especially as his church music is so much better in musical terms, and also perhaps, as an academic musician, more was expected of him!

The poets set to music by Bairstow mark him as a man of his time, with the balance evenly distributed between the early poets (Shakespeare, Jonson, Heywood and Herbert), the nineteenth century (Blake, Heine – via Thomson and Longfellow, Shelley and Whitman), and his contemporaries, known, like Edward Thomas, lesser-known but popular, like Alice Meynell and Winifred Letts, and what one might term 'the personal choice' – Richard Parker, Helen Sutherland, Eric Mackay and Reginald Arkell. Add to this an anonymous song and a folk-song, and one has the whole of Bairstow's output – just nineteen songs. Thus one can see that song-writing was not considered to be an important part of his total *oeuvre*, but rather an occasional 'divertissement'. Had he died young and left little, like William Baines or even George Butterworth, no doubt critics would have found originality and bemoaned the loss of its fulfilment. Had he left over a hundred and fifty songs, as did Bantock, then at least he might have to be taken seriously as a song composer. But as it is he did not die young, nor did he write many songs, and those that he did write span over thirty years of composition and so it is up to the individual, whether as performer or listener, to make up his or her own mind. The rest of this assessment offers a personal view of why at least some of the songs are worth rescuing from their present oblivion.

Six songs were published by Joseph Williams in 1903: Pack, clouds, away; The sea hath its pearls; The Pine Tree; I arise from dreams of thee; A prayer for light; and Daphnis and Chloë.

Pack, clouds, away (Thomas Heywood) has pace and the chromaticism typical of the Edwardian period, but the pedal notes, second inversions and inclinations from major to minor now hint more of the influence of Schubert than of Mozart. Add an operatic ending, an occasional infelicity of word-setting (e.g. 'Robin Redbreast') and a rather ordinary melody, and we have a song which relies on the performers' *élan* too much for its effect. Yet, given that *élan, i*t can be an effective piece for performers and listeners alike.

The sea hath its pearls finds Bairstow at his most Edwardian. The whole of the words of the first verse are repeated (with slight changes in the arpeggio accompaniment), and there are internal repeats as well. This continues into verses two and three: verse two has a rather solid accompaniment over a downward-striding bass, but verse three (addressing the 'little youthful maiden') attractively develops the melody of verse one, and has a light, whimsical accompaniment, which suddenly makes one wonder whether the earlier part of the song should be taken at all seriously. For me it is too much the sort of song one performs seriously with the underlying intent of poking fun at the style – though Claribel and Dolores did it better!

The third of this group of early songs is 'The Pine Tree', translated from the German of Heinrich Heine (the poet of *Dichterliebe*) by James Thomson, and those looking for echoes of Schumann will not be disappointed. It is a very short poem, considerably extended by Bairstow by means of repetition of the words. This is a pity, as he catches the atmosphere of the poem from the very beginning. There is a double introduction: the first a pre-echo of what will eventually be the climax; the second is an ostinato melody over which the voice enters. The second verse – for the 'dream' – goes into the major key, using a background of semiquaver arpeggios. The final page, reintroducing the first theme from the piano intro-duction, but now fortissimo, is musically satisfying (apart from the return to the major at the end), but whether the poem can stand this inflated treatment is another matter.

Shelley's Indian Serenade, *I arise from dreams of thee*, had already been set by Parry among others. Bairstow's version has a lilting melody with an octave leap at the climax of each verse. It has many of the compositional features of the songs already mentioned – chromaticism, pedal notes, syncopations – and the counter-melodies in the accompaniment to the second verse are skilfully done. The *allegro con fuoco* however (moderated quickly to *più lento e con passione,* and then back to *molto allegro e agitato)* seems too anxious and contrived, in spite of some Tchaikovsky-like bars in the accompaniment. There is a needless repetition of one line of the poem, and at the climax the composer seems more concerned with working out his enharmonic return. But the simple ending, quoting the opening ideas, works well. There is a manuscript ver-sion of the accompaniment in Bairstow's hand for full orchestra, including trombones, four horns and harp.

A Prayer for Light has words by Eric MacKay 'By kind permis-sion of Miss Marie Corelli', his sister. It is not a good poem, and Bairstow's inflated setting gives it everything it deserves. (There is an interesting comparison to be made with Holst's setting of the same poem). As a result we have what might be termed a true period-piece, rather like, but not as good as, Coleridge-Taylor's setting of the same poet's *Eléanore*. It is in C minor, and opens with a fortissimo Coleridge-Taylor-type of chromatic phrase on the piano. When the voice enters, over a typical descending bass, and to a rocking rhythm in the right hand, the melodic line is a disap-pointment, especially when it is deliberately set against the open-ing melody, first in the right hand, then in the left. We also have back Bairstow's habit of repeating words – as if they were not bad enough the first time! A short chromatic sequence leads into a *più mosso* section, with a climax in the dominant of the relative major. At this climax the introductory theme returns, leading to a passage of semiquaver *arpeggios* accompanying a vocal line still somewhat short of originality. Again this is broken by the opening theme, which quickly dies into the previously heard short chromatic theme, as the song comes to an end with the words (repeated, of course!), 'Kiss me to death!' (It is easy, perhaps, given present-day tastes, to poke fun at a period-piece such as this, but the combination of words and music makes it hard to resist. I should add that a solution I found for myself in order to perform Bairstow's music was to find a different poem and fit it to the music. Swinburne's *A Leave-Taking* works tolerably well, repeats and all!)

Daphnis and Chloë, to words by Richard Parker, is written in the style of Mozart's 'Das Veilchen' or 'Dans un bois solitaire'. There are a liberal number of chromatic appoggiaturas in the rather charming accompaniment, though Mozart might have been a little surprised at a few of the chords, and at the deliberate key changes in the *lento* section (which does however have an attractive 'cello' melody set against the syncopation in the right hand). As befits the period (Bairstow's, not Mozart's) there are a lot of instructions to the performers, my own favourite being *a tempo delicato* for the accompanist. In basically an AABA form, it has an air of lightness, or rather mock-seriousness, right up to the final, throw-away coda.

The fact that there are gaps in the composition of his songs does seem to indicate that Bairstow did not himself take his song-writing too seriously. The next song to be published was not, in fact, his own composition, but an arrangement of 'The Hostel'. This is a poem by Winifred M. Letts, the Irish poetess who, as one might expect, was a particular favourite of Stanford (e.g. 'The Monkey's Carol), and the melody is by a Colonel Alexander Ewing. Any success the song may have had is probably due to the contemporary taste for songs of a religious type, with a singable, easy melody, well within the capabilities of an amateur performer – or preferably a boy soprano, and Bairstow certainly knew all about them. His accompaniment for Colonel Ewing's melody is almost totally independent of the voice part, and works quite well as a piano solo.

But 'The Hostel' was followed in 1919 by the publication (by Enoch) of 'When I heard the Learn'd Astronomer' (Walt Whitman). The song was in existence ten years earlier, performed in the Steinway Hall in July 1909 by Mr. William Higley. In the first half of this song Bairstow shows his greatest potential as a song-writer. As in the best classical tradition the Whitman setting starts with a four-bar 'question and answer' introduction, and the two ideas are then used in both voice and piano parts – against each other, antiphonally, and in counterpoint. The whole effect is one of pace which is under total control. It reaches a climax in the relative major. It then modulates towards the tonic major, using the 'answer' phrase to take the music towards the second, *più tranquillo* half of the song. If this second half is less successful than the first, it still has a sense of purpose (only two words are repeated throughout the song) and comes across as a genuine attempt to achieve the poet's 'mystical perfect silence' in musical terms. A review in the Monthly Musical Record of November 19th 1920 must have afforded the composer some encouragement, and a performance of it at the Steinway Hall was written up in The Times of July 3rd 1909: 'It was a daring act for Dr. Bairstow to set these words to music, but his own big introspective style has proved him to be one of the few men who could have done it successfully. The song will appeal strongly to those singers who consider the message of music of more importance than the showing-off of their voices.' The Morning Post of the same date thought the song showed decided originality of conception.

The setting of Shakespeare's 'Orpheus with his lute' of 1919 was dedicated to E.S. (Elsie Suddaby?). It must have attracted immediate comparison with the versions by Sullivan and Vaughan Williams – and probably many others. In his version Bairstow brings all his very considerable skills into play, but as a result the poem is 'over set'. The vocal line is dramatic, making use of wide, usually falling intervals (the very first phrase has a minor seventh, an augmented fourth, a perfect fifth and a minor sixth), and changes of *tempo* (ignoring *accelerandi* and *ritenuti* there are four different *tempi*, not allowing for returns to '*Tempo 1*'). The accompaniment begins with 'strumming' effects, but quickly assumes a more pianistic style. In Bairstow fashion the harmonies do not settle until (effectively) the word 'sing' in bar 12; chromaticism abounds. The ABAC form is carefully worked out, the 'mountain-tops' are musically matched with the 'billows', and there is an attractive short canon between voice and piano at the start of the final *tranquillo* section.

But the chromatic descending bass, the modulating repeat and the final falling tenth all seem a little too deliberate.

In 1922 Stainer and Bell published a pair of Bairstow songs. The first was of the anonymous sixteenth century poem 'Come, lovers, follow me', and the second was an arrangement of the anonymous early seventeenth century setting of Ben Jonson's 'So sweet is she' (or 'Have you seen but a white lily grow?') In the first of these two miniatures Bairstow shows exemplary craftsmanship: the repetitions are there, but give the impression that they were there in the original poem; the vocal line has speed and variety, with some neat word-painting, and some breathless off-beat entries; the accompaniment toys with the various themes, sometimes independently, sometimes across the vocal line, sometimes antiphonally; there is a good climax – and suddenly it is over. The arrangement of the melody to the Jonson poem could almost belong to the early seventeenth century. Indeed Bairstow uses *arpeggiando* effects towards the end in harpsichord (or even virginal) style. He enjoys himself in the repeat by first making the bass line echo the voice, and then reversing that process. All in all a very charming setting, if a little anonymous compared to what Warlock was doing at that time.

Two years later Stainer and Bell published another pair of short songs by Bairstow: 'At Night' (Alice Meynell) and 'To Morning' (Blake). (Alice Meynell was a contemporary poetess who died in 1922; John Ireland also set two of her poems in the 1920s). After what has so far been said it may come as no surprise to learn that Bairstow sets the second song far more effectively than the first. 'To Morning', with its rushing triplets virtually throughout in the piano part, catches the breathless cry of Blake's poem exactly, slowed only by the hunting-horn climax. The accompaniment builds sequentially, echoes the trumpet phrases in the vocal line, and generally sweeps the song along to the final bar.

On the other hand, ' At Night', both as a poem and as a song, takes itself too seriously. It starts with an ambiguity of key that Bairstow often favoured; the triplet semiquavers in the second verse dutifully portray the birds; the word-setting of 'swiftest' is deliberately perverse, but much of the rest of the vocal line seems perfunctory, particularly in the use of semi-quavers. Yet the *tranquillo* motif of the opening bars of the accompaniment, used with variations throughout and repeated at the end, promised more.

Edward Thomas was one of the major poets of the early twentieth century, and was set to music by Finzi, Gurney and Cyril Scott among others. Bairstow's setting of 'The Oak Tree Bough' was the poem entitled 'The Gallows' by Thomas, but it may be that composer and publisher between them felt that this was not exactly a best-selling title! If there is such a thing as a *poème noir*, then this is it, and Bairstow finds exactly the right 'black humour' with which to set it. By marking it *scherzando* he also tells us that he knew exactly what he was doing. The melody swings along, with the odd lengthened bar, and with the jollity suddenly disappearing in the falling chromaticism at the end of each verse. The accompaniment's descending scale in the bass implies something more than the dancing figure in the right hand. The second and third verses have slight variations in both melody and accompaniment, while the chorus remains the same. The piano coda then takes it away *a niente*.

The arrangement of *The Hostel* in 1918 was advertised as being sung by 'Mr. H. Plunket Greene' (1865-1936), who was one of the greatest interpreters of English song of this period – many would say the greatest. It is therefore no surprise to find two later songs, *The Lonesome Girl* (W.M. Letts) and *The Buryin'* (Reginald Arkell) both headed 'Written for and sung by Mr. H. Plunket Greene'. In her poem *The Lonesome Girl* Winifred Letts shows that she can write in the best 'winsome' Irish tradition, and Bairstow matches her at every step. It is probably his best song. The voice is left to establish the scene, after a brief introduction, which it does in the minor key and in a beautifully shaped simple phrase, with the major seventh nicely pointing the word 'queerly' at the climax of the first verse. The accompaniment's triplets, which introduced the first verse, now continue into the second verse, while the vocal line remains the same. In verse three both melody and accompaniment work to a climax ending in the relative major. The melody in the fourth verse also rises to a climax, supported somewhat strangely by a descending sequence in the bass, and finds itself, via the dominant, in the relative minor. The gentle fifth verse (*più lento*), not in the compound time of the rest of the song, has a lovely counter melody in the right hand. Then the opening melody returns for the final verse, simply accompanied, with an extremely effective switch to the tonic major for the very last phrase. This is a perfectly crafted song, making allowance for the poem's sentiment without letting it become too sentimental.

'Two plodding beats in a bar' is how Percy Grainger might well have marked a song, and this is what we read at the top of *The Buryin'*, the second of the Plunket Greene songs. Like *The Lonesome Girl* it is in compound time, but it comes across as an attempt to follow the success of that song which does not quite come off. The folk-like melody is given the suggested plodding accompaniment, though the key (of C major) is never, as often, firmly established. The shift to B flat major towards the end of the verse works well, especially with the lengthening of the word 'rest' on which it occurs. The middle verse starts a fifth lower, with the plodding beats slightly syncopated, and with consecutive fifths in the bass. The third verse has lots of hesitation, as the singer gradually makes up his mind to wait until September as a more convenient time for his own buryin'. After the piece ends firmly – though gently – in C major, the piano plays as a coda a two-bar *arpeggio* in E major. Make what you will of that!

Bairstow's last published song appeared ten years later, and it is an arrangement of the English folk-song *The Frog and the Mouse*. This arrangement – again in compound time – sees him back at his best. The accompaniment is based on two pairs of three quavers in each bar. These stop occasionally, as at the nonsense chorus-line of the first verse; at other times they can 'ride' with a dotted rhythm for the hero; they can leave the second or third quaver out for variety; they can turn into a scale; or they can even become duplets. Against these basic quavers we find several different ideas – a falling (or rising) dotted crotchet theme, sometimes chromatic; a counter-melody in crotchets and quavers; even 'squeaks' of various kinds for 'Mistress Mouse'. All of this comes across very naturally, with a good sense of humour, and with no sense of contrivance, making sure that the folk-song style is maintained throughout.

In addition to the published songs and arrangements there are two manuscript songs. These are *Sweet Day* (George Herbert); and

Daffodils in the Grass (Helen B.G. Sutherland). Of these *Sweet Day* is probably the earliest, though there are no dates on any of these manuscripts. It also gives the impression of never being quite finished. The composer, it appears, did not like Herbert's final couplet. The poet wrote 'But tho' the whole world turn to coal, then chiefly lives'. Bairstow rewrote this couplet at the foot of the page as: 'And when this body turns to dust, In life immortal (he tried 'eternal' first) ever lives'. In a further correction under the music 'life' became 'realms'. The vocal line is pleasant enough, with a surprising leap of a tenth on the words 'so bright' in the first verse (it also works well on 'and brave' in the second verse, but less so for 'virtuous soul' in the final one). The accompaniment opens with an attractive sequential phrase, but as a whole contains far more perfect cadences than any other song. The change from E flat major to E major in the third verse seems rather forced, and the theme of dotted-quaver/semiquaver becomes repetitive. In the last verse some of the 'duetting' between voice and piano is effective, but one feels that quite a number of changes would have been made had Bairstow seriously considered publishing this song.

The final song is *Daffodils in the Grass*, which, like so many of his manuscripts, is undated, but which might be the song *Daffodils*, 'an effective little song with a dainty accompaniment' according to the Yorkshire Evening Post of 26 November 1909, as sung by Mr. Brearley in the Albert Hall, Leeds, in a concert in aid of the Parish Church choir fund. As with many of his better songs it is quite short – a 'miniature' in effect; it does not outstay its welcome by repetition, nor does it try to achieve too much within its twenty-seven bars. The one introductory bar merely provides the accompanying figure for the vocal line. The latter's descending opening phrase immediately establishes the key of A minor, but the F sharp in the third bar points to the Dorian mode. 'Restless trees' are conveyed by fluttering triplet semiquavers. The opening melody returns, lengthened, over a chromatic, descending bass, as the first half comes to a close in the tonic. As the second half starts, a third lower, the bass still prefers its chromatic descent, but is opposed to a syncopated rising theme in the right hand, though this soon gives way to a rocking, four-quaver idea, taken from the vocal line. This builds to a climax which leads directly to the opening melody as a *subito piano.* There is the inevitable modulation in the middle of the song (even reaching E flat major), but there is little sense of effort, merely of intensification. The song captures to perfection the atmosphere of a cold spring evening as twilight falls.

So – nineteen songs: where does that leave Bairstow as a song-writer? Certainly not in the first flight – or so Stephen Banfield would have us believe, as his book 'Sensibility and English Song' (CUP 1985) does not even mention Bairstow in passing. The same is true of most music dictionaries, though the article in the New Grove, written by Watkins Shaw, does mention 'a few songs', concluding 'all his vocal music shows a deeply serious approach and masterly craftsmanship, but although it has many beautiful and expressive moments it is not strongly personal. Most church musicians would agree with the first half of that statement, but for the many who perhaps only know Bairstow through *Blessed City* or the *Lamentation* the last five words would certainly not be true. My feeling is that the songs, in any case, are different. They certainly show the 'masterly craftsmanship' even if occasionally one feels it is being put to rather trivial use. But it is precisely when he is being 'deeply serious' that the songs are less good. The better songs come across as welcome light relief from the world of academe and the church. Why else would an eminent musician set *The Frog and the Mouse,* to take an obvious example? Bairstow's best songs are those which give the impression of a lack of inhibition, a feeling that the composer is not taking it too seriously, and that he is almost having fun; (there are others who will tell me if in fact he could do so!).

I myself have been pleased to find *Daphnis and Chloë* while writing this commentary, and look forward to trying it out on audiences. Meanwhile I would add it to *When I heard the learned astronomer, Come lovers follow me, To Morning, The Oak-Tree Bough, The Lonesome Girl, The Frog and the Mouse* and *Daffodils in the Grass* as songs which well repay study on the part of performers, and which do hold their own when compared to those of better-known song-writers of the period. Eight out of nineteen is not bad! And any composer who can write a scherzo-like piece such as *Come lovers* or *To Morning* or a whimsical piece like *Little Nellie Cassidy,* or catch the black humour of *The Gallows* is not one to be ignored or neglected.   G.P.

d. PART SONGS

Of the fourteen part songs only five are for all the four voices. Two are unison, one is for female voices and six for male voices – tenor, baritone, bass. The earliest, *Sweet day so cool*, for four-part choir, the words by George Herbert, was published in the year of his twenty-third birthday. Typical of its period and obviously a prentice work with certain infelicities and slight naiveties, it is not without charm. It is 'dedicated, by kind permission, to Lady Barttelot', a prime mover in the Petworth/Stopham choir (see page 25).

Four years later his grasp is more assured, with confident use of colourful harmony and a poetical reaction to the words. *The Dawn of Song,* published by Novello in 1901, had previously been printed by John Rinder of Farnley, Leeds, who also appears to have written the words. This edition bears the legend 'Ent. Sta. Hall.' which probably indicates that it was available for purchase by the public. The main difference is the substitution of *bouche fermée* accompaniment to the initial tenor melody whereas originally the other three voices sang the words. After this the altos continue the melody, which is then taken over by the sopranos who complete the first section. The whole choir then develops the theme, tossing it between the voices. The pulse changes from triple to quadruple time for a fugue which culminates in a triumphant statement of the final words 'In rapture sweet our voices join in singing Celestial songs, the music of the sky'.

After the lapse of seven years the first two of his male voice songs appeared, to words by Herrick and a key signature of six flats for both. *Her eyes the glow-worm lend thee* ('The Night-piece', To Julia) in the minor key, begins *scherzando* as it deals with glow-worms, shooting-stars, elves, snakes and will-o'-the-wisps, changing completely to a smooth *andante* for the final stanza ('Then, Julia, let me woo thee') and in the key of the tonic major. *I dare not ask a kiss* (To Electra), in the major key, follows the feelings of the poet, first his diffidence, then his ambition 'To kiss that air that lately kiss-ed thee'.

At the beginning of his York sojourn, *Where shall the lover rest,* to words of Sir Walter Scott, was Bairstow's most ambitious part-song so far. It begins in eight parts and has varying divisions as the piece progresses. It is in two sharply contrasted sections, the first concerning the lover, in a slow, rich texture ('under the willow soft be thy pillow') with the suggestion of cool, summer streams, boughs waving. Secondly, the traitor is dealt with, *allegro con molto fuoco e declamato*, the deceiver 'Who could win maiden's breast, Ruin and leave her?'). It is all expertly laid out for the singers who will need to be experienced and well drilled: a very good and searching test piece.

The Oak Tree bough was first published as a unison song in 1924, to be followed by a solo song version in a larger format two years later. (See page 287.) Its successor also concerns the oak tree and another as well. It is, of course, the familiar folk-tune *The Oak and the Ash,* arranged in an admirably straightforward manner for four-part choir. The tune is introduced by the altos against wordless accompaniment and is then taken over by the sopranos. For the refrain all voices sing the words 'O the oak and the ash and the bonny ivy tree, They flourish at home in my own country'. Suitable treatment is accorded bells and birds, and the final phrase of all is repeated nostalgically, by the altos with their wordless accompaniment as at the beginning. The fact that it was reissued fifty-five years later, in an Oxford University Press book of folk songs for choirs, is testimony to its enduring quality.

Shelley's words are used for the two pieces of 1929. *Music, when soft voices die,* for tenors and basses, both divided, is an uncomplicated setting, mostly in block chords. The word 'die' is subtly handled – with a sighing augmented triad – and the whole work depends for its success on the expressive powers of the performers. The other Shelley poem employs the upper voices – sopranos and altos in three parts. It is an opulent interpretation of the poet's enigmatic lines *On a poet's lips I slept* with a piano accompaniment that suggests an orchestra containing sounds such as those of flute, harp and strings. Lasting but two minutes it is intensely poetical, having characteristic word-paintings at the mention of 'aërial kisses' and deep chords for 'shapes that haunt thought's wildernesses'.

The Poacher, also from 1929, has failed to reveal itself despite exhaustive searchings.

COMMENTARIES 293

Three part-songs for tenor, baritone and bass appeared together in 1929 from OUP. Their assured writing shows Bairstow at his full maturity. Edgar Allan Poe's *Eldorado* begins in a galloping triple rhythm and the last verse conveys aptly the mysterious atmosphere of 'Over the mountains of the moon, Down the valley of the shadow, Ride, boldly ride, the shade replied, If you seek for Eldorado'. The favourite romantic triad recipe is employed for the last word (F A-flat F) as it is in *Listening*, the second of the three songs. John Freeman's beautiful poem depicts a peaceful evening scene which is captured in the music with subtle, sensitive word-painting. Deep basses are required. The third number sets *Gifts*, the poem of James Thomson: 'Give a man a horse he can ride' . . a boat, a pipe, a book, and 'a girl he can love', at which point a tenor solo is added to the three-voice texture and the harmony warms appreciably. The three songs together form a useful, imaginative and varied trilogy.

The attractive and deft arrangement of *The Frog and the Mouse* – his last song – is a masterpiece of craft. It can be used by a solo voice, though published as a unison song. (See page 288.)

The Schubert arrangements were no doubt undertaken with the object of bringing these songs, of which he thought so highly, within the scope of singers who had not the opportunity of performing them that came the way of the solo recitalist – an excellent notion, and one wonders how it was received by choral groups. Bairstow's craft, as usual, is of the finest quality and transforms these miniatures into their new medium leaving them as though this was Schubert's original intention.

e. CHORAL WORKS

It seems rather curious that Bairstow should have written so many male voice pieces – nine original and four Schubert arrangements – which exceed the number of part-songs that employ sopranos and altos. One does not imagine that this was his preferred medium. For the academic milieu in Durham, on its celebratory occasions, it is understandable and entirely appropriate, but for the rest it is likely that his target was the competitive festival, as could also be the case with many of the other part-songs.

The three Odes for Durham fall into a category of their own, even though two of them are of the same scale as the part-songs. For present purposes they are classed with his choral works despite their comparative brevity.

'*Salve, Salve (At the entry of the Chancellor)*' consists of 44 bars of 3/2 *maestoso* lasting less than two minutes, and begins with a bold welcome in E flat which soon gives place to a quiet passage in a sudden G flat at the mention of a sweet strain. 'Hail, hail again' runs the translation,'on a glad day not without rejoicing of men singing a sweet strain, Thou scion of a noble stock, appear thou noble chief'. The second stanza varies the main theme, and the third is a verbatim reprise of the first, the sudden key-change now referring to 'the Pierian maid near our Bears' (Great and Little, and thus northerly). Mostly in three parts, the texture increases to four as the tenors divide for the final phrase of each verse.

Orchestral accompaniment was evidently available for *Anxia quisquis gravitate mentis,* though no score or detail of instrumentation have so far come to light. The evidence is in the printed copy and its piano reduction. Again it is in bold, ceremonial style. After a four-bar introduction the voices enter with a bold unison theme, breaking into harmony at the words 'Gaudio pleni', and suggesting that any who are grown ill or tired with illness or heaviness of mind should keep their distance while, full of joy, the rest sing in homage to their *alma mater.* The words were written by John Wight Duff (1866-1944) who was Professor of Classics at Armstrong College, Newcastle upon Tyne 1898-1933 and then Professor Emeritus, among whose degrees was an honorary D. Litt. from Durham. He is undoubtedly the author of all three texts.

The longest of the three Odes is for four voices unaccompanied. It lasts some four-and-a-half minutes and has seven stanzas or strophes which tell (*Allegro maestoso*) of the high altitude of the city overlooking the River Wear; of medicine, craft, agriculture (pleasing to Ceres and Vulcan), of its light which will guide those who wander in darkness, chasing gloom away; and one of its most famous sons. 'Thou, remembering, honourest Bede, a name venerable to Englishmen, and thou leadest a throng of comrades to the founts which he unsealed in constant prayer'. The strong unison motif at the beginning, in a Dorian G minor, forms the basis of the odd-numbered verses, VII using the same music as I. The strophes are arranged symmetrically, II and VI, with their secondary theme, being related, respectively in the tonic major and the dominant. The fourth stanza, again in the tonic major, stands thematically independent as the central point.

Many years earlier (1894), the young Bairstow wrote his baccalaureate exercise, setting the words of Psalm 84 in four movements. The first movment, 'O how amiable are thy dwellings' is a cheerful *Allegro* 3/4 in A flat with a ten-bar introduction by the string orchestra. It is followed by the fourth verse, 'Blessed are they that dwell in thy house', an unaccompanied quartet *Andante con moto* in the current musical idiom, containing downward-moving semitones such as he later dubbed 'slithery'.

The third movement is a soprano solo, 'For the Lord God is a light and defence' in D flat *Andante grazioso*. Repetition is somewhat overdone, and the piece ends with two pizzicato chords. A Choral Fugue in five voice parts, using the words of the last verse of the psalm, is the last movement, in A flat *Allegro moderato*. The sopranos begin with 'Blessed is the man that putteth his trust in thee' and are succeeded by fugal entries by the altos, first tenors, second tenors and, finally, basses. There are the regulation artifices, including the obligatory dominant pedal near the end, and some attempts at inversion. The setting of 'O Lord God of hosts' allots two notes to the final word, constituting an upward leap of a major sixth. The title page is meticulously lettered in gothic script with a fine pen.

For his doctor's exercise Bairstow resorted again to the psalms, this time 137, 'By the waters of Babylon'. Again it is set in four movements, but the accompaniment is for full orchestra, with double woodwind, horns in G, horns in D, trumpets in E, 3 trombones, timpani and strings. It is signed at the end 'Ed. C. Bairstow 28.viii.1900'.

A substantial overture, begins *Adagio* with solemn chords in G minor by clarinets and bassoons who play the rhythm of the first five words, a figure several times made use of. After this introduction an *Allegro non troppo* dotted theme in 6/8 time follows and there are several changes of tempo before eventually the eight-part chorus enters, the men singing as far as 'we sat down' and the sopranos and altos adding 'and wept' in piteous tones. These same harmonies are used later for 'in a strange land' after the tenors and basses have asked 'How shall we sing the Lord's song?' The chorus continues on its own without accompaniment for a total of fifty-three bars.

A tenor solo 'If I forget thee, O Jerusalem' is the third movement, *Andante affetuoso* in G major. It becomes more turbulent at the words 'If I do not remember thee, let my tongue cleave to the roof of my mouth'. As in the earlier exercise there is much repetition.

The Finale is an Introduction, Fugue and Choral Recitative. The Introduction is for eight-part choir who sing 'Remember the children of Edom, O Lord' *molto maestoso*, and the fugue, with subject ('Down with it') and counter-subject ('Remember the children..') running concurrently, is an energetic three-in-a-bar at a speed of 108 crotchets to the minute. It is quite a formidable effort and must have commended itself to the examiners for its technical assurance. An impressive build-up is effected, to an exciting climax with a mighty unison F sharp on the word 'Down' and an octave drop to 'with it'. The Choral Recitative brings out the full drama of the psalm's peroration: 'Blessed shall he be that taketh thy children and throweth them against the stones'. The work concludes with twelve bars of *fortissimo* 6/8 *allegro con molto fuoco*, heard previously in the overture.

The Prodigal Son

Nearly forty years were to elapse before Bairstow was to produce a choral work that was intended for publication and performance. He called it a Choral Ballad and took the words from Chapter fifteen of Saint Luke's gospel, which tell the well-known story of the younger of the two sons who wasted his substance with riotous living; of the consequences of his excessive prodigality, his penitence on his return, the merrymaking to welcome him home, his elder brother's anger, his father's forgiveness. The forces employed are four-part chorus (with occasional divisions), small orchestra, no soloists (the chorus taking the part of the various characters – first basses representing the Prodigal Son, second basses the Father, and the elder brother sung by the tenors). Once, when asked why he had not given the principal protagonist's part to a tenor, his mischievous reply was "Who ever heard of a tenor leaving home". There being no female characters, the sopranos and contraltos are perforce confined to some of the narration. In this, the tenors and basses, as well as the full choir, participate as necessary.

The work opens with a quiet pastoral oboe theme in six-eight time, contemplative and with a touch of sadness. This mood turns to jollity at the son's thoughts of the good times he intends embarking upon. Soon, however, tragedy strikes, and with grave chords his desolation is portrayed, the contraltos, in a telling descending phrase relating his plight as feeder of swine – (the last word on a low G-sharp) – the shame and disgrace of it...! He then ponders on what he has left behind, and his thoughts of home are uttered in counterpoint against the pastoral theme in a warm major mode. The excitement of the reunion is undertaken by the upper voices *divisi*, and after the son has confessed his unworthiness, the father, in an expansive C-major tune, calls for the best robe, a ring for his hand, shoes, and for the killing of the fatted calf. The jubilations begin, and music (with a suitably archaic flavour) is heard, first in a light *allegro giocoso* then in a firm *risoluto*. Both these themes are employed as an accompaniment while the elder son confronts his father with his discontent. His father's reply is made against the expansive theme in the accompaniment, rising to a *fortissimo* at the words 'was lost and is found'.

Thus ends Saint Luke's chapter. At this point during the composition, Bairstow was for a time at a loss to know how to make a satisfactory ending. The solution was found earlier in the chapter, following the parables of the lost sheep and the widow's lost groats (Tyndale's word for coins). Softly the upper voices, led by the sopranos, begin singing 'There is joy in the presence of the angels of God over one sinner that repenteth'. The *risoluto* motif accompanies the succeeding phrase, 'more than over ninety and nine just persons which need no repentance'. The plaintive opening tune is then heard in full volume, played by the orchestra in its original key, and again quietly as the piece draws to its close.

The orchestra required has single woodwind and trumpet, two horns, timpani, percussion and strings. There is also a version for

strings and piano with optional organ, and an effective one employing organ and piano only.

Songs of the Spirit

Page 207 gives the genesis of this, his last and certainly one of
his best works. Written in his seventieth year, it contains the result
of a lifetime's experience and the full flowering of his composing
genius. The six numbers are well contrasted in every way, not only
in key (F-B flat minor – E flat – A flat – C minor – G) and thematic
material, but in mood and in the variety of forces employed, as his
letter of 28 July 1944 (page 210) explains – except that mixed voices
are used in three numbers rather than two.

Richard Crawshaw's *Come, lovely name* is set for the solo
baritone and three-part women's chorus with a rippling, rustling
triplet accompaniment. The soloist does not enter until he joins
the ladies in the second stanza. This is a cheerful, sunny movement, a total contrast to Mary Sidney's metrical version of Psalm
139, the second of the set. Only the first two stanzas are used. 'O
Lord, in me there lieth naught But to thy search revealed lies' is
introspective in a dark key. The second verse is introduced by a
canon in the accompaniment, and this continues as the soloist sings
'Thou walkest with me when I walk'. This movement is for the
soloist only.

Praise, the third number, is resolute and positive ('Lord, I will
mean and sing thy praise' George Herbert's words) and is for chorus
alone. Sir Walter Raleigh's poem *Purse and Scrip* follows. Its nine-
crotchets-in-a-bar *andante maestoso* and the ponderous chords
suggest the slow tread of the pilgrim. The first two verses are the
soloist's own, and in the second, after almost fourteen bars of mostly
the key of A-flat, there is a magical change to E major at the words:

> Whilst my soul, like quiet palmer,
> Travelleth toward the land of heav'n
> Over the silver mountains,
> Where spring the nectar fountains:

and the celesta makes its appearance in the orchestration. The
chorus enters for the third verse and accompanies the solo voice
with only hints from the orchestra at 'There will I kiss the bowl of

bliss; And drink mine everlasting fill Upon ev'ry milken hill'. The next phrase 'My soul will be a-dry before' is declaimed firmly by the solo voice and chorus together, in a mood of some desperation, but then there are warm, reassuring chords in the accompaniment bringing in the final words of confidence 'But after, it will thirst no more'. This and the final number are in Bairstow's most deeply-felt vein and are rarely equalled in the rest of his *oeuvre*.

The last number, entitled *L'Envoy* is a setting of another George Herbert poem: 'King of glory, king of peace, With the one make war to cease, With the other blesse thy sheep, Thee to love, in thee to sleep'. This first stanza and the second are given to the baritone who then leaves the third (which is a repetition of the first) to the chorus, the altos now singing the tune accompanied by a distant-sounding five-voice texture. Considering that this is almost certainly his last composition, the final line of the poem is especially poignant: he had but two years left to live. It breathes a spirit of contentment and peaceful resignation from its first notes which are, yet again and finally, the triad juxtaposition which he so loved, this time G major and B flat. The ending is a single strand of melody which fades away to nothing, suspended in mid-air.

These were published eight years after Bairstow's death and seen through the press by Sir Ernest Bullock. One number, however, was omitted on the grounds that it did not fit in with the others whose words are from the fifteenth and sixteenth centuries. Francis Thompson's poem *The Veteran of Heaven* came more than two hundred years later, and elicited from ECB a march-like conception employing a chorus of tenors and basses who effect a dialogue of question and answer alternately between themselves and the soloist, the latter in a different key and tempo. The inclusion of the whole-tone scale here and there is not his only use of it. It could be regarded as a further element of variety. Bairstow's plan, clearly, was to place this energetic movement as a foil between the gentle fourth and sixth, and certainly the contrast is valuable, not to say essential, from the musical angle.

All the movements are capable of performance by a solo voice alone, except for the third, *Praise*, which is for chorus only. The scoring is for normal symphony orchestra. Bairstow himself got no further with orchestration than the first two numbers: the rest is the work of Sir Ernest Bullock, who was present for the first performance of the five published movements in the Minster by the York Musical Society on 9 November 1955.

f. ORCHESTRAL

The music for the Pevensey Pageant has not been located.

Coronation March

In 1902 Bairstow entered a competition for a march for the impending coronation and used the *nom-de plume* 'Dum Spiro Spero'. The Musical Times of February 1902 announced the name of the winner: 'The prize of fifty guineas, offered by the Worshipful Company of Musicians for the best Coronation March for full orchestra, has been awarded to Mr. Percy Godfrey, Music-Master of King Edward's School, Canterbury. The prize winner was born at Croxall, Derbyshire, on August 16, 1859. He is no relation to the Godfreys of military music fame, nor does he hail from any of the schools of music. ...Mus. Bac. Durham 1897 ... No fewer than 190 compositions were sent in ... and the award of the examiners – Sir Frederick Bridge, Sir Hubert Parry and Sir Walter Parratt – was unanimous.'

Bairstow's entry inevitably followed the well-trodden 'Pomp and Circumstance' path and has echoes of Parry's own Bridal March from 'The Birds' of Aristophanes. It exists in Bairstow's full orchestral score (a laborious and time-consuming process, especially for such an uncertain outcome) and also in an arrangement for piano, a condition of entry to the competition. Both are, as always with ECB, admirably neat and clear. Whether or not it was ever performed in his lifetime is not known, but it was played by the York Symphony Orchestra in the Minster during his centenary year. It deserves to be heard, and an organ arrangement would help to that end.

g. CHAMBER MUSIC

Bairstow wrote two sets of variations; the first for two pianos in 1908 while he was at Leeds. It received its first performance by its dedicatees, Noel H. Bell and H. Percy Richardson, on 25 January 1911. (See page 3). This, according to the Musical News of 4 February, was at the weekly entertainment of the Leeds School of Music by members of the staff. It was not published until 1932 and the dedication by that time was 'To H. Percy Richardson'. A few days later (2 February 1911) it was played again, this time by the composer (Mr. Bairstow) and Mr. E. Bullock at the annual concert of Leeds Parish Church Choir in the Albert Hall (now part of the Leeds School of Music), an event which contained also ECB's part-song *Sweet day, so cool* and Stanford's *Songs of the Fleet*.

The eight-bar theme is in G minor and in triple time, *Andante serioso* , announced at the start by the first piano, accompanied by the second with off-beat chords. The four-bar middle section is a repeated upward scale covering the interval of a sixth. This, and the first part (with a kind of semiquaver turn) are germinal motives providing abundant scope which is amply realised in the seven variations. These are organised so that each leads into the following one, each sharply characterised and in a variety of key.

The first is in E-flat, *tranquillo*, with the theme gently heard over a softly-rippling accompaniment with some delicate flourishes which subside until a sudden chord of the dominant plunges both players into an active *molto vivace* 6/8 pulse which at one point becomes a cross-rhythm in 3/4.

Variation 3 is in G major, *andante con moto*, with the pianos answering one another at a bar's distance. This joins on to a delicate *Intermezzo* (Variation 4) which has a gossamer semiquaver texture with colourful chromaticism. The serious mood returns in variation 5 which, in C-minor, has contrapuntal imitation, the theme standing out in octaves as if by horns. A bridge passage – trying various possibilities – eventually plumps for the dominant of A flat, in which key a busy *scherzo* (the sixth variation) in an *allegro vivace* 6/8 plies its exciting course, giving the players plenty to do, including the simultaneous hand-crossing which provides an intriguing visual element in performance.

A *smorzando* leads to the final variation, the seventh, '*Tempo della Tema*' as it is entitled, which is a return of the theme, this time in fine style and magnificence, with a great deal of elaboration in the shape of double octaves and arpeggios and chromatic scales in thirds. One could imagine something added on, as with Elgar and the Enigma Variations which his friends persuaded him to add after the first performance. It can, nevertheless, be made imposing enough to provide a convincing conclusion to what is a splendid piece affording enjoyment and challenge to two pianists possessed of a fairly advanced technique. It is written in true pianistic style.

Idiomatic, also, is the writing in the 'Six Variations on an Original Theme for violin and piano, written for and dedicated to Sybil Eaton' at York in 1916. It was published fifteen years later by Oxford University Press. Similar to the earlier set, it contains the concentrated essence of Bairstow's style; more so, if possible.

The 6/8 theme is in a modal D-minor *andante*, descending through an octave and rising again with a sequence of falling fourths and a contrasting four bars for a central section, all features which are made good use of later. The first variation, *(allegro con grazia)* is, surprisingly, in the major key – so soon. It is in canon almost throughout, calling to mind César Franck's famous last movement. In some other respects also the spirit of Franck could be said to enter into this work, though without his extreme chromaticisms.

The piano begins the second variation *(allegro molto, scherzando 3/8)* with a menacing figure in the bass while the violin inverts the theme. The falling-fourth motif is given out in firm octaves and longer notes by the piano, which is later joined in this by the violin in close canon. It is intensely rhythmical and vital, and sputters out at the end. Number three *(andante espressivo)* is a contrast, warm and expansive, with much imitation in the middle section, here expanded to twenty bars. Its mood is contented, slightly nostalgic, and very English.

The fourth, *maestoso,* begins with high *risoluto* chords of the seventh and bare fifths on the piano while the violin, on its lowest string, gives a variant of the theme. In the middle section the piano chords have become a softer, bell-like version of the main theme against which the violin weaves arabesques. A passionate climax is reached, strong and meaningful, which subsides to a somewhat unquiet *pianissimo*, two beats rest and a loud final chord.

Number five, a second *scherzo (Allegro non troppo, Giocoso)*, is once more in the tonic major, full of life and mischief, with a good deal of semiquaver activity and attractive rhythmic figures. All this ceases on a loud discord which sets off a solo cadenza in which the violin does a dramatic descent, again to the lowest string. This leads into the final variation, number six. This *adagio* is back again in the minor key and the original six-eight, but intensely serious and regretful with only snatches of the downward theme in nostalgic recollections and with passionate *crescendi*, the crisis being reached in the piano's forceful solo tenor line of the theme in a whole-tone guise. Thereafter, regrets become almost too hard to bear, but peace comes in the end in the major key as both instruments gradually rise to the calmness of 'realms supernal' high in their compass.

It is difficult to describe this work without appearing to over-state its virtues. Its deep feeling, variety of invention, drama, humour and playfulness, all served by an unerring technique, are some of the ingredients which help to form a work of consummate beauty such as Bairstow spent his whole life in pursuing. It is more than a pity that it is never heard. Any English composer – even Elgar – could have taken pride in acknowledging its authorship. Beautiful though the two-piano set is, the one for violin and piano is even more so, eight years later. Perhaps he found more inspira-tion in the theme, or in the expressive qualities of the violin – and the violinist dedicatee whose playing he so admired. It is certainly music which, far from being written out of duty, came forth from his innermost being as a spontaneous expression of his emotions: this, as we have seen, he considered to be the prime purpose of all music.

h. LITERARY WORKS

Handel's Oratorio 'The Messiah', O.U.P. 1928

This, in the small format of the Musical Pilgrim series, is a product of the pre-authentic performance era, taking as its main theme the advisability of adding to and altering Handel's orches-trations, praising particularly the trombone parts added by the mysterious Mr. Smithies. The book undoubtedly filled a need at the time, receiving encouraging reviews, the Musical Times commenting on the freshness, enthusiasm, and discrimination which the author brings to his writing. *Everyman's* opinion was that 'one searches his prose in vain for verbal felicities and epigram-matic flashes, but in his plain dealing with the reader he not only furnishes all the information that can possibly be desired, but contrives to raise a good many points which show a freshness of conception no amount of familiarity has been able to stale'.

Counterpoint and Harmony, Macmillan 1937 (second edition 1945)

This was written at the suggestion of Stanford whose idea was that counterpoint and harmony should be studied simultaneously – rather than harmony first and then counterpoint (hence the reversal of the more normal order of these two subjects in his title of the book) – and that the modes should be fully explained, and exercises given, in modal counterpoint. The book is designed 'to be of service to all, from the executant, who has to learn a little harmony and counterpoint to obtain a diploma, to the embryo composer'. Fine tunes are used in the exercises, and instruction is given in writing for the pianoforte. Stanford's plan of making students write 'over' a classical model has been adopted. Bairstow hoped that study of the book would produce freedom and ease in place of the 'stiff, cramped, and unimaginative' work that the old method of teaching tended to produce. He is firmly of the opinion that 'the acquisition of line, shape and movement in part-writing is of far more importance to the beginner than the knowledge of harmonic colour. (See pages 125 and 131)

All this and more is set out in the preface. There follows throughout the book a detailed and highly informative account of every aspect of music likely to be required by any music student. It was well received. Harvey Grace's idea (in Musical Times) was that, with its 400 pages, the book was expensive, but that 'the guinea will soon show itself to have been not spent but well invested'.

A detailed review by R.H. Walthew is largely appreciative. He quotes paragraph 271 which deals with a kind of music Bairstow disliked. 'Of chromatic passing notes we are told that they are very easy to write, and like all things which cost little, they are not worth much; and if used for long together and without an admixture of diatonic passing notes, may sound very cheap and give the impression of much ado about nothing. A shining example of this type of music is the prologue to Sullivan's *Golden Legend*' – and the reviewer adds that this remark might well have been omitted. But it is the only criticism in the article. Edmund Rubbra's review in *Music and Letters* stated firmly that 'Emancipation cannot commence until species counterpoint, given prominence in Sir Edward's book, is thrown over as useless academic lumber'. Opinions have certainly differed on this subject, but Bairstow's book treats it with every respect and obviously believes in its worth as a discipline. The book was revolutionary and unique in its day, and there is little doubt that, over the years, it has fulfilled its purpose handsomely in the hands of many of the right kind of students.

The Evolution of Musical Form, O.U.P. 1943 (See page 199)

This is based on the six Ferens Fine Art Lectures at Hull University College. The first chapter deals fully with the Cadence; then follows the Form of a Melody; instrumental forms in the seventeenth and eighteenth centuries, the fugue and the choral prelude, sonata and rondo form, and finally, modern developments. '...the fundamental ideas, from which all rules came, have not been lost in the best modern music, for they originated in human nature, which is unchangeable. Love is still the only thing which can cast out fear'. A familiar theme. And another one, the last word of all – the principles which develop from the cadence into great symphonic movements 'were founded on human nature, which never changes, and which demands variety and contrast, excitement and tranquillity, and, above all, beauty'.

Singing learned from speech, Macmillan/Stainer & Bell 1945

This 'primer for teachers and students' is developed from papers of Harry Plunket Greene who had been Bairstow's friend since around 1904 and from whom he learned his ideals 'and the sound and logical, natural principles which gave birth to them'. 'Sing as you speak' is a watchword. Silver is often pronounced *seelver*, lovely as if it were *lovelee*. Mountain should be sung, not as spelt, but as *mounten*. Particularly valuable are his thoughts on the insertion of an extra syllable between the consonants of two adjacent words, a principle which is still not always held to by some of the best singers. Bairstow sets the *reductio ad absurdum* to music: 'Bad dog Bob bit that cat, And got scratched grievously...' This, as with most of the other exercises in the book (presumably composed by ECB) has piano accompaniment for one hand, making repetition pleasanter, and easier than using two hands. Plunket Greene's imaginative style of writing does not always make his meaning clear, but Sidney Northcote in a Musical Times review spoke of the book's vigorous common sense and found it refreshing and enlightening. Bairstow's lion's share of the authorship evinces a deep knowledge of singing in all its aspects and he takes great care to convey his meaning in a more down-to-earth style than that of his friend. Bairstow was very successful as a singing teacher, with his great affection for the human voice. Two of his enormous number of pupils attained national fame – Elsie Suddaby and George Parker.

Recollections of Sir Edward

by David Hird

MY FIRST MEETING WITH Sir Edward was in the autumn of 1936 when I met him at his studio in Leeds to discuss the possibility of training as a professional musician. As a result of that meeting I started lessons which continued until I was called for military service in November 1940. Typical of Sir Edward's kindness and interest was the arrangement of my lessons. I visited him in York each week on Tuesday. My timetable started at the Song School at 8.45 a.m. with the boys' practice followed by full choir at 9.0 until 9.45. Often the music being rehearsed was for the weekly broadcast of Evensong in the afternoon. Occasionally the choir crossed to the Minster to rehearse in the choir stalls for the benefit of the BBC engineers, and sometimes I was asked to play the organ whilst Sir Edward listened from different positions. Rehearsal over, fully choral Matins followed at 10.0, after which we went across to Minster Court where glasses of milk and buns were always waiting on the music room table.

Half-hour lessons started at 11.0 and continued until 1.0 o'clock.and I was usually allowed to stay right through, listening to each lesson. My own lesson was at 12.30 and consisted of either piano-playing or written work in preparation for university degree. At 1.0 p.m. I went out into York for lunch. Sir Edward did not usually give lessons during the afternoon, but often he would say 'Come back at 2.0 p.m.' Between then and 3.30 he was engaged in various ways and he would often discuss and talk about the work he was doing. When he had compositions submitted as exercises for Durham degrees he would put the score on the music desk of the piano and go through it, discussing details. Similarly, when he was engaged in composing works of his own he would go through them at the piano. Works which I remember looking at with him are the introit *Let my prayer come up*, written for the coronation of George VI, his cantata *The Prodigal Son*, his setting of the evening canticles in G, and especially the organ sonata. I particularly remember the sonata. Most of it was written during his summer holiday on the Isle of Arran, but when he came home he still had much of the final fugue to write. On one visit to York soon afterwards, I spent the afternoon with him, playing the organ pedal part on the piano whilst he played the manual parts of the completed sections of the sonata. He spoke of his plans for the fugue, particularly his idea of making the entries of the subject at the interval of a third instead of the usual fourths and fifths.

Sir Edward's free accompaniments to unison verses of hymns were always very fine. When OUP asked him to provide accompaniments for the unison verses of hymns in the English Hymnal some of his improvisations were crystallised and written down. During the time that he was writing these he used to talk about them and play them on the piano. His written accompaniment to *Aeterna Christi Munera* closely resembles what I recollect of his improvised accompaniment to this hymn.

When he was preparing lectures he would discuss his plans. One of these was given to the Royal College of Organists on Brahms' fourth symphony, and the Ferens series of lectures for Hull University were later published as a book with the title *The evolution of musical form*. He spent a lot of time preparing examples for these lectures and I remember him showing me various 'visual aids' that he had prepared. He was very concerned that he should not speak above the heads of his audience.

He often talked of Plunket Greene and the book on singing that they were to have written together. This was eventually published as *Singing learned from speech*. Incidentally, singers figured prominently in his music room. Over the fireplace hung a photograph of his friend, the singer Gervase Elwes, and on the wall near the piano was a print of Byrd's *Reasons for singing*. Sometimes Tuesday afternoon was spent in preparatory work for a Leeds Philharmonic

Society concert. One work that I remember going through with him was Stanford's *Stabat Mater*.

Sir Edward often insisted that a musician's training should range widely over all aspects of music, that organists should listen to and study chamber music and other branches of the art not directly connected with their professional work. His own interests were wide, and he passed this on to his pupils.

Continuing the timetable of my weekly visits to York: – after spending the afternoon in his music room in the various ways described, at 3.30 we went along to his drawing room to join Lady Bairstow for afternoon tea. At 3.45 we went across to the Minster for Evensong (usually broadcast) at 4.0. In connexion with the broadcasts, I remember that in general he chose pedal stops of the violone type rather than bourdons, as he said these broadcast better in the lower registers. I think he said he had not to use the Tuba Mirabilis, as it was too powerful for the BBC equipment, but he often used the 8' and 16' small tubas on the Solo Organ. If the anthem was unaccompanied he would go downstairs and robe after the Nunc Dimittis and I would give the note. On one occasion I remember my consternation when the boys did not take the note I gave. Sir Edward immediately stopped them and I gave the note again.

During the first few months of my lessons, I joined Norman Gilbert who was already going to York each Tuesday. Occasionally there were visitors or other pupils in the organ loft during service, but for most of the time I was there I was the only pupil present on that day of the week. Sir Edward rarely played the voluntary after service. (I can remember him playing his own prelude on *Veni Emmanuel* from a very decrepit manuscript copy, and the prelude in G minor from the first book of preludes and postludes by Stanford). He always said that he did not have time to practise, and any pupil present might as well play the voluntary. Sir Edward kept at the console a record of the voluntaries played, and sometime during the service he would ask what I was going to play, duly entering it in his record, and on the organ voluntary notice, which I would then take and pin on the notice board at the south-east corner of the nave. (*Service was in the Choir, and with the screen curtains drawn, it was possible to leave the organ loft without being seen by the congregation).*

When evensong was over, it was time for my organ lesson. Very occasionally another pupil would be present and would play before me. Pupils that I remember playing in this manner at various times include H.K. Andrews who played the Bach Toccata in F for ECB's comments. He was to play it at an interview at New College, Oxford. Francis Jackson played an organ arrangement of the slow movement of Debussy's String Quartet, and Ernest Hopkinson, Bach's Trio Sonata 5. My organ lesson consisted of organ pieces which I had prepared, and when I was preparing for the RCO examinations, each week I had to do a past paper of 'Tests at the Organ'. Sir Edward never set any pattern of pieces to be learnt, and so far as I can remember, he never suggested that I should practise any particular piece. This applied also in my study of piano, harmony and composition with him. What work I did he left entirely to me. By the time my organ lesson was over it was usually between 5.30 and 6.0, I having spent most of the day from 8.45 in the morning with Sir Edward for a 'half-hour lesson'.

During the four years that I carried out this weekly routine I had many interesting conversations with him. This extended contact with him has undoubtedly influenced the whole of my musical career. However, details of his actual teaching have now for the most part faded and been absorbed into my subconscious mind. My paperwork commenced by working through his book 'Counterpoint and Harmony' which was not published but was in proof stage. Each week he would give me a few sheets of corrected proof to work through at my own speed. He hoped his book was self-explanatory and that an intelligent student would be able to use it without the aid of a teacher. Nevertheless, his comments and suggestions were always illuminating. He believed in extensive use of models, and his book carries out this plan. In this he was much influenced by Stanford, of whom he often used to speak. Beyond the stage of text-book harmony he still used models, though I cannot remember him suggesting any particular one, except perhaps Debussy's String Quartet, and Sibelius. I remember writing a string quartet based on Beethoven's opus 95, but I don't think he suggested the model. At the time that I was writing a string quartet for the Durham B. Mus. exercise, he examined my work each week and showed a keen interest in how the work was progressing.

In his organ teaching he insisted on good legato playing and in this connexion I remember particularly the Vaughan Williams prelude on *Rhosymedre* which I prepared with him for A.R.C.O. He insisted that the inner parts should be legato, often helping out the left hand with the thumb of the right hand. This cost me many hours of practice before he was satisfied. In connection with the use of the thumb, I remember that he played the Charles Wood prelude on 'York Tune' soloing the tune and assisting the left-hand accompaniment on a lower manual with the right-hand thumb. I once played Brahms' *Es ist ein Ros' entsprungen* for him, too quickly he thought. His comment was something like 'If you race through the countryside in a fast car you miss many of its beauties'.

Sir Edward was well known for his often sarcastic and biting comments, though I never remember him saying anything offensive to me. He was often amused, and particularly so if he thought he was one up on the Dean or clergy. On one occasion when his anthem "The King of Love" was being performed, he related, with evident amusement, that he wrote it when he was on holiday and had no hymn book available, so had to write the words from memory. When he returned to York with the completed anthem, he discovered that he had not followed the hymn book order of verses, having put verse three after verse five of the hymn book, and none of the clergy had noticed it!

During the period when I was visiting York for lessons, Sir Edward was invited to adjudicate at the Summerscale Festival in Keighley, my home town. It was therefore arranged that he would come to Keighley on the Friday evening and stay overnight at my home in readiness for an early start on the Saturday morning. At the Festival he insisted that I should sit with him and learn something of the job of adjudicating – a most interesting experience.

My lessons terminated in November 1940 when I was called up for military service, but his interest did not cease. During the whole of the time that I was away he regularly wrote to me, and some of his letters I have preserved. I last saw him about

July-August 1945 when I came home on leave from the Middle East. The decline in his health during the years I had been away was very marked. His last letter to me was written only three weeks before his death, and would, I imagine, be one of the last letters he wrote.   D.H.

Appendix

Chants

From the Westminster Abbey Chant Book 1894.

From the All Saints, Norfolk Square, Chant Book.

From the York Minster Chant Book 1916/1929.

PSALM XLII, *Verses 6 and 7, 14 and 15; PSALM XLIII,verses 5 and 6.*

S. Wesley, harmonised by E.C.B.

PSALM LVIII.

E. C. Bairstow.

PSALM LXXII.

E. C. Bairstow.

PSALM LXXVIII.
Verses 66 to end, and Gloria.

E. C. Bairstow.

PSALM LXXXV.

E. C. Bairstow.

PSALM CVII.
Verses 1 to 3, 8 and 9, 15 and 16, 21 and 22,
31 to end and Gloria.

E.C. Bairstow.

This setting was written (for the 1929 edition of the Chant Book) to accord with the pointing of the English Psalter, as follows.

PSALM CXIV. – *In exitu Israel.*

{ WHEN Israel came out of Egypt, and the house of Jacob from a- | mong the . strange | people,
{ 2   Judah was his sanctuary and | Isra-el | his do- | minion. | |

{ 3   The sea saw that and fled; Jordan was | driven | back. | |
{ 4   The mountains skipped like rams, | and the . little | hills like young | sheep. | |

{ 5   What aileth thee O thou sea that thou fleddest? ⋆ and thou Jordan that | thou wast . driven |
          back? | |
{ 6   Ye mountains that ye skipped like rams? ⋆ | and ye. little | hills like young | sheep? | |

{ 7   Tremble thou earth at the presence of the Lord, ⋆ at the presence of the | God of | Jacob; | |
{ 8   Who turned the hard rock into a standing water, ⋆ and the | flintstone . into a | springing |
          well. | |

216   PSALM CXXXIX.   E. C. Bairstow.

See page 280.

*In addition there are eight chants (three of them single) in the Novello
chant books of 1909. Three of them are also in the York book bearing the
acknowledgement of the publisher's copyright.*

*There are also, in manuscript, four ATB chants, two single (for psalms
124 and 150) and two double (for psalms 6, 7 and 8).*

*Probably there were others by ECB in what appears to be a 'Men Only'
collection assembled in his early York days.*

*Other composers represented were: R.S.M. Akerman, P.C. Buck,
G.F. Cobb, Walford Davies, H.A. Harding, G.F. Huntley,
C.J. King, C.H. Lloyd, G.C. Martin, C.F. Musgrove, C.L. Naylor,
E.W. Naylor, C.B. Rootham, G.A. Scaife, B.L. Selby,
E.H. Thorne, J.E. West and C.L. Williams.*

Descants

Reproduced from Diocesan Musical Festival Service Books.

"LONDON NEW."

3. Ye   fear-ful Saints, . . fresh cour-age take,
6. Blind   un - be - lief . . is sure to   err,

The clouds ye   so   much dread, Are big with mer - cy, with
And scan His work in   vain. God is His own,   His

1. He   plants His foot- steps, His

foot - steps in   the sea, And rides . . up - on the storm.
mer - cy, and shall break, In   bless   - ings on your head.
own in - ter - pre - ter, And He . . will make it   plain.

W. COWPER.

PRAISE MY SOUL

DESCANT.

4. An · gels, help . . us to a · dore . . Him; Ye be-hold Him face to face;

Sun and moon, bow down be - fore Him; Dwel -lers all in time and space.

Praise Him, Praise Him, Praise Him, Praise with us the God of grace.

O GOD OF LOVE

Descant by E. C. Bairstow.

A - MEN.

MOSCOW

Descant by E.C. BAIRSTOW.

MOSCOW.
Adapted from F. GIARDINI 1/16- 96.

1. Thou whose Al- migh-ty Word | Cha - os and darkness heard, | And took their flight; Hear us we hum- bly pray, | And where the Gos - pel-day Sheds not its glo - rious ray | Let there be light!

* *Descant to verses 1 and 3.*

EBORACUM

(Count in minims)

Tune written for 'Through the night of doubt and sorrow'.

*The autograph of Dr. Bairstow's accompaniment for brass, timpani
and organ, arranged for the enthronement of
Archbishop Temple in 1928.
The first trumpet part later became used as a descant,
starting on B flat simultaneously with the tune, rising then to
the first of two E flats.*

Hymn

Let us sing out our praises to the Lord

(formerly Lift up, O Lord, 1911)

Copyright Caryl Micklem.

Words: Rev'd Caryl Micklem
Metrical adaptation of the Venite (Psalm 95)

Music: Sir Edward Bairstow
from Coronation Hymn Collection, 1911; *Tune:* Huntington

1. Let us sing out our prais-es to the Lord, the rock of our sal-va-tion.
2. So let our voi-ces shout a-loud God's worth and tell a-new the sto-ry:

Let Him by thou-sand thou-sands be a-dored as God of His cre-a-tion.
How the Good Shep-herd loves us from our birth till death dis-clos-es glo-ry.

His care en-folds the Earth's re-mot-est hills; He cups the o-ceans in His hands;
No power can seize the jew-els from His crown or take our her-it-age a-way.

All hu-man joy and hope, all fears and ills, His bound-less wis-dom un-der-stands.
Heart of the world, put your de-fen-ces down and hear His liv-ing voice to-day.

By kind permission of Mr. S. G. B. Brown and the Reverend Caryl Micklem.

Bibliography

Bairstow, Sir Edward Cuthbert (in addition to Literary Works, p. 303)

Common Sense in choir training (lecture 9 April 1932)
RCO calendar 1932/3

Brahms's Fourth Symphony (lecture 13 March 1937)
RCO calendar 1937/8

Four presidential addresses 1929/30   RCO calendars

The organist as musician (address to the IAO)
RCO calendar 1938/9

Articles in the Music Student: 1913-20

    Anglican chanting
    Another book for singers
    Atmosphere in church music
    Elgar's songs
    Expression in counterpoint
    A few thoughts on speech in song
    Good advice for choirmasters
    Graded lists of English church music
    Grieg transcribed for organ
    MacDowell's music on the organ
    A new French symphony (Vierne 4)
    Obituary of G. S. Talbot
    Our consultant's desk
    Physiology and the voice
    Plunket Greene on 'Economy in diction'
    Voice production – misconceptions
    The value of simple things
    The vocal works of Beethoven

The anthems of S. S. Wesley   Musical Times 1926

Music in Yorkshire   Music and Letters 1920 vol. 1 pt. iv
Vocal and unvocal   – do–   vol. 10 pt. iii
The future of music   Music Journal (ISM) vol. 6 No. 2
                                        February 1935
Practical choir training   Study Notes No. 13   R.S.C.M.
The church organ: Importance of pure tone
                                The Times, 25 June 1930
Modern French and German organ music
            The Musical Standard, 2, 9 and 16 June 1917
The Music of the Minster
            York Minster Historical Tracts No. 28   S.P.C.K.
The Musical Education (of the chorister)
    in 'Us and our Song School'   York Minster 1927
York Minster – Restoration of the Organ: history,
    specification, and programmes of opening recitals   1931
Bradbury, Ernest
    Sir Edward Bairstow – A Birthday Tribute
                        Musical Times, August 1944
Bullock, Sir Ernest
    Sir Edward Bairstow. Seventieth Birthday –
        An Appreciation   Yorkshire Post, 22 August 1944
'Dotted Crotchet' –
    Leeds Parish Church   Musical Times, January 1906
Holt, Charles
    Edward Cuthbert Bairstow – His Times, His Work, His Works
        carbon typescript, undated, but post-1946
Jackson, Francis
    Sir Edward Bairstow: Paper delivered to the Church Music
        Society, 5 July 1986   CMS
    Sir Edward Bairstow: article based on a broadcast talk of 22
        August 1974 in the magazine of the Friends of Cathedral
        Music   Cathedral Music, FCM November 1995
    Sir Edward Bairstow: Address to the Friends of York Minster
                        Friends Annual Report 1975

Presidential address to the Incorporated Association of
Organists 1961   The Quarterly Record, October 1961
Lindley, Simon
Bairstow – The Leeds Legacy
Church Music Quarterly, RSCM April 1996
Stevens, Robert
A Bibliography of Sir Edward Bairstow – diploma thesis
at Loughborough Technical College   MS 1971

Addenda

Simplified genealogical tree showing the descent of
Edward C. Bairstow from James Watt (1736-1819) who used
steam as energy

James Watt

Richard Watt = Mary Denton
1777-1822

Hannah = Oates Bairstow
1816-1862   d. 1889

John Thomas Hobson   James Oates Bairstow = Elizabeth Watson
= Harriet Dewhurst   b. 1844

Edith Harriet Hobson   =   Edward Cuthbert Bairstow
22.viii.1874-1.v.1946

Stephen = Mary Lampard   Nancy = George BROWN   Peter = Kay
1904-   b. 1907   b. 1917   Hodgkins
1950

1 Ruth (div.)   1 Stephen George Bairstow BROWN =   Simon
2 Elizabeth (div.)   2 Elizabeth =   Eliz. Pouncey
3 Anthony   John Gibbs
                 3 Richard   =   Rosemary Corbett

James   1 John Edward   1 Helen   Scott   Jacquie
Brown   2 Thomas   2 Edward
                3 Joseph   3 Michael
                4 Mary   4 Mary
1 Ruth = Nicholas Bellord   5 Ruth

Frances   Elizabeth = Nicholas Froy

Martha Cecilia

2 Elizabeth = Trevor Eden   1 Julian = Belinda Phillips
                                    2 Jonathan
                                    3 James

Letter from ECB to Elsie Suddaby, dated 11th May but no year: probably early 1940s.

> My dear Elsie,
> I listened to you on Sunday. You amazed even me who knows your singing so well. I'm quite sure there is no-one in the country who can sing like that. I have heard and still hear so many, that I know. Your voice is as good and fresh, beautiful as ever, but I think you have matured and got a broader background. It is not often I am really moved, but you gave me a lump in my throat all right. With love, Yours, ECB.

The organist of St. Paul's Cathedral, Dr. Stanley Marchant had sent a Te Deum, written by his assistant, Douglas Hopkins, for comment by ECB. This brought forth a detailed reply, including a diagram pointing out that his climaxes did not reflect those of the words. '... personally I think there are only two things in the world more difficult to write than a service – one is a hymn-tune and the other a chant. The restrictions are so great and so many people have done it before – good musicians too. Yet what is the good of putting forth immature work that has practically nothing fresh or nothing of one's own personality in it? I tried for six years to write a Te Deum (the one in D) and really I don't think very much of it now.' (Minster Court, 12 February 1933). Nevertheless the Te Deum was sung regularly at York to the end of his days and for many years afterwards, both at Sunday matins (with the Benedictus) and at the end of evensong on Easter Day and other festivals.

Gordon Slater, organist of Lincoln Cathedral, on the day after Sir Edward's seventieth birthday concert: 'ECB got as much colour from the organ in half an hour as all other organists in England put together would get in a year.' (3 September 1944)

At an Elgar concert by the Leeds Philharmonic Society on 18 November 1944, ECB had 'a young contralto' as the angel in

Gerontius, along with Eric Greene (tenor) and William Parsons (bass). Taking the part for the first time, she sang it entirely from memory. Her name – Kathleen Ferrier.

After his consecration as Bishop of Manchester on 25 January 1921, William Temple wrote to express his deep appreciation of the music at the service. Dr. F. A. Iremonger in his life of Temple records that Bairstow replied that, though he had been an organist for many years, he seldom received such letters, and he was therefore all the more grateful for the bishop's considerate thought for the Minster organist and choir.

The Three Short Preludes for the organ were published posthumously in 1947 and were seen through the press by Sir Ernest Bullock. They cannot be dated, but the third was in existence during the nineteen-thirties and probably well before then. They are simple and uncomplicated, especially the first two, showing the composer in contemplative and undemonstrative mood. The result is music that is more accessible to the less accomplished player than are many of his other works. They have contrapuntal interest as well as harmonic colour and will profit from varied registration. Veni Emmanuel is episodic in its treatment of the oft-heard plainsong melody, and what at first might seem unpromising cumulative rising arpeggios in the accompaniment yield some pleasing and attractive harmonic shifts.

John Thomas Hobson, ECB's father-in-law, was a Government Inspector of Alkali Works.

Index